Diverse Sexuality and Schools

●◆ A REFERENCE HANDBOOK

Diverse Sexuality and Schools

A REFERENCE HANDBOOK

David Campos

A B C CLIO

Santa Barbara, California • Denver, Colorado • Oxford, England

Library of Congress Cataloging-in-Publication Data

Campos, David.
  Diverse sexuality and schools : a reference handbook / David Campos.
    p. cm. — (Contemporary education issues)
  ISBN 1-85109-545-4 (hardcover : alk. paper) ISBN 1-85109-550-0 (e-book)
  1. Homosexuality and education—United States. 2. Gay
students—United States. 3. Lesbian students—United States. 4.
Bisexual students—United States. 5. Transsexual students—United
States. I. Title. II. Series.

  LC192.6.C26 2003
  371.826'6—dc21
                              2003003574

07 06 05 04 03   10 9 8 7 6 5 4 3 2 1

This book is also available on the World Wide Web as an e-book. Visit abc-clio.com for details.

ABC-CLIO, Inc.
130 Cremona Drive, P.O. Box 1911
Santa Barbara, California 93116-1911

This book is printed on acid-free paper ∞.
Manufactured in the United States of America

To my mother and father,
Guadalupe S. and Agapito D. Campos,
whose love, wisdom, and strength
helped me believe that
earning an education
could become a reality

✎ Contents

☙ Series Editor's Preface

The Contemporary Education Issues series is dedicated to providing readers with an up-to-date exploration of the central issues in education today. Books in the series will examine such controversial topics as home schooling, charter schools, privatization of public schools, Native American education, African American education, literacy, curriculum development, and many others. The series is national in scope and is intended to encourage research by anyone interested in the field.

Because education is undergoing radical if not revolutionary change, the series is particularly concerned with how contemporary controversies in education affect both the organization of schools and the content and delivery of curriculum. Authors will endeavor to provide a balanced understanding of the issues and their effects on teachers, students, parents, administrators, and policymakers. The aim of the Contemporary Education Issues series is to publish excellent research on today's educational concerns by some of the finest scholars/practitioners in the field while pointing to new directions. The series promises to offer important analyses of some of the most controversial issues facing society today.

Danny Weil
Series Editor

❧ Preface and Acknowledgments

If you are truly right within your heart and with Christianity, you know in advance that you do not know enough about other people's lives to judge them.

—Joycelyn Elders, former U.S. surgeon general
(*The Advocate*, March 22, 1994)

Some of the most controversial and emotionally charged discussions in education today are about gay, lesbian, bisexual, and transgender (GLBT) youth. Reading about these youth or about this population in general is sure to make some people uncomfortable and uneasy. This is understandable considering that our society is heterosexist—that is, we presume that persons are heterosexual. Everywhere, it seems, we see heterosexuals—heterosexual teachers, doctors, sales clerks, ministers, newscasters, families, and so forth. Moreover, most parents and youth-serving professionals assume that their youth are heterosexual. Consequently, most people find gay and lesbian issues foreign, frightening, and contrary to the norm, and will do everything possible to protect themselves from what seems to be gay and lesbian propaganda. But there is no gay and lesbian propaganda. There is no recruitment scheme. There is no ulterior motive. The goal of this text is to educate the general public that these youth exist in our schools today and that they need acceptance, support, and protection.

I discovered this topic while writing one of the chapters for an earlier book for ABC-CLIO titled *Sex, Youth, and Sex Education*. Prior to this, I believed that the growing incidence of gay and lesbian characters on television corresponded to a heightened acceptance of the community. Moreover, I was amazed when I discovered that a Borders bookstore in a small, conservative Midwest town carried eleven different magazines for and about the gay and lesbian community. I thought for sure that this type of exposure meant the community had won an arduous battle and was finally accepted and that GLBT youth now had complete support in schools. I thought the days of teasing and name-calling—fag and dyke—was a thing of the past. I could not have been more mistaken.

I started my research and found painful testimonies of gay, lesbian, bisexual, and transgender youth harassed, beaten, stabbed, and kicked in school. One gay boy had been lassoed and threatened that he would be hitched to the back of a truck. A gang of boys urinated on another gay boy. Another gay boy had an antigay slur carved on his back. The girls at one lesbian's school refused to talk to her. Even more disturbing, school administrators and teachers did very little to protect these youth. I started reading more about them and their plight and discovered they have defining moments in their lives of isolation and alienation. I was reminded of Hillary Rodham Clinton's remark, "No human being is immune to adversity or personal setbacks." But when you think about how tumultuous adolescent life is, factor in that gay and lesbian youth must also contend with these possibilities:

- Their sexual attractions and desires are contrary to those of their peers
- They often cannot share their adolescent milestones (such as a first crush)
- Derogatory remarks and messages are made about gays and lesbians each day
- Everyone around them believes that it is bad and wrong to be gay or lesbian
- There is no help or solace from their teachers and counselors

One cannot help but wonder how much more adversity and how many personal setbacks these youth will endure before schools take a proactive stance and reach out to them.

This book discusses the current status of gay, lesbian, bisexual, and transgender youth. The introductory chapter explains some terminology associated with the population, describes the development of diverse sexual orientations, and concludes with legal implications for schools. Chapters 2 and 3 follow with a chronology of events and a historical survey of the literature from the mid-1960s to the mid-1990s. Chapter 4 shares the life histories of five youth today, and Chapter 5 is an overview of three schools devoted to these gay, lesbian, bisexual, and transgender youth. Chapter 6 highlights organizations, associations, and government agencies serving this population, and Chapter 7 outlines print and nonprint resources. A final reflection concludes the text in Chapter 8.

More than anything, I hope this text enables readers to see that these youth deserve more than a cursory judgment. More importantly, as A. Damien Martin wrote in his letter to the young people of the

---

The Hetrick-Martin Institute
Promoting Growth and a Positive Self-Image

Dear Reader:

I remember going to the library when I was 13 years old trying to see if I could learn something about homosexuality. I knew I was gay, but I wasn't sure just what that meant. The only things I had heard about homosexuals were terrible and just did not apply to me. But I was afraid that maybe my feelings meant that I was going to grow up into one of those "terrible people."

I remember being afraid to look into the library's card catalogue at first for fear that someone would see me and know what I was looking up. Then I was faced with the problem of getting the books once I found the titles. Most of them were not in the open stacks and I felt that I couldn't ask the librarian for them. The books that I did find were not very positive, telling me that I was sick, maldeveloped, unhappy, neurotic, and worse.

I didn't have much luck with friends, either. I was afraid to let anyone in school know how I felt. I was afraid to ask teachers questions. I avoided those other kids who were gay for fear someone would know I was "queer" if I made friends with them.

Things are still rough for gay and lesbian teenagers. But they are just a little better. This series of comic books is meant to help with some of the problems still faced by our young people. We hope that they let you know that you are not alone and that there are answers.

Sincerely,
A. Damien Martin, Ed.D.
Executive Director and Publisher

Source: "Tales of the Closet: Graphic Book Two, Falldown" [letter], by A. Damien Martin, 1987. In *Tales of the Closet* 1(2): 32.

---

nation, I hope that every gay, lesbian, bisexual, or transgender youth reader learns that he or she is not alone; others share a similar fate, and some advocates work tenaciously to transform the way youth are received in schools.

ACKNOWLEDGMENTS

A number of people supported me and were incredibly helpful throughout the writing of this text. I am grateful to the teachers at

Harvey Milk School, OASIS, and the Walt Whitman Community School who invested so much of their valuable time to answer my many questions. Thank you so much, Christopher R. Rodriguez, Deborah E. Smock, Joe Salvemini, and Becky Thompson. Greater society has no real appreciation of your tireless efforts. I commend you. I am also indebted to the courageous youth who were willing to share their life histories with me. Do not let the fact that your full names do not appear in the text dishearten you in any way; you know who you are and know that you will inevitably provide a reader some hope. I only wish you the best in life.

My editor Danny Weil was ever encouraging and believed in this book from the very beginning. Thank you so much for seeing this through. I extend my gratitude to the wonderful and efficient folks at ABC-CLIO, Alicia Merritt, Melanie Stafford, and Jan Kristiansson. Your eye for details made bringing this together easier. My colleague Dr. Valerie Janesick provided me much motivation. Thanks for your wisdom and humor. A special thank you to my confidant and colleague Dr. Kenneth A. Perez, who initially encouraged me to write this book. Your unwavering support and the insight you provide from the physician's perspective are much appreciated.

My mother and father, Guadalupe S. and Agapito D. Campos, continue to be steadfast pillars in my life. You have unfailingly given me love, spirituality, encouragement, and support and assigned my needs a great priority in your lives. Thank you for so much. My brothers, Ernie and John, inspire me in so many unspoken ways. You two are the smartest, nicest, and most humble guys in the world.

David Campos
Chicago, Illinois

Chapter One

●→ **Introduction**

One summer while I was visiting my grandparents, I went into a bodega with my cousin. I must have been seven years old; my cousin was three years older. He went to the coolers for some drinks; I headed for the candy aisle. We shouted back and forth, deciding how to stretch our money as much as we could when I heard the voice of another rougher-looking kid say to me, "Fucking fag." Looking back at me was a twelve-year-old boy who sported a look of disgust. I knew what "fucking" meant, and although I had heard fag before, I wasn't quite sure what it meant; I knew it wasn't good though. . . .A few years later, my family and I were watching *Murphy Brown*. Miles [one of the show's characters] looked directly at the camera, and I let it slip that I thought he was cute. Everyone turned toward my direction. My father yelled: "What the hell's the matter with you? What are you, a goddamn queer?" My brothers gave me a stern look: "You're sick! You're not our brother." The statements scored right through me. Thereafter, I was very careful about the way I acted and talked.

—Mark, Seventeen, Hartford, Connecticut

GAY, LESBIAN, BISEXUAL, AND TRANSGENDER YOUTH

Many persons, like Mark in the vignette, who are gay, lesbian, bisexual, or transgender have countless experiences where they were degraded, censured, and made to feel guilty for who they are. Some have sustained emotional pain, others have endured physical violence, and still others have lost their lives simply because they did not behave to the norm. Although contemporary society is seemingly becoming more progressive, gay, lesbian, bisexual, and transgender youth are still victim to ridicule, harassment, and condemnation.

We know from history that gay, lesbian, bisexual, and transgender people have always existed in society. The Bible has certainly made

1

references to homosexuality, some of the great Greek philosophers were known homosexuals, nineteenth-century psychologists discussed the etiology of homosexuality, and homosexuals were among the 6 million killed in the Holocaust. In the last thirty years, however, American society has witnessed a visible growth of the gay, lesbian, bisexual, and transgender community. The community as a whole has become politically powerful, and distinct communities have emerged in San Francisco (Castro), New York (Chelsea; Greenwich Village), Chicago (Lake View), Houston (Montrose), and Los Angeles (West Hollywood). In fact, U.S. Census 2001 demographics suggest that there are more same-sex couples living in the United States than ever before (abcnews.com 2002b). Since 1990, the population of same-sex couples has increased 700 percent in Delaware and Nevada. Vermont, Indiana, Nebraska, and Louisiana have witnessed this population grow 400 percent. And the number of same-sex couples in Connecticut, Illinois, Massachusetts, and Montana has increased 200 percent. Researchers indicate that these figures do not necessarily reflect a growth in the actual number of gay, lesbian, bisexual, and transgender people, but instead reveal that they are more comfortable in disclosing their relationships.

The entertainment industry has equally adapted to the political and social times. Gay, lesbian, bisexual, and transgender characters are incorporated into more story lines than ever before. Prior to the sitcom *Ellen*, where Ellen DeGeneres disclosed that her character was lesbian, very few prime-time television shows featured gay or lesbian characters. Even though *Ellen* was cancelled, many believe that her sitcom paved the way for shows that involve gay or lesbian characters such as *Will & Grace, Dawson's Creek, Friends, The Simpsons,* and *South Park.* At the same time, the premium cable channels have embraced gay and lesbian characters and story lines. HBO features a gay character on the critically acclaimed *Six Feet Under;* gay men, lesbians, bisexuals, and transgender persons have been included in the hit comedy *Sex and the City;* and Showtime is the first to showcase a drama about the camaraderie of gay men, lesbians, and a gay youth in *Queer as Folk.*

Many Americans are supportive of the community of gay, lesbian, bisexual, and transgender people. In June 2001, a Gallup Poll found that among those polled,

- 85 percent believe that GLBT people should have equal job opportunities
- 55 percent believe that same-sex relationships between consenting adults are not morally wrong

- 45 percent believe that these persons cannot change their sexuality
- 57 percent believe insurance coverage should extend to domestic partners
- 52 percent believe that homosexuality should be accepted as an alternative lifestyle (abcnews.com 2002b)

To some degree, public acceptance has also extended to gay and lesbian youth. The Gay, Lesbian, and Straight Education Network (GLSEN 2001), for instance, estimates that since 1989, students in public and private schools across the nation have formed more than 1,000 gay-straight alliances (GSAs) that promote tolerance, celebrate differences, and eliminate sexual orientation discrimination. One school community in particular has been overwhelmingly supportive of a lesbian couple. In December 2001 in Dover, New Hampshire, 77 percent of the senior class at Dover High School voted a lesbian couple "class sweethearts." Although there was some dissent and the principal declared the vote invalid, the classmates encouraged the couple to fight for the superlative title. One classmate responded: "I think it's wrong that they can't be free about how they [the class] feel. They should be able to express that. If people think they are the cutest couple in the school, then why not? Not everything is traditional. . . .People do things their own way" (GLSEN 2002b).

Although gay, lesbian, bisexual, and transgender people are becoming more accepted, the fact remains that contemporary society is conservative and somewhat homophobic. For example, in the summer of 2000, a lesbian couple kissed at a Los Angeles Dodgers–Chicago Cubs game at Dodger Stadium. To their dismay, they were thrown out of the stadium with no initial explanation other than "someone complained and said children should not be exposed to 'those people'" (acbnews.com 2002a). As another example, Ken Connor of the Family Research Council responded to the American Academy of Pediatrics (AAP) 2002 official endorsement of adoption of children by same-sex partners by exclaiming, "The sad fact is that promiscuity, domestic violence, and other problems endemic to the homosexual lifestyle makes these relationships inherently unstable, and thus unsuitable for the raising of children" (Family Research Council 2002). But perhaps the most spiteful comment about the community of gay, lesbian, bisexual, and transgender people was a remark made by Jerry Falwell in an exchange with Pat Robertson regarding the World Trade Center tragedy. The following was taken from "You Helped This Happen," an ABC News commentary on their *700 Club* discourse:

"God," he told Robertson, had protected America "wonderfully these 225 years. And since 1812, this is the first time that we've been attacked on our soil and by far the worst results. Throwing God out successfully with the help of the federal court system, throwing God out of the public square, out of the schools," he said. "The abortionists have got to bear some burden for this because God will not be mocked. And when we destroy 40 million little innocent babies, we make God mad. The Pagans and the abortionists and the feminists and the gays and lesbians who are actively trying to make that an alternative lifestyle, the ACLU, People for the American Way—all of them who have tried to secularize America," Falwell continued, "I point the finger in their face and say, 'You helped this happen.'

"Well, I totally concur," responded Robertson. (abcnews.com 2002c)

In their defense, Falwell released a statement that indicated that his comments were taken out of context, and a spokeswoman for Robertson mentioned that he did not blame gays and lesbians for the terrorist attack. Be that as it may, these types of statements do absolutely nothing for the ultimate acceptance of gay, lesbian, bisexual, and transgender persons, and reinforce the notion that theirs is an alternative "lifestyle" that is evil, distasteful, and deserving of God's wrath.

Despite the increase in the number of gay-straight alliances, homophobia often appears to permeate school communities. One study of 168 adolescents receiving services from a gay and lesbian social agency found that 73 percent of gay youth and 71 percent of lesbian youth reported encountering physical abuse, threats of physical abuse, demeaning jokes and comments, and profanities written on their lockers (Telljohann and Price 1993). Some youth are harassed in ways unimaginable. Nearly fifteen students backed up one gay youth against a fence and began to punch and kick him, all the while chanting: "Kill the faggot. Kill the faggot" (cnn.com 2002b). One lesbian youth was barred from wearing a suit and tie in her yearbook picture. At another high school, students voted on "Who is the biggest faggot in school?" by placing a tally mark next to a list of student names printed on a bathroom wall (GLSEN 2002a).

In the last century, the population of gay, lesbian, bisexual, and transgender youth was overlooked, and their plight was often dismissed or trivialized. However, a number of events have underscored the need to attend to this population. First, empirical research reports that these youth experience intolerance and harassment more often than any other group of youth. Second, school districts have been sued for their failure to protect these youth. Third, there is a nationwide initiative to have safe school environments free of bullying and sexual harassment. As a result, more gay and lesbian youth are starting to disclose their sexuality at younger ages than previous generations. This chapter begins the discussion of their lives by looking at terms associated with these youth, what characterizes this population, the challenges presented to these youth, and what legal recourse they have.

TERMS ASSOCIATED WITH THESE YOUTH

Many terms are associated with the population of gay, lesbian, bisexual, and transgender people. Some terms are politically accurate and respectful, whereas others are pejorative and damaging. The following terms and their definitions are used throughout the chapters.

Homosexual

The term describes persons who are sexually attracted to, sexually desire, or have sex with members of the same gender. German Hungarian journalist Karoly Maria Kertbeny coined the term in 1868 and again in 1869 in his letter opposing a Prussian antisodomy law (Fone 2000). He used the term *Homosexualitat* (sexual attraction and desire for persons of the same sex) to distinguish it from *Normalsexualitat* (sexual attraction and desire experienced by the general population). The term became widely used in Germany in 1907 when rumors circulated about a "homosexual clique" involved in an espionage scandal (Hogan and Hudson 1998). The term apparently became a convenient moniker for the Kaiser's court. The term often has medical connotations, with implications for pathology and etiology (Kaplan and Sadock 1998).

Gay

The term has varied meanings. In some instances, it is synonymous with homosexuality and connotes sexual attractions to, romance with, and behaviors toward persons of the same sex. Other times the term is used to describe homosexual men, although the American Psychological Association (1995) suggests that the terms gay men and lesbian be used instead of homosexual. The term can be used broadly to describe modern homosexual life—the social culture, community, and concepts associated with the population considered nonheterosexual. The term has a significant history, with meanings ranging from "merry" same-sex love songs in the thirteenth century to prostitution in the nineteenth century (Hogan and Hudson 1998). The American Heritage College Dictionary (1993) elaborates: "Gay may be regarded as offensive when used as a noun to refer to particular individuals, as in *There were two gays on the panel;* here a phrase such as *gay people* should be used instead. But there is no objection to the use of the noun in the plural to refer to the general gay community" (565).

Lesbian

The term is used to define women who have sexual desires or strong emotional affinities for other women. The term is derived from Lesbos, an island east of Greece and the birthplace of woman poet Sappho (circa 600 B.C.), whose lyrics suggest her passion for other women. Sapphist, tribade (derived from "to rub"), and gay gal were some of the words historically used to describe the passion, romance, sex, or affinity shared between two women (Hogan and Hudson 1998). *Lesbian* has become more accepted and readily used since the 1970s.

Bisexual

The term denotes persons who are emotionally and sexually attracted to and desire romance or coitus with either gender. Ruth Westheimer (2000) adds, "Some persons have sexual relationships with men and women at the same time, while others alternate with male and female partners, one after the other. Some persons engage in bisexual behavior for relatively short periods of their lives, while for others it is a more stable behavior pattern" (53).

Transgender

The term describes people whose gender identity does not complement their biological anatomy. These are mentally healthy persons whose core existence is the opposite gender. Such people can be heterosexual, homosexual, or bisexual and may cross-dress or pursue sex reassignment surgery if they have no emotional attachment to their body. A male youth could identify himself as a woman, occasionally dress as a woman, and yearn to have romantic and sexual relationships with women; he would be considered transgender, not gay.

Queer

The term has an interesting history. At the beginning of the last century, homosexual men who did not consider themselves effeminate used the term to distinguish themselves from the fairies, faggots, and pansies (Fone 2000; Hogan and Hudson 1998). Apparently, the term befitted the unconventional, masculine homosexual. The term was eventually replaced by *gay,* and *queer* became offensive slang by the 1930s and 1940s. In the 1980s, however, a political activist group known as Queer Nation transformed the meaning of the word. It is responsible for the mantra "We're here! We're queer! Get used to it!" The term now describes gay, lesbian, bisexual, and transgender people and what they embody. Albeit offensive to some and at times politically charged, queer has become a term of empowerment and is more socially acceptable. Many universities now have Queer Studies programs, and some academic discourse is appropriately assigned under Queer Literature.

Sexual Orientation

The term describes a person's sexual interest for members of the opposite gender, the same gender, or either gender. Janis Bohan (1996) added, "While the term emphasizes the sexual component of interpersonal relationships, in reality any sexual orientation involves a wide range of feelings, behaviors, experiences, and commitments" (xvi). *Sexual orientation* should be used instead of *sexual preference* because the latter suggests that people prefer—or choose—the direction of their sexual interest. Some conservative factions believe that a person can change his or her sexual orientation through religious guidance or psychoanalysis. However, most reputable organizations maintain that sexual orientation is unchangeable. As such, youth cannot be "recruited" to become gay, lesbian, bisexual, or transgender.

Come Out

The phrase indicates the process by which an individual realizes and/or accepts his or her sexual orientation and acknowledges or reveals this to others. Historically, homosexual people used this phrase to indicate that a person had accepted her or his sexual orientation and/or disclosed this to other members of the homosexual community. The term has taken on an additional meaning that represents political and public declaration of one's sexual orientation and suggests a sense of pride and bravery in the direct line of social rebuke and censure (D'Emilio and

Freedman 1997). Gay, lesbian, bisexual, or transgender people *come out* every time they disclose their sexual orientation to others.

Out

The term translates to being open about one's sexual orientation. When a youth announces before her peers that she is lesbian, she is considered *out*. *Outed* or *outing,* however, is the act of publicizing a person's sexual orientation regardless of the person's desire to conceal that orientation. If the same youth had had another peer exclaim, "Luann is lesbian because we saw her making out with Maricela at Friday's party," she would have been outed.

In the Closet

The phrase means to conceal one's sexual orientation regardless of whether this is "a state of conscious overt, tacit, or implicit denial of being primarily attracted to the same sex" (Hogan and Hudson 1998, 140). People can be out about their sexuality, live their life completely *in the closet,* or be in the closet in various social contexts. For instance, a lesbian youth could be in the closet with her parents and school peers, but out to her siblings and coworkers.

Homophobia

The term denotes a fear or hatred of gay, lesbian, bisexual, or transgender people, their community, or what they embody. The term also encompasses the prejudice or discrimination experienced by such persons based on their sexual orientation or gender identity. Researchers have refined this definition to include "the dread of being in close quarters with homosexuals" and "extreme rage and fear reaction to homosexuals" (Fone 2000, 5). *Homophobia* manifests in a variety of ways, from offensive jokes made about such people or their community to such people being threatened, harassed, or physically assaulted. Social institutions are considered homophobic whenever they deny GLBT people the opportunity to maintain equal rights that ensure a legal recognition of same-sex marriages, adoption of children, and health benefits extensions to same-sex households.

A DISTINCT POPULATION

Not by chance has the population of gay, lesbian, bisexual, and transgender youth been called the forgotten, invisible minority (Savin-Williams 1990). For much of the last century, adult issues have dominated the gay, lesbian, bisexual, and transgender research agenda, and much of the community's social justice activism has overlooked these youth, schools, and curriculum. Moreover, educational research has ignored this group despite the fact that literature abounds on the classroom justice or lack thereof experienced by girls, youth of color, and youth with disabilities. It was not until the 1970s that research started to emerge on this population of youth. In 1988, the Society of Adolescent Medicine devoted a *Journal of Adolescent Health Care* issue to this population. The literature included discussions and empirical research to demonstrate that a significant number of these youth exist and that they have needs that warrant national attention. Since then, more research has surfaced on this population, although the literature is moderately limited.

Albeit a definite population, these youth often remain invisible because of the severe stigma attached to being known as gay. Children are exposed to homophobic comments early on by parents, siblings, peers, and the media (van Wormer, Wells, and Boes 2000). They may hear disparaging words such as fag and lesbo and not know their inherent meaning but know that these words are powerful enough to be used as verbal assaults. As youth develop into adolescents, words long associated with negative or aberrant behavior and other slurs are introduced—gay rod, queen, homo, queer bait, and so forth—and are just as emotionally loaded. Such words are certainly humiliating, and when these are exchanged in the classroom, hallway, or playground, the lesson reinforced is that it is heinous to be gay or lesbian. No youth wants to be thought of or known as gay; they just want to conform to their peer group rather than risk alienation. It is not surprising to find that youth who are gay, lesbian, or bisexual conceal their sexual identity for fear that they will be discovered and suffer reprisals. Many of these youth keep their sexual identity secret even from their closest confidants.

Because most people do not disclose their sexual orientation until adulthood (Haffner 1998) and it is common for youth to experience and act on same-sex attraction (American Academy of Child and Adolescent Psychiatry 1999), it is difficult to determine the population size of youth who are gay, lesbian, bisexual, or transgender. The exact figure is unknown, but demographic data demonstrate a population ranging from 1 to 10 percent of adolescents in the United States. In some instances, such as a study conducted by Ritch Savin-Williams and

Richard Rodriguez (cited in PERSON Project 2000), youth will report that they have homosexual attractions or behaviors, but indicate that they are heterosexual. One percent of the junior and high school youth in their study reported they were gay, lesbian, or bisexual, yet 6 percent reported having homosexual attractions and engaging in homosexual behaviors. Gary Remafedi, Michael Resnick, and Robert Blum (1992) found in a sample of seventh through twelfth graders that 1 percent were gay, lesbian, or bisexual, and 11 percent were unsure of their orientation. Another study found that 5 percent of boys and girls between the ages of thirteen and fifteen had had sex with a member of the same sex (American Academy of Child and Adolescent Psychiatry 1999). This is consistent with a University of North Carolina study that estimates that from 5 to 6 percent of youth seventeen or younger are gay, lesbian, or bisexual (GLSEN 2002c). The percentage rate was higher in the 1996 Safe Schools Coalition Anti-Violence Report (cited in National Coalition for Gay, Lesbian, Bisexual, and Transgender Youth 2000); 9 percent of high school youth considered themselves nonheterosexual. Robert Deisher (1989) estimates that about 10 percent of youth are gay, lesbian, bisexual, or transgender. Roberta Ginsberg (1996) has deduced that roughly 6 percent of youth, or 2,610,515, are gay or lesbian. The National Education Association's (NEA) Task Force on Sexual Orientation supports this figure (GLSEN 2002c), which translates to 1 in 20 youth likely to have same-sex attractions. Youth Pride (2001) has underscored that nearly 1 to 3 of every 10 youth is nonheterosexual or has a family member who is. The demographic inconsistencies should not trivialize the population size because a conservative estimate of 1 percent of the 24.6 million youth between the ages of thirteen and nineteen living in the United States would mean that 246,000 youth encounter challenges associated with their sexuality.

Although most youth choose to remain silent about their sexual orientation, some do come out while in school. In fact, more youth are finding it easier to come out, which has resulted in a record number of youth revealing their sexual orientation at earlier ages than ever before (Rofes 1997; Jordan, Vaughan, and Woodworth 1997). Karen Jordan, Jill Vaughan, and Katharine Woodworth (1997) suggest that this is the result of an increased visibility of gay, lesbian, bisexual, and transgender people. Youth may also feel safer about coming out than ever before because schools are now legally obligated to protect this population from harassment and bullying. Mike Glatze and Benjie Nycum (2001) have discovered: "It's a fact that people are coming out younger and younger, as early as 11 or 12 in some cases, and they aren't so concerned with whether being gay is OK. They seem more comfortable with their sexuality than previous generations. Coming out still raises many challenges, but rather than being discouraged, most gay kids are pissed that the world treats them the way it does and are driven to do something about it" (56).

Most youth first become aware of their sexual orientation around the age of 10 (D'Augelli and Hershberger 1993), with some research samples suggesting 9.7 years (Herdt and Boxer 1996) and 12.2 years of age (National Coalition for Gay, Lesbian, Bisexual, and Transgender Youth 2000). Although some youth come out as early as fifth or sixth grade (Rofes 1997), most who come out to their family and peers are about sixteen years old (National Coalition for Gay, Lesbian, Bisexual, and Transgender Youth 2000). Bruce Shenitz (2002) finds that "Adults who came out in the 1970s and early 1980s first became aware of same-sex attraction around age 13, while adolescents who came out in the late 1980s and early 1990s experienced this as early as age 9; self-identification as lesbian or gay occurred between ages 19 and 23 for the adults and between ages 14 and 16 for the adolescents" (103).

Gay, lesbian, bisexual, and transgender youth are a heterogeneous group. Despite the fact that they share a common bond, they are as diverse as can be. They are white, black, Latino, or Asian, and they live in urban, suburban, and rural areas. Some come from wealthy households, some come from middle-class families, and others come from households barely making ends meet. Some have families that accept them as they are; others are beaten and disowned. These youth can be found in almost every imaginable subculture (church groups, honors cohorts, detention programs, athletic teams, and so forth). When Glatze and Nycum (2001) set out to interview gay youth across the country they knew full well that gay youth thrived everywhere including the smallest communities. What they did not anticipate was the support available to these youth:

> Our travels have revealed some great things about being young and gay in America. For one, no matter where you are, chances are you're probably within 100 miles of a youth group or some kind of support.
> . . .Truckloads of kids caravan from the most rural parts of Arkansas and Mississippi to Memphis Area Gay Youth in Tennessee. The fortunate ones have parents willing to drive them around or friends to hitch a ride with to places like the Jacksonville Areas Sexual Minority Youth Network, Boise's Youth Alliance for Diversity, or Halifax, Canada's, Lesbian, Gay, and Bisexual Youth Project. (56)

CHALLENGES ENCOUNTERED BY THESE YOUTH

The process of human development is tumultuous with its periods of unstable skills, interests, and defenses (Isay 1997). For adolescents, this process is complicated by their need to fit in with their peers; rarely do adolescents risk alienation. Imagine, then, how difficult it is for youth contending with the normal challenges associated with growing up to wrestle with feelings that seem to contradict everything their peers believe in. Everywhere these youth turn—to their parents, their peers, their teachers, at church, at the mall, at the grocers, on TV, on the newsstands—they encounter images of what society deems a "normal" life. Moreover, whenever gay, lesbian, bisexual, or transgender issues arise, society's responses are usually unfavorable. For instance, teachers and school officials often do nothing when youth call each other faggot or dyke. It is no wonder that youth who are gay, lesbian, bisexual, or transgender are often quiet about their sexual orientation. Why should they risk alienation, hatred, or verbal and physical violence from their peers, family, and community?

Speaking metaphorically, Susan Morrow (1997) describes growing up in America today as treading a rocky road, but growing up in America gay, lesbian, bisexual, or transgender as traveling through a minefield. These youth face particular challenges that deserve some attention. Among them are homophobia and violence, especially as evidenced in the climate in schools, the actions of the Boy Scouts of America (BSA), and the murder of Matthew Shepard; unique developmental needs; lack of role models and emotional support; and variable risks.

Homophobic Harassment and Physical Violence

Homophobia exists in every country, but negative reactions to gay, lesbian, bisexual, and transgender people are severe in the United States (Savin-Williams 1990). Although the severity of homophobia could be debated, the fact remains that some Americans would be overjoyed if all gay, lesbian, bisexual, and transgender people disappeared. These Americans simply despise everything that the community embodies and will disparage and degrade gay, lesbian, bisexual, and transgender people by

- perpetuating stereotypes
- making crude jokes
- suggesting that they are disgusting, shameful, and abnormal

•• using the Bible and religion to support antigay sentiment
•• verbally and physically assaulting them
•• suggesting that they deserve to die of AIDS
•• calling others fag, lesbo, and so forth

All too often the image of the homophobe is of a white, middle-aged, beer-guzzling, blue-collar, pickup-driving man from the South. Homophobia, however, is expressed by many powerful role models, including parents, relatives, teachers, preachers, peers, and media personalities. In 1981, for instance, former First Lady Nancy Reagan remarked to the *Boston Globe:* "It is appalling to see parades in San Francisco and elsewhere proclaiming 'gay pride' and all that. What in the world do they have to be proud of?" (Hogan and Hudson 1998, 292). In 1989, the Bush administration attempted to remove a study on gay, lesbian, and bisexual adolescent suicide from a larger national survey because elements of the study contradicted traditional family values (Geh 1989, cited in van Wormer, Wells, and Boes 2000). Byrne Fone (2000) has referred to homophobia as "the last acceptable prejudice" (3), and Harvard University professor Peter Gomes (cited in Baker 2002) has called homophobia "the last respected prejudice of the century" (2). This perspective is the result of intense inquiry into society's behavior and attitude toward gay, lesbian, bisexual, and transgender people. Some of the prejudice experienced by African Americans, Jewish Americans, Latino Americans, women, and people with disabilities has been eliminated through the work of various movements for civil rights. In the last four decades or so, many people have adjusted their attitudes and behaviors and now respect and accept these groups as deserving of social justice. If a young person were to call an African American a nigger, a Latino American a spic, or person with a disability a retard, he or she would be subjected to public censure. But if that same youth called a gay youth faggot, no reprimand, stern look, or lecture would ensue. Rarely do public role models ever discount ethnic or racial minorities, people with disabilities, or women. But gay, lesbian, bisexual, and transgender people have not been afforded this luxury and are often victim to prejudice. Public role models make homophobic comments and rarely apologize for offending the community. Jean Baker (2002) has outlined overt instances of homophobia. Here are a few:

•• In the early 1990s, General Colin Powell believed that openly gay personnel serving in the armed forces would demoralize and jeopardize the military's effectiveness.
•• Religious groups urged the public to boycott Disney

because as the parent company of ABC, it allowed Ellen DeGeneres's character in her show *Ellen* to come out as a lesbian.

•→ Columnist and radio and TV personality Dr. Laura Schlesinger wrote, "I see homosexuality as a biological faux pas—that is, an error in proper brain development with respect to potential reproductivity" (originally cited in Rutenberg and Elliot 2000, A-22).

•→ U.S. Senate Majority Leader Trent Lott stated that homosexuality is a sin. He declared, "You should try to show them a way to deal with [homosexuality] just like alcoholism . . .or sex addiction . . .or kleptomaniacs" (originally cited in Lacayo 1998, 34).

•→ Religious organizations such as the Christian Coalition and Family Research Council advertised that homosexuality is a sinful choice that can be cured (originally cited in Leland and Miller 1998).

•→ Arizona considered legislation to ban gay student support groups because some believed that such groups would recruit members. One legislator remarked that homosexuality is "disgustingly disturbing" and another declared, "Gays want to sodomize and I don't want them recruiting for that" (50).

•→ At the 1999 annual meeting, the Southern Baptists denounced President Bill Clinton for proclaiming June Gay and Lesbian Pride Month.

An endless supply of homophobic incidents could be provided, but one particular case elucidates some of the hatred toward this community: the recent U.S. Supreme Court decision upholding the Boy Scouts of America ban on homosexual members.

The Boy Scouts of America

The image of the Boy Scouts of America (BSA) is a wholesome one with members purportedly learning to become fine, upstanding citizens of the United States. Scouts are supposed to live according to virtues that society upholds and values (trustworthiness, courtesy, loyalty, respect, and so forth) and take the Boy Scout Oath—"On my honor I will do my best to do my duty to God and country and to obey the Scout Law; to help other people at all times; to keep myself physically strong, mentally awake, and morally straight" (Donohue 1994). Moreover, the BSA curriculum is educational, practical, and meaningful.

As of 1990, Boy Scouts (including Tiger Scouts, Cub Scouts, Boy Scouts, and Explorers) membership comprised nearly 4.3 million youth and about 1.2 million adults (Salzman 1992). Being a Boy Scout is evidently beneficial because a glance at notable professions finds that many of their members were former Boy Scouts. For instance, 65 percent of U.S. congressman, 85 percent of all FBI agents, 75 percent of military academy graduates, and eleven of the twelve astronauts who walked on the moon were Boy Scouts (Salzman 1992).

Boy Scouts are supposed to be role models and future pillars of society. Why, then, would any one accuse the BSA of homophobia? The answer is that gay youth or men are not tolerated in the Boy Scouts. No matter how great a scout he is, no matter how successfully he rises through the ranks or even becomes an Eagle Scout (the highest honor), if he is openly gay, he cannot be recognized as a Boy Scout. Scout officials maintain that homosexuality "is immoral behavior and has no place in Scouting;" "homosexuals do not provide the proper role model for youth membership"; and "inclusion of a homosexual Scoutmaster who has publicly acknowledged his or her homosexuality would either undermine the force of the Boy Scout view that homosexuality is immoral and inconsistent with the Scout oath and law, or would undermine the credibility of the Scoutmaster who attempts to communicate this view (Donohue 1994, 60).

Timothy Curran, James Dale, Chuck Merino, and Keith Richardson shared a similar fate when they were dismissed from the Boy Scouts and/or denied the opportunity to work with the BSA because they are gay. Believing their civil rights violated, these men pursued litigation. James Dale's case reached the U.S. Supreme Court in spring of the year 2000. Dale, who had been an exemplary Boy Scout for twelve years, was expelled from the BSA when it learned that Dale was copresident of Rutgers University's Lesbian/Gay Alliance. He sued the BSA, and the New Jersey Supreme Court ruled in his favor. The BSA appealed, and the U.S. Supreme Court ruled in its favor. The Boy Scouts now have the constitutional right to bar gay youth or men from becoming scoutmasters. The BSA does not have permission to bar gay youth from membership, but the ruling left room for interpretation (cnn.com 2002a).

In support of Dale and in an attempt to penalize the BSA, many national businesses (such as Levi Strauss, the Bank of America, and Wells Fargo) no longer contribute to the BSA, the United Way no longer supports the BSA, and some school districts throughout the nation no longer allow the Scouts to meet on campuses. Film director Steven Spielberg has even declined to serve as an honorary board member (Bull 2001). However, there still remains an equal and sometimes greater support of the BSA's convictions on homosexuality. Dale has been called a "revolutionary sodomite" who works in metaphoric sewers (Grigg 1999), and legislation has been introduced to prevent local governments from withholding funding from the Scouts. The most powerful message that resonates from the *Boy Scouts of America v. Dale* case is that homosexuality is morally wrong and that there is no place for it in an organization as wholesome as the Boy Scouts. In short, this perpetuates the belief that to be gay is inherently un-American, and nearly 5 million members are indoctrinated in this ideology.

Homophobic Climate in Schools

Schools mirror the homophobic climate in general society. As early as kindergarten and first grade, youth begin calling each other fag, queer, and sissy and the name-calling progresses as they get older. This type of name-calling reinforces the message that to be gay or lesbian is awful. This can be painful for youth who may have some homosexual tendencies, but on a larger scale youth learn very quickly to follow strict sex-role behaviors or risk ridicule (Gordon 1994). Youth who are gay, lesbian, or bisexual or have transgender tendencies are pressured to suppress their true sexual identity and take on a heterosexual one. Moreover, all of the name-calling reinforces false negative stereotypes about gays and lesbians—if you are gay, then you must also be feminine; if you are lesbian you must like masculine things. Don Johnson (1996) has noted that it is virtually impossible to grow up in our society and not absorb some level of homophobia.

This argument is significant considering that large, empirical studies on sexual harassment have underscored that name-calling is pervasive in schools. The American Association of University Women (1993; 2001) conducted two sexual harassment studies, one in 1993 and the other in 2001. The 2001 study revealed that four out of five students experienced some form of sexual harassment (largely by other students) that ranged from sexual innuendoes to unwanted groping and removal of clothing. In that same study, 36 percent of the 2,064 students in eighth through eleventh grades reported that they had been called gay or lesbian. This figure was markedly higher than the 17 percent reported in 1993. Boys in both studies were more likely to be called gay or lesbian than girls. In 2001, boys were twice as likely to be called gay or lesbian than in 1993, and girls were three times more likely to be called gay or lesbian in 2001 than in 1993. Although youth may not recognize the fact that name-calling is emotionally damaging, studies suggest otherwise. Nearly 86 percent of the 1993 sample and 73 percent of the 2001 sample indicated that they would become "very upset" if someone called them gay or lesbian. Apparently, the adage "Sticks and stones may break my bones, but words will never hurt me" is not internalized by youth.

The Gay, Lesbian, and Straight Education Network (GLSEN 2002d) conducted a study to assess the homophobic climate in schools. The study of 904 gay, lesbian, bisexual, and transgender high school youth revealed that they frequently heard homophobic comments such as "faggot," "dyke," "That's so gay," or "You're so gay" in the proximity of faculty and staff. Overwhelming numbers indicated that these professionals never intervened or did so only occasionally, and nearly one quarter of those surveyed indicated that they had heard faculty and staff make homophobic remarks. Over 81 percent of the youth in the sample reported being verbally harassed because of their sexual orientation. More results of the study are found in Sidebar 1.1.

Charol Shakeshaft et al. (1997) conducted a three-year observational study of the sexual harassment experiences of youth in middle, junior, and high schools. The results of the study revealed that boys who did not fit the masculine norm were often targets of harassment. They were often called queer, old lady, girl, sissy, or any name associated with girls or feminine behavior. If any boy appeared weak—silent or maladroit in sports—he was called gay or faggot. The boys in this study, much like the youth in the AAUW study, feared being labeled gay and worked hard to behave and conform to the traditional boy image.

Other studies also confirm that youth harass other youth with homophobic remarks. The Massachusetts Governor's Commission on Gay and Lesbian Youth (1993) found that 97 percent of youth reported hearing homophobic comments made by peers. The National Coalition for Gay, Lesbian, Bisexual, and Transgender Youth (2000) Internet survey found that 64 percent of the respondents had been verbally assaulted. In a sample of twenty-nine gay or bisexual boys between the ages of fifteen and nineteen, 55 percent reported they had experienced some form of verbal abuse (Remafedi 1987).

Verbal harassment is effective in suppressing a youth's spirit. But when the harassment is physical and a youth is assaulted because of his or her sexual orientation, the spirit and physical body are critically altered. Take the example of Nevada youth Derek Henkle.

Derek came out to his mother when he was twelve years old. He had endured some verbal harassment at school, and given that no support system was available to him there, he began hanging around the gay, lesbian, and bisexual student union at the University of Nevada, Reno. The students were older, some as old as twenty-eight, but he enjoyed the camaraderie and community nonetheless. His ordeal began when a local cable access show came to video the group's discussion on coming out.

Sidebar 1.1 Results from the GLSEN
"2001 National School Climate Survey"

- 84.3% of lesbian, gay, bixexual, and transgender students reported hearing homophobic remarks, such as "faggot" or "dyke," frequently or often
- 90.8% reported hearing the expression "That's so gay," or "You're so gay," frequently or often
- 23.6% reported hearing homophobic remarks from faculty and staff at least some of the time
- 81.8% reported that faculty and staff never intervened or intervened only some of the time when present when homophobic comments were made
- 83.2% of LGBT students reported being verbally harassed (name calling, threats, etc.) because of their sexual orientation
- 48.3% of LGBT students of color reported being verbally harassed because of both their sexual orientation and their race/ethnicity
- 65.4% of LGBT students reported being sexually harassed (sexual comments, inappropriately touched, etc.)
- 74.2% of lesbian and bisexual young women reported being sexually harassed
- 73.7% of transgender students reported being sexually harassed
- 41.9% of LGBT students reported being physically harassed (being shoved, pushed, etc.) because of their sexual orientation
- 21.1% of LGBT reported being physically assaulted (being punched, kicked, injured with a weapon) because of their sexual orientation
- 31.3% of LGBT reported experiencing physical harassment based on their gender expression
- 13.7% of LGBT students reported experiencing physical assault based on their gender expression

Source: "The 2001 National School Climate Survey: Lesbian, Gay, Bisexual, and Transgender Students and Their Experiences in Schools," by Gay, Lesbian, and Straight Education Network, 2002. Available at http://www.glsen.org/ binary=data/GLSEN_ARTICLES/pdf_file/ 1029.pdf (cited February 28). Reprinted with permission.

Knowing that the show would only be on cable access Derek was not worried about how much more harassment he might have to endure. He participated in the discussion, although he said very little. Shortly thereafter, a fellow student saw Derek on the show "with a bunch of fags" and asked him if he was gay. Derek answered in the affirmative.

The severity of the harassment escalated. On his forty-five-minute bus ride to school, he was constantly assaulted and taunted with "butt muncher" and "butt pirate." The assaults grew to being shoved in a locker and being spit on. But perhaps the scariest event for Derek was when a group of boys took a lasso and said, "Let's lasso the fag and tie him to the back of the truck and drag him down the highway" (Shenitz 2002, 99). The boys managed to put the lasso around his neck three times.

To contend with the situation, Derek, his parents, his therapist, and school administrators decided that he should write a letter indicating that other students had violated the sexual harassment policy, but the administrators then decided to drop the entire matter. Thereafter, Henkle emphasizes, "everyone knew in the school that this was going on . . . and it overwhelmingly opened the doors to constant violence. I was being pushed into lockers on a daily basis; people were pushing me in the hallway; people were throwing stuff at me. And it was so terrifying because I would literally walk around the corner in my school and not know whether this time I was going to have to be bashed up against the locker or whether I was going to be able to get where I needed to go" (Shenitz 2002, 102–103). Henkle was transferred to an alternative high school (for delinquent students, pregnant students, or teenage parents) where he was told to not talk about being gay. Most shockingly, his principal told him, "I will not have you acting like a fag in my school" (103).

Derek Henkle is not alone. Other youth—Jamie Nabozny, Mike LeVasseur, Timothy Dahle, among others—have experienced similar situations only to have school officials turn their backs. Ellen Bass and Kate Kaufman (1996) emphasize that gay, lesbian, bisexual, and transgender youth are often blamed for provoking their tormentors and asked to change their appearance and behavior, but the tormentors are excused or their behavior is rationalized (Martin and Hetrick 1988; Uribe and Harbeck 1991, cited in Hunter, Shannon, Knox, and Martin 1998). A 1997 Massachusetts Youth Risk Behavior Survey found that gay, lesbian, and bisexual youth were four times more likely to report being threatened with a weapon while at school than their heterosexual peers (Safe Schools Coalition of Washington 1999). The Gay, Lesbian, and Straight Education Network (2002d) survey of school climates revealed that about 42 percent of gay, lesbian, bisexual, and transgender youth were physically harassed (shoved, pushed), and nearly 21 percent were physically assaulted (punched, kicked, injured with a weapon) because of their sexual orientation. This finding is consistent with that of Joyce Hunter (1990, cited in Hunter, Shannon, Knox, and Martin 1998), who found that 40 percent of the gay and lesbian youth in her sample reported that they had been physically assaulted at least once. The National Coalition for Gay, Lesbian, Bisexual, and Transgender Youth (2000) survey revealed that of its sample, 28 percent had been threatened with physical violence; 14 percent had been punched, kicked, or beaten; and 4 percent had been raped. It is not surprising that a 1999 GLSEN study found that almost half of the gay, lesbian, bisexual, and transgender youth did not feel safe in their schools.

Schools tend to have varying degrees of homophobic climates. Sidebar 1.2 presents some news headlines from around the country that capture the extent of homophobia in our schools. These types of climates impact our youth on various levels. For those who are heterosexual, these environments reinforce the stigma and prejudice associated with homosexuality. Openly gay, lesbian, bisexual, or transgender youth, or those who appear to be, are overtly impacted—they endure harassment. Homophobia also affects those youth who are in the closet—they are encouraged to appear heterosexual. They will do whatever it takes to fit in, often studying their peers and copying their gestures, body language, and fashion so that they are not perceived as gay or lesbian (Johnson 1996). These youth force themselves to keep their sexual orientation a secret for fear that they will be discovered and subjected to similar harassment (Bass and Kaufman 1996; van Wormer, Wells, and Boes 2000). Some youth will go so far as to participate in harassment to appear as heterosexual as their peers.

Matthew Shepard's Murder

On October 7, 1998, Matthew Shepard was beaten, tied with a rope, pistol-whipped, and left out in the cold in Wyoming to die. Shepard's murder could have very well been an everyday homicide statistic in our society; however, twenty-one-year-old Shepard suffered a gruesome murder at the hands of two young, self-proclaimed homophobes, Aaron McKinney and Russell Henderson. Shepard was living as openly gay in Laramie, Wyoming, when he encountered the two high school dropouts at a local bar. Police records indicate that Shepard told McKinney and Henderson that he was gay, and the two told him they were gay to lure him into leaving with them. They drove Shepard to a desolate field outside of Laramie, beat him, and left him hanging on a fence. The murderers then proceeded back into town, where they got into an altercation

Sidebar 1.2 Gay, Lesbian, Bisexual, and Transgender Youth in the News

Title	Date	Source
"Young, Gay, and Scared to Death at School," by Maria Hinojosa	September 23, 1999	cnn.com
"Teen Gets Anti-Gay Slur Carved into Stomach," by Jack Nichols	October 17, 1999	Gay Today
"LGBT Youth Persecuted in Schools," by Nancy Guerin	July 4, 2001	*Metroland Weekly,* New York
"Gay Student Leaves Town after Coming Out," by Scott Finn	July 29, 2001	*Charleston Sunday Gazette Mail,* West Virginia
"Escambia High Ignores the Needs, Rights of LGBT Students," by Sara Cohan	December 30, 2001	*Pensacola News-Journal,* Florida
"School Prevents Student from Forming Gay-Straight Alliance," by Matt Frazier	January 6, 2002	*Fort Worth Star-Telegram,* Texas
"Lesbian Student Barred from Wearing a Tie in Senior Photos," by Melanie Ave	January 25, 2002	*St. Petersburg Times,* Florida
"Hallways Present Threat for LGBT Students," by Kate Stone Lombardi	January 27, 2002	*New York Times,* New York
"Student Editorial Condemning Homosexuality Causes Controversy," by Molly Dugan	February 5, 2002	*Sacramento Bee,* California
"School Defends Trip to Avoid Gay Days Festival," by Clark Kauffman	February 6, 2002	*Des Moines Register,* Iowa
"Mother Sues School District over Son's Harassment," by Ellen Cronin	February 7, 2002	*Caledonian Record,* Vermont
"Gay Teens Ignored by High School Sex Ed Classes," by Carol Lee	February 10, 2002	Women's E-News
"Town Up in Arms over LGBT Schools Item," by Meggan Clark	February 19, 2002	*Brattleboro Reformer,* Vermont

with two other men. Police were called in and discovered a bloody .357 Magnum and Shepard's wallet in their pickup truck. McKinney's girlfriend, who lied about being an alibi for the two, excused her boyfriend because Shepard had embarrassed him.

In a matter of days, thousands gathered in Laramie; thousands more gathered in Washington, D.C., and other cities; and candlelight vigils were held to grieve Shepard's death. Hundreds of radical, conservative Christians countered the vigil because they believed that Shepard had deserved to die. A Kansas minister, Fred Phelps, prepared to dance on the grave at the funeral. Many others held signs that read: "AIDS Cures Fags," "God Hates Fags," and "Your Parents May *Accept* You, Your Religion May *Tolerate* You, Science May *Excuse* You, Society May *Include* You, Gov't May *Protect* You, But God Will Throw You in HELL" (the word SIN duplicated as a border). Other conservatives responded to the national attention with "wage war against the homosexual agenda" and "the acceptance of homosexuality is the last step in the decline of Gentile civilization" (Lacayo 1998). Time/CNN conducted a poll shortly after the Shepard murder and found that despite an increased societal acceptance of gay, lesbian, bisexual, and transgender people since 1978, one third of the sample still did not accept them and nearly half believed that homosexual relationships are morally wrong (see Sidebar 1.3).

Unique Developmental Needs

Gay, lesbian, bisexual, and transgender youth share the same developmental struggles as youth who are heterosexual. They are concerned with their social context and they have crises when events fail to unfold as planned. They have acne, they talk on the phone, they argue with their siblings and parents, they want to be popular, they want to fashionable, and they want to experience physical and emotional intimacy (Lerner, Lerner, and Finkelstein 2001). But even though they are outwardly the same as their peers, as gay, lesbian, bisexual, and transgender youth, they have some unique common challenges (Ryan and Futterman 1998).

Perhaps the greatest challenge is the fact that youth are caught in heterosexism—the assumption that people are heterosexual (Lasser and Tharinger 2000). Growing up, youth see heterosexist behavior and hear heterosexist comments. Girls may hear early on that they will have a beautiful wedding and marry a tall, dark, and handsome young man, and boys are encouraged to pursue good, beautiful girls. Everything surrounding them is presumed to be heterosexual from their parents to their teachers to their peers (Durby 1994). Savin-Williams (1990) writes:

**Sidebar 1.3 *Time*/CNN Polls Taken before and after
Matthew Shepard's Murder**

How do you feel about homosexual relationships?

	1998	1978
Acceptable for others, but not for self	52%	35%
Acceptable for others and self	12%	6%
Not acceptable at all	33%	59%

Are homosexual relationships between consenting adults morally wrong or not a moral issue?

	1998	1978
Yes, morally wrong	48%	53%
Not a moral issue	45%	38%

Do you have a family member or close friend who is gay or lesbian?

	1998	1994
Yes	41%	32%
No	57%	66%

Is homosexuality something that some people are born with, or is it due to factors such as how they were raised or their environment?

	1998
Born with	33%
How raised or environment	40%
Both	11%

Can people who are homosexual change their sexual orientation if they choose to do so?

Yes	51%
No	36%

Do you favor or oppose permitting people who are openly gay or lesbian to serve in the military?

Favor	52%
Oppose	39%

Do you favor or oppose permitting people who are openly gay or lesbian to teach in schools in your community?

Favor	51%
Oppose	42%

Note: "Not sure" answers were omitted from the original table
Source: "*Time*/CNN Poll" insert in "The New Gay Struggle," by Richard Lacayo.
1998. In *Time*, October 26, p. 36. Reprinted with permission.

"Most youth are raised in heterosexual families, associated in heterosexual peer groups, and are educated in heterosexual institutions. Youth who are not heterosexual often feel they have little option except to pass as 'heterosexually normal'" (1). In the minds of some youth, other gay, lesbian, bisexual, and transgender youth do not exist and a community of such adults is as accessible as the nearest galaxy. In a heterosexist world, youth simply cannot be gay, lesbian, bisexual, or transgender; for those who claim they are, they are in a phase they will outgrow, or so society tells them.

Based on work with adults, various scholars have proposed models for the identity development of gay and lesbian people. Arthur Lipkin (1999) has outlined some of these models and integrated them into a five-stage model. A more in-depth investigation of the fascinating work of Eli Coleman (1982), Vivienne C. Cass (1984), Richard Troiden (1989), Henry L. Minton and Gary J. McDonald (1984), and Arthur Lipkin (1999) can be found in Anthony D'Augelli and Charlotte Patterson's work (2001). For the purposes of this text, however, the models' skeletal structures are presented in Sidebar 1.4; here we look at pivotal moments—those revelations throughout a lifetime that shape sexual identity.

Awareness of Stigma

Youth know that there are negative connotations associated with being gay or lesbian. They are familiar with the epithets. They may not know what they mean, but they know that these epithets are powerful and destructive.

Realization that They Are Different

Youth know that they are different from their same-gender peers and often marginalize their own feelings. They may find themselves thinking, "I'm just not like the others." Whatever same-sex feelings they have are gender-focused rather than sexuality-based. A young boy, for instance, may like to play with dolls, enjoy ribbons and flowers, and refrain from playing traditional boy games or sports. He may believe that these feelings are "bad and wrong" and work to suppress his tendencies. Most youth at this moment have not even considered the words *gay* or *lesbian* or entertained thoughts that they might be. One gay youth remarks: "There was always something I knew was a little bit different about me. I didn't know exactly what that might have been. It was just something that was there and I learned to accept it" (Owens 1998, 16).

Sidebar 1.4 Models of Identity Development for Gay and Lesbian Youth

Continuum of Pivotal Moments	Coleman's Five Stage Model	Cass's Six Stage Model	Troiden's Four Stage Model	Minton and McDonald's Three Stage Model	Lipkin's Five Stage Model
Awareness of stigma	1) Pre-coming out		1) Sensitization	1) Egocentric	1) Presexuality
Realization that "I am different"		1) Identity confusion;			
Sexualization of sense of difference		2) Identity comparison	2) Identity confusion		2) Identity questioning
Denial and resistance	2) Coming out			2) Sociocentric	
Realization		3) Identity tolerance			
Acceptance of sexual identity		4) Identity acceptance			3) Coming out;
Exploration of the GLBT community	3) Exploration		3) Identity assumption;		4) Pride
		5) Identity pride	4) Commitment	3) Universalistic	
Opening up	4) First relationships;				
Recognition of sexuality's place as a part of the whole person	5) Integration	6) Identity synthesis			5) Postsexuality

Source: Adapted from developmental models in *Understanding Homosexuality: Changing Schools,* by Arthur Lipkin. 1999. Boulder, CO: Westview Press.

Sexualization of the Sense of Difference

The feeling of being different is now sexualized. At this pivotal moment, these youth are consciously aware that they have same-sex attractions. A gay youth recounts: "In every grade, there was at least one boy that I had a certain fondness for. . . . And later on, . . . I recognized this as crushes. I wanted to spend as much time as I could with them" (Owens 1998, 20).

Denial and Resistance

They resist answering the question, "Can I be homosexual?" They may begin to rationalize their feelings and behaviors—"I'm not lesbian. I love her because she's my best friend." They avoid labels and struggle with their same-sex attractions. They trivialize their sexual interests. They are unable to identify with or are confused by false negative stereotypes. They may prefer to be apart from others to avoid questions about their interests. Richard Isay (1997) adds, "Some homosexual adolescents are more withdrawn or more uncomfortable in peer interactions than their heterosexual counterparts" (65). They may even date members of the opposite sex to give the impression that they are heterosexual and/or to conform to social expectations. They cannot accept their sexual orientation, perhaps because they could be "subjected to verbal abuse, physical cruelty, condemnation by organized religion, overt discrimination, or outright rejection in response to suspicion or disclosure of their homosexuality" (Durby 1994, 5).

Realization That They May Be Gay, Lesbian, or Bisexual

They tolerate the fact that they may be homosexual. Some may temporarily define themselves as bisexual or asexual. Others may excuse their behavior with, "I was so drunk last night; I had no idea what was going on." They begin to realize that they have no community to identify with. They feel isolated, with no sense of belonging. They keep their feelings secret and act heterosexual to avoid homophobia. According to Don Johnson (1996), "One of the extraordinarily consequences of living in a homophobic environment for the gay/lesbian youth is the internalized belief that acceptance becomes based upon how well one can hide (lie about) who one really is" (40). One youth mentions: "I felt like I had to be ultra-careful in the dressing room. I couldn't let my eyes wander; I couldn't let anyone suspect the slightest thing. I found myself putting up more of a front in sports than anywhere else. I felt like it was such a proving ground—proving my manhood to my father, to other guys, to myself" (Owens 1998, 26). All of these factors begin to affect self-concept, and some demonstrate self-hatred. Roberta Ginsberg (1996) writes, "Gays/lesbians appear to be doubly damned: by the hostility shown them by society at large and by the self-hate and self-questioning that results from their sharing the dominant attitudes and values of that society" (11).

Acceptance

They accept the fact that they are gay or lesbian. They begin to identify with or associate with other members of the gay, lesbian, bisexual, and transgender community. This is the pivotal moment when they start to come out. "The coming out experience is so powerful for the gay/lesbian person that it will be remembered in great detail by most for the rest of their lives. For the first time, the words about this core piece of identity have been spoken out loud to another human being. The universe, for that gay or lesbian individual has changed forever" (Johnson 1996, 40). Initially, they come out to other gay and lesbian people. Then they progressively come out to (in the general order) close heterosexual friends, close family members such as siblings, parents, and close friends at work (Ryan and Futterman 1998). Dennis Durby (1994) elaborates: "Persons able to accept their sexual orientation are able to resolve many of the conflicts they had been experiencing. They seek out more information and self-understanding about their thoughts and feelings, and may experience relief at finally gaining an understanding about who they are" (8). A youth writes: "The hardest part about coming out is telling something that's so deep in your heart with the realization that at any point they could say, 'You're immoral; you're wrong.' . . . But what's wonderful is that finally you're not lying. You're being completely honest and they're sharing that joy with you" (Owens 1998, 41).

Exploration of the Gay, Lesbian, Bisexual, and Transgender Community

They socially immerse themselves in this subculture. They develop a social network, have sexual experiences, share emotional and physical intimacy, and have romantic relationships. They are selective about disclosing their sexual orientation.

Opening Up

They contemplate the question, "why pretend?" They realize that there is nothing disparaging about their orientation or way of life. They comprehend the importance of living an open life. They do not fear the prejudice or stigma associated with their sexual orientation.

Recognition of Sexuality as a Part of the Whole Person

They begin to understand that sexual orientation is one facet of many in a person's life. Their sexuality does not define who they are.

The sidebar on page 25 shows these pivotal moments as steps that most gay and lesbian people take. They progress through the steps at various rates—some reach the highest stages, others never do, and others progress through the steps and regress following horrifying experiences. Various elements in a person's life—personality characteristics, psychosocial turmoil, social network, and so forth—affect how he or she travels through the stages. Gay, lesbian, bisexual, and transgender youth must contend with these issues as well as with issues that all youth experience—feeling unattractive because they have to wear glasses or braces, feeling inferior because they are not as smart as the others, feeling awkward because they are too tall or too short or overweight, and wanting to fit in. Far too often they contend with these issues alone.

Lack of Role Models and Emotional Support

Growing up gay, lesbian, bisexual, or transgender is further complicated by the fact that these adolescents have very few immediate role models in their social milieu and almost no social support. Positive gay and lesbian role models exist in our society—rock singer Melissa Etheridge, Olympic swimmer Greg Louganis, Stanford University football player Dwight Slater, talk-show host Rosie O'Donnell, and ABC News correspondent Jeffrey Kofman, to name a few. But for the most part, these youth have few healthy role models to emulate, and some youth may have a hard time relating to the gay men and lesbians available to them (Isay 1997). Conceivably, a white, young lesbian adolescent could relate to the school's white lesbian guidance counselor. But a gay African American boy may have a harder time relating to the same counselor.

Johnson (1996) hypothesizes that many healthy gay or lesbian teachers, neighbors, relatives, and so forth cannot afford to be visible in our culture. They simply cannot risk everything they have to homophobia and prejudice. Many teachers are even forced to conceal their sexual orientation because they risk being dismissed from their jobs if they open up about their sexuality (Hunter, Shannon, Knox, and Martin 1998). In *The Advocate*, a national magazine on gay and lesbian issues, one fifth-grade teacher concludes his editorial on bullying with, "I did not sign my name to this letter because in Oklahoma, a teacher can still be fired for being gay" ("Bully Pulpit" 2001, 4). Many potential gay and lesbian role models also fear that if they advocate on behalf of these youth they will be perceived as pedophiles. The risk of being labeled with this stereotype or even considered "guilty by association" is too great (Savin-Williams 1990). One teacher volunteers, "If you portray gay/lesbian relationships unbiasedly, students will label you as one of them" (van Wormer, Wells, and Boes 2000, 68). Role models for these youth are few and far between. Because of this absence, many of these youth will often perceive gay, lesbian, bisexual, and transgender adults according to false negative stereotypes.

Rarely do gay, lesbian, bisexual, and transgender youth sustain a support network. Susan Telljohann and James Price (1993) found in their study of gay and lesbian adolescents that fewer than one in five could identify someone who was very supportive of them. Whenever heterosexual youth have a developmental milestone, such as their first die-hard crush, they can confide in their friends, siblings, and even their parents, teachers, and school counselors (if they feel the need to), but most gay, lesbian, bisexual, and transgender youth have no such confidants. If they share their milestones with their closest friends, they risk losing the friendships. Some youth simply cannot handle the stigma and do not want their association to lead others to believe that they, too, are gay or lesbian (Hunter and Schaecher 1987). Many studies consistently reveal that as many as one half of these youth will lose their friends after coming out to them (D'Augelli and Hershberger 1993; Remafedi 1987; Ryan and Futterman 1997).

The family, the primary source of support for most youth, can very well work against the mental and spiritual development of youth who are gay, lesbian, bisexual, or transgender. So often and understandably, parents who for their lifetime have been steeped in negative, anti-gay stereotypes are unsupportive of their children. One father captures this sentiment the best:

> On reflecting about homosexuality, I've learned that: my religious tradition taught me to believe that my son was a sinner; my medical support system taught me to believe that my son was sick; my educational system taught me that my son was abnormal; my legal system views my son and his partner in an unsanctioned relationship without legal rights and protection that are afforded my married daughter; my family, immediate and extended, provided no acknowledgment of support for having a gay relative in the midst; my major communications sources treated homosexuality as deviant. (GLSEN 2001, 1)

Some parents react violently by throwing their children out of their homes or attacking them (one study revealed that nearly one third of gays and lesbians were abused by family members [Philadelphia Lesbian and Gay Task Force 1996]), others permanently end their relationships with their children (Baker 2002), and others learn to accept them. A. Damien Martin and Emery Hetrick (1988) found that nearly one half

of gay, lesbian, bisexual, and transgender youth seeking help from a social agency had been physically assaulted by their parents or siblings.

Teachers are not much of an option for these youth either, given
that teachers rarely intervene in the hallways and rarely discuss gay
and lesbian issues. As evidenced in the Gay, Lesbian, and Straight Education Network (2002d) national study, most teachers do very little to
intervene when they hear other youth make homophobic comments.
Other studies seem to confirm this pattern (Massachusetts Governor's
Commission on Gay and Lesbian Youth 1993; National Coalition for
Gay, Lesbian, Bisexual, and Transgender Youth 2000). Moreover, teachers use very little of their instructional time to talk about gay or lesbian
issues. The National Coalition for Gay, Lesbian, Bisexual, and Transgender Youth (2000), for instance, found that only 10 percent of the
1,960 sample reported that their teachers had ever discussed homosexuality in a positive manner. Moreover, Telljohann, Price, Mohammed
Poureslami, and Alyssa Easton (1995) found that less than one half of
their secondary health teachers sample discussed gay, lesbian, bisexual, or transgender issues, and many teachers were uncertain about or
believed in stereotypes. For the most part, studies have revealed that
many teachers

- do not teach about homosexuality
- do not feel comfortable or competent enough to teach about
  homosexuality
- feel the need to update the knowledge in order to teach
  about homosexuality
- discuss homosexuality in the negative (SIECUS 2002)

Despite being trained to work with youth who are struggling over
emotional issues, many school counselors are not comfortable or competent enough to work with gay, lesbian, bisexual, and transgender
youth. Price and Telljohann (1991) found that of 289 secondary school
counselors, one in six believed that there were no gay students in the
school, and one in five responded that they were incompetent to counsel gay students and would not find counseling such personally gratify-
ing. Telljohann and Price (1993) later found that only about one quarter
of all gay and lesbian youth in their study mentioned they were able to
talk to their counselor about their sexual orientation.

In short, these youth are not afforded the same opportunities as
their counterparts to affirm their milestones. They probably

- do not have a gay and lesbian support group despite an

increase in the number of gay-straight alliances to 800 by
2001 (GLSEN 2001)

➥ do not have role models they can interact with and do
not feel comfortable enough to turn to their teachers,
counselors, or families

➥ do not have gay, lesbian, bisexual, and transgender
resources in their school libraries

➥ do not have access to the nearest gay and lesbian
community

Variable Risks

Research has revealed that gay, lesbian, bisexual, and transgender youth
report feeling isolated and alone. From this cognitive, social, and emotional isolation, youth can develop a number of severe problems.

Depression, Low Self-Esteem, and Anxiety

The social stigma attached to homosexuality can leave many gay, lesbian, bisexual, or transgender youth depressed. The stigma alone takes
its toll on how they feel about themselves (Lasser and Tharinger 2000).
Anthony D'Augelli and Scott Hershberger (1993), for instance, found
that 77 percent of gay boys and 62 percent of lesbian girls had experienced some form of depression. They also found that 73 percent of the
boys and 53 percent of the girls had suffered from anxiety. But how can
we expect these youth to feel good about themselves if everyone around
them is indirectly reinforcing how bad they are? In addition, they have
to deny who they really are to their closest friends, all the while worrying about what could happen if their secret was out. It should not surprise anyone that feeling lonely, unhappy, anxiety ridden, and powerless
accompanies being gay, lesbian, bisexual, or transgender.

School Failure

How can these youth be expected to excel at school when they have so
much stress to contend with? One gay youth writes, "Because people
gave me such a hard time, school was really miserable for me. And I had
no concept of how important education was. I didn't realize that it was
going to be important later. Earning money wasn't a concept to me at
the time. I just had no desire to go back to school and suffer anymore"
(Bass and Kaufman 1996, 195). Morrow (1997) indicates that many of
these youth are truant, and Ginsberg (1996) underscores that these

youth have to work harder to achieve academic and social success because their lives are relatively tumultuous.

Alcohol and Chemical Abuse

Many times persons turn to alcohol or drugs to help them cope with the challenges presented in their lives. The situation is no different for the community of gay, lesbian, bisexual, and transgender people. In fact, research has found that many of these adults are far more affected by alcoholism than the general public. James Herbert, Brandon Hunt, and Gina Dell (1994) found that the community of gay, lesbian, bisexual, and transgender persons was affected by alcoholism at rates ranging from 20 to 33 percent as compared to 10 percent of the general population. The rates for these youth are just as compelling. The Safe Schools Coalition of Washington (1999, cited in GLSEN 2000) found that 35.8 percent of these youth reported substance abuse whereas their heterosexual counterparts reported 22.5 percent (61). Another study found that 68 percent of gay youth used alcohol and 44 percent had used drugs. The lesbian youth in that study revealed that 83 percent had used alcohol, 56 percent had used drugs, and 11 percent had experiences with crack/cocaine (Rosario, Hunter, and Rotheram-Borus 1992). Alcohol abuse is about 50 percent higher and marijuana use is three times higher for youth who are gay, lesbian, or bisexual than for their heterosexual counterparts (Telljohann, Price, Poureslami, and Easton 1995).

Running Away

Unable to cope with the added pressures of being gay, lesbian, bisexual, or transgender, some youth leave their homes and others are forced out. Most of the research on street youth is outdated, but nonetheless critical. Savin-Williams (1988), for instance, found that one in four gay or bisexual males was forced out of his home because of his sexual orientation. A 1986 study found that as many as 40 percent of the street youth living in Seattle were gay, lesbian, or bisexual (Orion Center 1986). The National Gay and Lesbian Task Force (1984, cited in PERSON Project 2000) and the U.S. Department of Health and Human Services (Gibson 1989, cited in PERSON Project 2000) reported that nearly one quarter of all youth living on the streets are gay, lesbian, bisexual, or transgender. Gabe Kruks (1991) conducted one of the most recent investigations on street youth. He found that about 25 to 35 percent of the youth living on the streets of Los Angeles were gay, and about 80 percent of these cited homophobia and victimization as the main reason for running away from home.

Suicide

Some gay, lesbian, bisexual, and transgender youth unfortunately perceive suicide as an option for ending the chronic problems in their lives. One lesbian youth recounts the events that led her to attempt suicide: "Due to societal fear and ignorance, my teachers and counselors labeled my confusion as rebellion, and placed me in the category of a troubled discipline problem. But still I had nothing to identify with and no role models to guide me, to help sort out this confusion, and I began to believe that I was simply alone. A few weeks into my sophomore year, I woke up in a psych hospital after taking my father's camping knife violently to my wrists and hoping for success" (GLSEN 2000).

Suicide has been a critical problem among this youth population ever since a U.S. Department of Health and Human Services (Gibson 1989) study revealed that gay, lesbian, bisexual, and transgender youth attempt and commit suicide more often than any other group of youth. The youth in the study were two to three times more likely to attempt suicide than their heterosexual counterparts, and they constituted as much as 30 percent of the annual youth suicide. Since then, other studies have confirmed that these youth are at high risk for suicide. Gary Remafedi, James Farrow, and Robert Deisher (1991), for instance, found that of 137 gay and bisexual males between the ages of fourteen to twenty-one, 29 percent had attempted suicide and 50 percent of these youth had attempted suicide more than once. Kruks (1991) reported that 57 percent of gay youth seeking services from a Los Angeles social service had attempted suicide once, and 47 percent had indicated multiple attempts. In a more recent study, the 1995 Massachusetts Youth Risk Behavior Survey found that gay, lesbian, and bisexual youth were nearly four times more likely to have attempted suicide in the previous year than their heterosexual peers (cited in SIECUS 2002, 5). The National Coalition for Gay, Lesbian, Bisexual, and Transgender Youth (2000) survey found that of its sample, nearly 25 percent had attempted suicide with most attempts occurring around the age of fourteen. According to Patrick Healy (2001), the Massachusetts Department of Public Health found that of 4,000 students, nearly 40 percent of gay, lesbian, bisexual, and transgender youth had attempted suicide compared to 10 percent of their heterosexual peers. These are alarming statistics given that other studies consistently find that the range for suicide attempts is 6 to 10 percent for heterosexual youth (Garland and Zigler 1993).

Sexually Transmitted Diseases

Youth who do not practice safe sex (such as condom or dental dam usage) are at risk for acquiring sexually transmitted diseases (STDs), including the human immunodeficiency virus (HIV), which causes AIDS. Gay, lesbian, bisexual, and transgender youth are at a greater risk than other groups of youth for becoming infected with an STD, and gay young men are especially vulnerable. Lipkin (1999) indicates that these youth tend to acquire more STDs than their heterosexual counterparts (Remafedi 1987); a significant number in some urban areas are living with HIV (Russell 1997); gay male youth of color have higher rates of HIV infection than their white counterparts (Russell 1997); and AIDS is spreading particularly fast among urban gay and bisexual males (those between the ages of fifteen and nineteen had a 5 percent infection rate) (Haney 1996). It is not difficult to surmise why these youth encounter such risks. For one, many of these youth have such low self-esteem that they do not care what their future holds and will engage is risky sexual behaviors.

In all, feelings of isolation—actual or perceived—affect how gay, lesbian, bisexual, and transgender youth sustain themselves emotionally. Some youth adapt quite well and are empowered by a support network, role models, and so forth. Others hope for a more understanding social context. These social and school contexts are slowly evolving, and in the past decade or so schools have started to address the needs of this population. This could not have happened without the courage of those youth who pursued justice through the legal system.

LEGAL PERSPECTIVE

Since the mid-1990s, significant legal strides have been made for the social justice of gay, lesbian, bisexual, and transgender youth. Up until this point, these youth were not represented in the court system despite the injustices they encountered at school (Buckel 2000), and there is now a growing number of lawsuits filed against school districts for their failure to protect these youth from harassment and bullying (Jones 1999). In addition to notable legislation, the federal government has issued recommendations to schools on safe school environments; attorneys have more than one recourse in defending gay, lesbian, bisexual, and transgender youth, and youth groups have filed lawsuits under First Amendment protections.

Notable Litigation

The first such lawsuit was filed on behalf of gay student Jamie Nabozny in *Nabozny v. Podlesney.* Jamie was living with his family in Ashland, Wisconsin, when in middle school a peer asked him if he was gay. Jamie answered yes, and there immediately began his long and arduous battle with homophobia. Jamie was an unfortunate victim of continued verbal, physical, and sexual harassment by his peers, and school officials did little to intervene on his behalf. He was beaten, urinated on, humiliated with antigay slurs, and once wrestled to the floor and mock-raped by two boys while other students watched and laughed. He was even knocked to the floor and kicked so badly that he was hospitalized with internal bleeding. Jamie and his parents met with school officials, and he identified his attackers. His parents pleaded for intervention, yet school officials made no meaningful attempt to protect him or discipline his tormentors. According to the lawsuit, one school official even claimed that Jamie had to expect this sort of behavior because he was gay. Needless to say, Jamie was in poor shape—he suffered from posttraumatic stress disorder, he had run away from home, and he had attempted suicide multiple times. Unable to cope with the humiliation and violence, Jamie dropped out of school and moved to Minneapolis. In 1995, Jamie sued the Ashland School District for its failure to stop the harassment. A trial court initially threw out the suit, but the Seventh U.S. Circuit Court of Appeals held that Jamie was entitled to a trial. Jamie won the trial and was awarded $900,000 in punitive damages. The message was clear: "A school's failure to stop antigay abuse was unlawful...[and] students learned they were equal under the law and deserved protection from abuse so that they could finish high school" (Buckel 2000, 392).

Derek Henkle was another youth who legally challenged his school district. Derek's ordeal was very similar to Jamie's in that he endured relentless harassment to the point of being lassoed by his tormentors. Despite meetings between school officials and his parents, Derek was shuffled from school to school as if *he* were the problem. Derek filed a lawsuit against the Washoe County School District "for allowing years of merciless abuse to drive a gay student from completing high school" (Lambda 2001e). In particular, the suit charges "principals and administrators at Galena, Washoe, and Wooster High Schools, with violating the constitutional guarantee of equal protection because they refused to act decisively against the anti-gay harassment" (Lambda 2001e). As of this writing, Derek is awaiting his trial.

Timothy Dahle, another gay youth, dropped out of high school because he could no longer endure the antigay harassment at school.

He had been taunted, attacked, and pushed down a flight of stairs. He and his had parents pleaded with school officials for some protection but to no avail. Timothy's parents filed a lawsuit against the Titusville Area School District for its negligence in eradicating the verbal and physical harassment directed toward Timothy. The district argued that Timothy had brought the problems on himself because he had been "verbally aggressive toward other students" (Weiss 2002). The parties settled out of court in January 2002, and the district agreed to pay Timothy $312,000 in damages.

Several other youth are following in the footsteps of Jamie, Derek, and Timothy. In fact, lawsuits involving gay, lesbian, bisexual, and transgender youth and their school districts have been filed in California, Illinois, Minnesota, Missouri, New Jersey, and Washington (Buckel 2000). Despite how controversial, lengthy, and complicated these cases may get, these youth are courageous enough to fight to make the lives of future gay, lesbian, bisexual, and transgender youth easier. Fearing lawsuits and damages awards up to $1 million, many school districts are becoming more responsive to this population (Adriano 2002). These landmark cases clearly demonstrate that districts can no longer dismiss or trivialize any physical, verbal, or sexual harassment directed toward these youth.

Federal Guidelines and Recommendations

If school districts were unsure of how to protect gay, lesbian, bisexual, and transgender youth in the past, they should now have a better understanding since the federal government has clearly delineated how to protect all students. In January 1999, the U.S. Department of Education, Office of Civil Rights distributed *Protecting Students from Harassment and Hate Crimes: A Guide for Schools* to school districts throughout the country. (The document is available online at the department's website.) School districts were to use the report to develop sexual harassment policies and create a safe learning environment that "expects appropriate behavior and promotes tolerance, sensitivity to others' views, and cooperative interactions among students" (5). The report includes statistics on sexual harassment; criteria for identifying incidents of harassment and violence and responding to them, including working with law enforcement agencies; and procedures for establishing a supportive school environment.

Sexual orientation is addressed throughout the document. In the introductory paragraphs, for instance, the document mentions, "The Guide may also be of assistance in protecting students from harassment based on sexual orientation, religion, or other grounds that are covered by state and local laws or that schools recognize as particularly damaging to their students" (U.S. Department of Education 1999, 1). Gay and lesbian youth are specifically mentioned in the harassment section of the document:

> Sexual harassment directed at gay or lesbian students may constitute unlawful sexual harassment. For example, targeting a gay or lesbian student for physical, sexual advances may constitute sexual harassment. However, nonsexual harassing behavior directed at a student because of the student's sexual orientation does not constitute sexual harassment under the federal discrimination laws enforced by OCR. . . . A district's policy may include a statement that harassing conduct of a sexual nature, which is otherwise prohibited, is not exempted based on the sex or sexual orientation of the harasser or target of harassment. (U.S. Department of Education 1999, 5)

In a section on other types of harassment, the document specifies:

> Some state and local laws may prohibit discrimination on the basis of sexual orientation. Also, under certain circumstances, courts have permitted a remedy for harassment on the basis of sexual orientation under other federal legal authority. For example, a 1996 federal court of appeals case held that a gay student could recover for discrimination based on both sex and sexual orientation under the Equal Protection Clause of the United States Constitution in a case in which school district officials allegedly failed to protect the student to the same extent that other student were protected from harassment due to the student's sex and sexual orientation. School districts should consult appropriate state and local officials and legal counsel regarding the extent of their responsibility to address harassment of students based on sexual orientation. . . . School officials should consider whether adopting specific statement or policies regarding harassment based on sexual orientation will help to protect students from violence and damaging behavior of this sort. (8)

Hate crime is defined in the document with sexual orientation in mind: "Depending on the jurisdiction, hate or bias crimes involve criminal acts in which the victims are selected based on characteristics such as . . . sexual orientation" (U.S. Department of Education 1999, 7). The document further provides a list of probable motivation for engaging in a hate crime. These include "attacks in which the victim and perpetrator are of a different race, religion, national origin, gender, or sexual orientation, especially of such attacks; and victim's known association with activities relating to his or her race, ethnicity, religion, disability, sex, or sexual orientation (for example, attacks on participants in Black History Month programs)" (2).

Legal Recourse

When gay, lesbian, bisexual, and transgender youth encounter harassment and/or violence and school administrators ignore or dismiss their tribulation, these youth can challenge them in a court of law. David Buckel (2000) mentions that attorneys generally have several avenues for pursuing justice for their clients.

Equal Protection under the U.S. Constitution

Under the Equal Protection Clause of the U.S. Constitution all youth must be ensured their safety. School officials cannot arbitrarily decide that only girls will be protected because boys can defend themselves; in fact, they are violating the clause when they trivialize the harassment directed toward a boy because "he's a boy" or "he can take care of himself because he is a boy." Schools are in further violation when they do not offer protection to a youth because of his or her sexual orientation. Dismissing a student's plight with "She's such a tough lesbian; she can fight them off" or "All that rough play just might cure him" runs contrary to the spirit of the clause. All youth deserve equal treatment. The American Counseling Association (1999) states that "The Supreme Court has made clear that public officials may not impose discriminatory burdens or unequal treatment on gays and lesbians. . . . In the public school setting, this means, among other things, that a school district must protect students from anti-gay harassment just as it protects students from other kinds of harassment" (8).

State and Local Civil Rights Protections

Some state, city, and county laws (known as civil rights or human rights laws) prohibit discrimination toward people because of their sexual orientation. As of May 2000, eleven states prohibited sexual orientation discrimination: California, Connecticut, Hawaii, Massachusetts, Minnesota, Nevada, New Hampshire, New Jersey, Rhode Island, Vermont, and Wisconsin. A school within the jurisdiction of a law protecting gay, lesbian, bisexual, and transgender students from discrimination would

be liable if school administrators failed to intervene during some antigay harassment.

State Tort Law

Tort laws are most widely associated with personal injury lawsuits. They
are invoked to address "damage, injury, or a wrongful act done willfully,
negligently, or in circumstances involving strict liability" (*American Heritage College Dictionary* 1993, 1429). A principal, for instance, may be liable under a state tort law if he knowingly failed to protect or intervene
on behalf of a lesbian youth and she was subsequently injured in an
antigay assault.

Criminal Law

The body of laws that deal with crimes, known collectively as criminal
law, can be invoked whenever one student has assaulted another student. If some youth assaulted a transgender youth in Maine, for instance, his parents could bypass school officials and file a complaint directly with the police. The local district attorney could then prosecute
the assailant.

Title IX

Title IX of the Education Amendments of 1972 (P.L. 92-318) mandates
that schools cannot discriminate against youth based on gender.
Schools must treat all youth equally and fairly. Thus boys and girls
should have equal access to academic and extracurricular programs
whether they involve math and sciences programs, home economics,
driver's education, or athletics. Moreover, boys and girls are to have
comparable locker rooms and bathrooms. Under the law, sexual harassment is considered a source of sexual discrimination and therefore
illegal. If a student or school faculty/staff member engages in, condones, allows, or tolerates sexual harassment, he or she is facilitating
sexual discrimination and thereby violating the law (U.S. Department
of Education 1999). Most gay, lesbian, bisexual, and transgender youth
experience sexual orientation discrimination, but sometimes their experiences can be defined as sexual discrimination. Buckel (2000)
writes, "Sex discrimination may be at work when school officials respond to complaints of antigay abuse merely by observing that the targeted girl is too masculine or the targeted boy is too feminine (which is
sex stereotyping)" (394).

First Amendment Violation

Students have a right to freedom of speech. As such, school administrators cannot silence youth if they are openly gay or retaliate against them for failing to "tone it down." In Derek Henkle's case, he was openly gay and was told to stop behaving like a fag. His attorneys argued that Derek had the right to express his sexuality and that the school had violated the First Amendment. School administrators responded that they did not know that expression of sexual orientation was a constitutional right. A Nevada court ruled that "education officials should have known that high school students have the right to speak out and express their sexual orientation in school settings"(Lambda 2001c). *Protecting Students from Harassment and Hate Crimes* asserts schools must be mindful of the First Amendment and cannot regulate the content of their students' speech.

Youth Groups, the Equal Access Act, and Litigation

With the increase in the number of extracurricular clubs that focus on enhancing the dynamics between heterosexual and nonheterosexual youth has come some resistance to allowing these clubs to be created, let alone meet. Some school officials and community members simply resist the idea of youth gathering to discuss social and gay, lesbian, bisexual, or transgender issues. One group of high school students in Orange County, California, for instance, decided to form a gay-straight alliance, but school officials denied them the right to meet; they could not so much as set up a table or hang a banner at a school fair (Lambda 2001b). Their club application was denied at the school level despite the board's antidiscrimination policy, and later the students' plea was subjected to hostility. The students eventually filed a lawsuit against Orange County Unified School District officials and in less than three months a U.S. district judge ordered the district to allow the club to meet at the high school while the case proceeded (Lambda 2001b). The attorneys reached a settlement a few months thereafter, and the gay-straight alliance club members were able meet just as the other clubs did. A director for the attorneys representing the youth emphasized, "With this case, the students have been forced to teach a big lesson to the very school officials who should be helping them protect their learning environment" (cited in Lambda 2001d).

Under the Equal Access Act, high schools cannot pick and choose which clubs will be allowed to meet (Lambda 2001a). Schools officially endorse clubs that have an academic nature (curricular), and although other clubs may not have such a basis (noncurricular), they are nonetheless allowed to meet. Curricular clubs include the math club, the student council, the school band, and the German club; the chess club, the bowling club, and the skateboard club are examples of non-curricular clubs. If a district allows just one noncurricular club to meet, it must allow any group of students to meet as a club. However, if a district allows only for curricular clubs, it can institute a ban on all non-curricular clubs. Essentially a school district cannot keep youth from creating a gay-straight alliance if the district allows for a car club, the Young Democrats, and so forth.

A group of youth in Salt Lake City, Utah, met a similar fate as the youth in Orange County, California. The youth had formed the East High Gay-Straight Alliance, and shortly thereafter the school board began to ban dozens of noncurricular clubs to avoid compliance with the Equal Access Act and ultimately disband the alliance. The district went so far as to reclassify some of the clubs as "curricular" to allow their continuation, and other clubs were not reclassified at all and were still allowed to meet. For two years the district imposed a ban on noncurricular clubs. Even after the students renamed/reclassified the Gay-Straight Alliance as a curricular club (People Respecting Important Social Movements), they were denied recognition. After a long court battle, the Salt Lake City School Board changed its policy, and students were allowed to create gay-straight alliances and meet.

In sum, litigation has clearly established that school districts must intervene on behalf of gay, lesbian, bisexual, and transgender youth who have encountered sexual, physical, or verbal harassment. School officials who dismiss or trivialize a student's encounter with violence or do little to eradicate a hostile learning environment are likely to be named in a lawsuit. The federal government has been proactive and has offered recommendations to assist districts in developing policies that ultimately enhance safe school climates. A district that promotes all forms of diversity and implements a clearly articulated, antiharassment policy (such as the one found in the Appendix) that is embraced by faculty and students alike is a district that has children's best interests at heart.

SUMMARY

In the last thirty years or so, society has witnessed a visible growth of the gay, lesbian, bisexual, and transgender community. Much of this community's attention, however, has been focused on adult issues—gays in the military, adoptions by gay and lesbian adults, same-sex marriages, and so forth. The growth of the community and its attention to these issues have had a definite impact on youth who are gay, lesbian, bisexual, or transgender. In the past, these youth were silent about their sexual orientation, but now many are boldly coming out. Those who do will either be accepted by their school community or subjected to verbal, physical, or sexual harassment. Some will be humiliated. As one youth recalls: "I was pulled away from the urinal by two people. . . . My eyes were covered, and I was kicked and hit, and then they threw me in a corner, crying. I didn't even look up. At that point, I was so frightened that they were going to hit me again that I rolled over and stayed there" (Jones 1999, 29).

At one time, school administrators could ignore the needs of these youth and shirk their responsibilities to protect them. Clearly, this is no longer an option. School communities must now make a concerted effort to establish a safe and healthy climate where all youth are protected from harassment or violence regardless of their sexual orientation.

REFERENCES

abcnews.com. 2002a. "Kiss and Make Up: Dodgers Apologize to Lesbian Couple," http://more.abcnews.go.com/sections/sports/DailyNews/dodgers000824.html (cited February 2, 2002).

———. 2002b. "Out of the Closet: This Gay Pride Day, Homosexuals Have Something to Cheer About," http://abcnews.go.com/sections/wnt/DailyNews/onmymind010623.html (cited February 2, 2002).

———. 2002c. "You Helped This Happen: Falwell's Controversial Comments Draw Fire," http://abcnews.go.com/sections/politics/DailyNews/WTC_Falwell010914.html (cited February 2, 2002).

Adriano, Joneil. 2002. "A New Battle to Protect Gay Students," http://www.lambdalegal.org/cgi-bin/iowa/documents/record?record=676 (cited March 11, 2002).

American Academy of Child and Adolescent Psychiatry. 1999. *Your Adolescent: Emotional, Behavioral, and Cognitive Development from Early Childhood through the Teen Years.* New York: HarperCollins.

American Academy of Pediatrics. 2002. "Coparent or Second-Parent Adoption by Same-Sex Parents." *Pediatrics* 109(3): 339–340.

American Association of University Women. 1993. *Hostile Hallways: The AAUW Survey on Sexual Harassment in America's Schools.* Washington, DC: AAUW.

———. 2001. *Hostile Hallways: Bullying, Teasing, and Sexual Harassment in School.* Washington, DC: AAUW.

American Counseling Association. 1999. *Just the Facts about Sexual Orientation and Youth: A Primer for Principals, Educators, and School Personnel.* Alexandria, VA: American Counseling Association.

American Heritage College Dictionary. 1993. Boston: Houghton Mifflin.

American Psychological Association. 1995. *Publication Manual of the American Psychological Association.* Washington, DC: American Psychological Association.

Baker, Jean M. 2002. *How Homophobia Hurts Children: Nurturing Diversity at Home, at School, and in the Community.* Binghamton, NY: Harrington Park Press.

Bass, Ellen, and Kate Kaufman. 1996. *Free Your Mind: The Book for Gay, Lesbian, and Bisexual Youth—And Their Allies.* New York: HarperPerennial.

Bohan, Janis S. 1996. *Psychology and Sexual Orientation: Coming to Terms.* New York: Routledge.

Buckel, David S. 2000. "Legal Perspective on Ensuring a Safe and Nondiscriminatory School Environment for Lesbian, Gay, Bisexual, and Transgendered Students." *Education and Urban Society* 32(3): 390–398.

Bull, Chris. 2001. "Spielberg Yells 'Cut.'" *The Advocate* (22 May): 49.

"Bully Pulpit." 2001. *The Advocate* (28 August): 4.

Cass, Vivienne C. 1984. "Homosexual Identity Formation: Testing a Theoretical Model." *Journal of Sex Research* 20 (2): 143–167.

cnn.com. 2002a. "High Court Allows Boy Scouts to Exclude Gays," http://www.cnn.com/2000/LAW/06/28/scotus.gay.boyscouts.01/index.html (cited February 2, 2002).

———. 2002b. "Young, Gay, and Scared to Death at School," http://www.cnn.com/US/9909/23/hate.crimes.gays/index.html (cited February 2, 2002).

Coleman, Eli. 1982. "Developmental Stages of the Coming Out Process." In *Homosexuality: Social, Psychological, and Biological Issues,* edited by William Paul, James D. Weinrich, John C. Gonsiorek, and Mary E. Hotvedt. Thousand Oaks, CA: Sage.

D'Augelli, Anthony R., and Scott L. Hershberger. 1993. "Lesbian, Gay, and Bisexual Youth in Community Settings: Personal Challenges and Mental Health Problems." *American Journal of Community Psychology* 21(4): 313–318.

D'Augelli, Anthony R., and Charlotte J. Patterson. 2001. *Lesbian, Gay, and Bisexual Identities and Youth: Psychological Perspectives.* New York: Oxford University Press.

Deisher, Robert. 1989. "Adolescent Homosexuality: Preface." *Journal of Homosexuality* 17 (1–2): xiii–xv.

D'Emilio, John, and Estelle B. Freedman. 1997. *Intimate Matters: A History of Sexuality in America.* Chicago: University of Chicago Press.

Donohue, William A. 1994. "Culture Wars against the Boy Scouts." *Society* 31(4): 59–68.

Durby, Dennis D. 1994. "Gay, Lesbian, and Bisexual Youth." In *Helping Gay and Lesbian Youth: New Policies, New Programs, New Practice*, edited by Teresa DeCrescenzo. Binghamton, NY: Harrington Park Press.

Family Research Council. 2002. "FRC Opposes Pediatricians' Endorsement of Homosexual Adoption," http://www.frc.org/get/p02b01.cfm (cited February 6, 2002).

Fone, Byrne. 2000. *Homophobia: A History.* New York: Metropolitan Books.

Garland, Ann F., and Edward Zigler. 1993. "Adolescent Suicide Prevention." *American Psychologist* 48 (2): 169–182.

Gay, Lesbian, and Straight Education Network. 2000. "Just the Facts: A Fact Sheet That Summarizes Important Statistics about the Impact of Homophobia on Gay and Lesbian Youth," http://www.glsen.org/pages/sections/library/ references/015/article (cited August 11, 2000).

———. 2001. "Gay-Straight Alliances," http://www.glsen.org/templates/issues/ index.html?subject=3 (cited July 20, 2001).

———. 2002a. "Hallways Present Threat for LGBT Students," http://www. glsen.org/templates/news/record.html?section=12&record=1148 (cited February 2, 2002).

———. 2002b. "Lesbian Couple Remains 'Class Sweethearts' after Protests," http://www.glsen.org/templates/news/record.html?section=12& record= 1082 (cited February 2, 2002).

———. 2002c. "Schools Face Challenges as More Teens Come Out," http:// www.glsen.org/templates/news/record.html?section=12&record=1151 (cited February 25, 2002).

———. 2002d. "The 2001 National School Climate Survey: Lesbian, Gay, Bisexual, and Transgender Students and Their Experiences in Schools," http:// www.glsen.org/binary-data/GLSEN_ARTICLES/pdf_file/1029.pdf (cited February 28, 2002).

Geh, J. 1989. "Sullivan Tosses Suicide Report." *The Sentinel,* 2 November.

Gibson, Paul. 1989. "Gay Male and Lesbian Youth Suicide." In *Report of the Secretary's Task Force on Youth Suicide.* Washington, DC: U.S. Department of Health and Human Services.

Ginsberg, Roberta. 1996. "Silenced Voices Inside Our School." *Initiatives* 58(3): 1–15.

Glatze, Mike, and Benjie Nycum. 2001. "Youthquake: San Francisco–Based Journalists Mike Glatze and Benjie Nycum Hit the Road to Document the State of Young Gay America—A Joyful, Heartbreaking, and Sometimes Harrowing Adventure." *Out* (October): 54–62.

Gordon, Lenore. 1994. "What Do We Say When We Hear 'Faggot'?" In *Rethinking Our Classroom: Teaching for Equity and Justice,* edited by Bill Bigelow,

Linda Christensen, Stan Karp, Barbara Miner, and Bob Peterson. Milwaukee, WI: Rethinking Schools.

Grigg, William Norman. 1999. "Drawing 'Straight' with Crooked Lines." *New American* (27 September): 44.

Haffner, Debra W. 1998. "Sexual Health for American Adolescents." *Journal of Adolescent Health* 22 (6): 453–459.

Haney, Daniel Q. 1996."Study: AIDS Still Spreading Fast amongst Young Gay, Bisexual Men Having Unsafe Sex." *Bay Window,* 15 February.

Healy, Patrick. 2001. "Massachusetts Study Shows High Suicide Rate for Gay Students." *Boston Globe,* 28 February.

Herbert, James, Brandon Hunt, and Gina Dell. 1994. "Counseling Gay Men and Lesbians with Alcohol Problems." *Journal of Rehabilitation* 60(2): 52–57.

Herdt, Gilbert, and Andrew Boxer. 1996. *Children of Horizons: How Gay and Lesbian Teens Are Leading a New Way Out of the Closet.* Boston: Beacon Press.

Hogan, Steve, and Lee Hudson. 1998. *Completely Queer: The Gay and Lesbian Encyclopedia.* New York: Henry Holt.

Hunter, Joyce. 1990. "Violence against Lesbian and Gay Male Youths." *Journal of Interpersonal Violence* 5 (3): 295–300.

Hunter, Joyce, and Robert Schaecher. 1987. "Stresses on Lesbian and Gay Adolescents in Schools." *Social Work in Education* 9 (3): 180–186.

Hunter, Ski, Coleen Shannon, Jo Knox, and James I. Martin. 1998. *Lesbian, Gay, and Bisexual Youths and Adults: Knowledge for Human Services Practice.* Thousand Oaks, CA: Sage.

Isay, Richard A. 1997. *Becoming Gay: The Journey to Self-Acceptance.* New York: Henry Holt.

Johnson, Don. 1996. "The Developmental Experience of Gay/Lesbian Youth." *The Journal of College Admission* 152/153: 38–41.

Jones, Rebecca. 1999. "'I Don't Feel Safe Here Anymore': Your Legal Duty to Protect Gay Kids from Harassment." *American School Board Journal* 186(11): 27–31.

Jordan, Karen M., Jill S. Vaughan, and Katharine J. Woodworth. 1997. "I Will Survive: Lesbian, Gay, and Bisexual Youths' Experience of High School." *Journal of Gay and Lesbian Social Services* 7(14): 17–33.

Kaplan, Harold I., and Benjamin J. Sadock. 1998. *Synopsis of Psychiatry: Behavioral Sciences/Clinical Psychiatry.* 8th ed. Philadelphia: Lippincott, Williams, and Williams.

Kruks, Gabe. 1991. "Gay and Lesbian Homeless/Street Youth: Special Issues and Concerns." *Journal of Adolescent Health* 12(7): 515–518.

Lacayo, Richard. 1998. "The New Gay Struggle: The Wyoming Lynching Is Enraging, But It Hides a Deeper Truth—Gay Life, and Gay Politics, Has Changed." *Time* (26 October): 32–36.

Lambda Legal Defense and Education Fund. 2001a. "The Equal Access Act: What Does It Mean?" http://www.lambdalegal.org/cgi-bin/pages/documents/record?record=78 (cited July 27, 2001).

———. 2001b. "Gay/Straight Alliance Students Sue Orange County High School," http://www.lambdalegal.org/cgi-bin/pages/documents/record?record= 529 (cited July 27, 2001).

———. 2001c. "Henkle v. Gregory: Preliminary Victory," http://www.lambda legal.org/cgi-bin/pages/cases/record?record=128 (cited July 27, 2001).

———. 2001d. "Judge Rules El Modena High Gay-Straight Alliance Must Be Allowed to Meet," http://www.lambalegal.org/cgi-bin/pages/documents/record?record=566 (July 27, 2001).

———. 2001e. "Lambda to Sue Reno School Officials for Failing to Protect Gay Student," http://www.lambdalegal.org/cgi-bin/pages/documents/record?record=560 (cited July 27, 2001).

Lasser, Jon, and Deborah Tharinger. 2000. "Sexual Minority Youth." In *Children's Needs II: Development, Problems, and Alternatives,* edited by George C. Bear, Kathleen M. Minke, and Alex Thomas. Bethesda, MD: National Association of School Psychologists.

Leland, John, and Mark Miller. 1998. "Can Gays Convert?" *Newsweek* (17 August): 47–50.

Lerner, Jaqueline V., Richard M. Lerner, and Jordan Finkelstein. 2001. *Adolescence in America: An Encyclopedia.* 2 vols. Santa Barbara, CA: ABC-CLIO.

Lipkin, Arthur. 1999. *Understanding Homosexuality: Changing Schools.* Boulder, CO: Westview Press.

Martin, A. Damien, and Emery S. Hetrick. 1988. "The Stigmatization of the Gay and Lesbian Adolescent." *Journal of Homosexuality* 15 (1/2): 163–183.

Massachusetts Governor's Commission on Gay and Lesbian Youth. 1993. *Making Schools Safe for Gay and Lesbian Youth.* Boston: Author.

Minton, Henry L., and Gary J. McDonald. 1984. "Homosexual Identity Formation as a Developmental Process." *Journal of Homosexuality* 9 (2/3): 91–104.

Morrow, Susan L. 1997. "Career Development of Lesbian and Gay Youth: Effects of Sexual Orientation, Coming Out, and Homophobia." *Journal of Gay and Lesbian Social Services* 7(14): 1–15.

National Coalition for Gay, Lesbian, Bisexual, and Transgender Youth. 2000. "Out-Proud/OASIS Internet Survey of Queer and Questioning Youth," http://www.outproud.org (cited October 11, 2000).

National Gay and Lesbian Task Force. 1984. *Antigay/Lesbian Victimization.* Washington, DC: NGLTF.

Orion Center. 1986. *Survey of Street Youth.* Seattle: Author.

Owens, Robert E., Jr. 1998. *Queer Kids: The Challenges and Promise for Lesbian, Gay, and Bisexual Youth.* Binghamton, NY: Harrington Park Press.

PERSON Project. 2000. "Fact Sheet on LGBT Youth Health Education Needs," http://www.youth.org/loco/PERSONProject.html (cited July 20, 2001).

Philadelphia Lesbian and Gay Task Force. 1996. *Discrimination and Violence toward Lesbian Women and Gay Men in Philadelphia and Commonwealth.* Philadelphia: Author.

Price, James H., and Susan K. Telljohann. 1991. "School Counselors' Perceptions of Adolescent Homosexuals." *Journal of School Health* 61 (10): 433–438.

Remafedi, Gary. 1987. "Male Homosexuality: The Adolescent Perspective." *Pediatrics* 79 (3): 326–330.

Remafedi, Gary, James Farrow, and Robert Deisher. 1991. "Risk Factors for Attempted Suicide in Gay and Bisexual Youth." *Pediatrics* 87 (6): 869–875.

Remafedi, Gary, Michael Resnick, and Robert Blum. 1992. "Demography of Sexual Orientation in Adolescents." *Pediatrics* 89 (4) 714–721.

Rofes, Eric. 1997. "Schools: The Neglected Site of Queer Activists." *Journal of Gay and Lesbian Social Services* 7(4): xv–xx.

Rosario, M., Joyce Hunter, and M. J. Rotheram-Borus. 1992. "Unpublished Data on Lesbian Adolescents." New York: HIV Center for Clinical and Behavioral Studies, New York State Psychiatric Institute.

Russell, Sabin. 1997. "AIDS Rate Drops for Young Gays." *San Francisco Chronicle*, 23 January.

Rutenberg, Jim, and Stuart Elliot. 2000. "Advertisers Shun Talk Show as Gay Protest Gains Power." *New York Times*, 19 May, A-22.

Ryan, Caitlin, and Donna Futterman. 1997. "Lesbian and Gay Youth: Care and Counseling." *Adolescent Medicine, State of the Art Reviews* 8(2): 221.

———. 1998. *Lesbian and Gay Youth: Care and Counseling.* New York: Columbia University Press.

Safe Schools Coalition of Washington. 1999. *Eighty-three Thousand Youth: Selected Findings of Eight Population-based Studies as They Pertain to Antigay Harassment and the Safety and Well-being of Sexual Minority Students.* Seattle: Safe Schools Coalition of Washington.

Salzman, Allen. 1992. "The Boy Scouts under Siege." *American Scholar* 61 (4): 591–597.

Savin-Williams, Ritch C. 1988. "Theoretical Perspectives Accounting for Adolescent Homosexuality." *Journal of Adolescent Health Care* 9(2): 95–104.

———. 1990. *Gay and Lesbian Youth: Expressions of Identity.* New York: Hemisphere Publishing.

Shakeshaft, Charol, Laurie Mandel, Yolanda M. Johnson, Janice Sawyer, Mary Ann Hergenrother, and Ellen Barber. 1997. "Boys Call Me Cow." *Educational Leadership* 55(2): 22–25.

Shenitz, Bruce. 2002. "Fighting Back." *Out* (March): 98–113, 118–120.

SIECUS. 2002. *Lesbian, Gay, Bisexual, and Transgender Youth Issues.* SIECUS

Report Supplement 29 (4): 1–5. Available at http://www.siecus.org/pubs/ fact/fact0013.html (cited February 23, 2002).

Telljohann, Susan K., and James H. Price. 1993. "A Qualitative Examination of Adolescent Homosexuals' Life Experiences: Ramifications for Secondary School Personnel." *Journal of Homosexuality* 26(1): 41–56.

Telljohann, Susan K., James H. Price, Mohammed Poureslami, and Alyssa Easton. 1995. "Teaching about Sexual Orientation by Secondary Health Teachers." *Journal of School Health* 65(1): 18–22.

Troiden, Richard R. 1989. "The Formation of Homosexual Identities." In *Gay and Lesbian Youth,* edited by Gilbert Herdt. Binghamton, NY: Harrington Park Press.

U.S. Department of Education, Office of Civil Rights. 1999. *Protecting Students from Harassment and Hate Crimes: A Guide for Schools.* http://www.ed.gov/pubs/Harassment/harass_intro.html (cited July 6, 2001).

van Wormer, Katherine, Joel Wells, and Mary Boes. 2000. *Social Work with Lesbians, Gays, and Bisexuals.* Boston: Allyn and Bacon.

Weiss, Gerry. 2002. "Youth to Get Landmark Settlement on Anti-gay Harassment Case." *Erie Times News,* 17 January.

Westheimer, Ruth K. 2000. *Encyclopedia of Sex.* New York: Continuum.

Youth Pride Inc. 2001. "Creating Safe Schools for Lesbian and Gay Students: A Resource Guide for School Staff," http://members.tripod.com/~ twood/guide.html (cited July 20, 2001).

Chapter Two

✒ Chronology

I've never really had a hard time being lesbian. I know some gay kids go through phases where they're scared and all that, but I didn't. I'm lucky I guess. . . . My mom was okay with it, my dad doesn't even know who I am, and my friends were like "whatever." I like being a black lesbian in 2002. . . . My uncle is gay—he's way old, like 44—and he reminds me that times used to be way hard. I could say "whatever" but I'm not stupid and mean. We've come a long way, and I guess I'm smart enough to know that there are a lot of gay people who fought some nasty fights so that I could be the way I am today.

—Jasmine, Seventeen, Detroit, Michigan

Many events in the last thirty years have shaped the way gay, lesbian, bisexual, and transgender people are perceived by society today. Unsurprisingly, these events unfolded in a conservative climate, and only in the last few years has society become more tolerant of diverse sexualities. Presented here is an outline of some of the events that impacted the community, forced its members to react deliberately, and ultimately paved the way for future generations.

1960s

1967   The gay and lesbian publication *The Los Angeles Advocate* premieres. The editors write: "Homosexuals, more than ever before, are out to win their legal rights, to end the injustices against them, to experience their share of happiness in their own way. If *The Advocate* can help in achieving those goals, all the time, sweat, and money that goes into it will be well spent" ("Happy Birthday to Us" 1967, 1).

1967,
cont.
The Marines refuse to release an eighteen-year-old man who identifies himself as homosexual. He is restricted to a unit with thirty other homosexuals. Guards, attorneys, and others refer to these men as man-eaters and members of the Peter Puffer Platoon.

New York City employment applications no longer ask applicants if they are homosexual.

1968
The American Civil Liberties Union (ACLU) demands that anti-gay laws be banned. In a different matter, the ACLU defends a teacher who was fired because he (in his own home) engaged in mutual masturbation with another teacher.

At a church conference, ninety Episcopalian priests agree that homosexual acts are not morally wrong. They assert, "A homosexual relationship between two consenting adults should be judged by the same criteria as a heterosexual marriage—that is, whether it intended to foster a permanent relationship of love" ("Homosexual Acts Morally Neutral, Priests Say" 1968, 4).

The governor of California, Ronald Reagan, states that homosexuality is a "tragic disease" and should be made illegal.

The California Senate passes a bill that fires teachers who are convicted of a sexual felony, including sodomy.

Homosexual copulation is illegal in every state except Illinois.

1969
Connecticut repeals its antihomosexual laws.

The children's book *I'll Get There. It Better Be Worth the Trip,* by John Donovan is published. It is the first children's book that describes a sexual experience between two thirteen-year-old boys.

Police raid a gay bar in Greenwich Village called the Stonewall Inn. The patrons vehemently protest, and the gay rights movement begins.

Dr. Evelyn Hooker heads a task force on homosexuality for the National Institute of Mental Health. The report issued by the task force emphasizes that there is nothing inherently dangerous about homosexuality and that antigay/antisodomy laws should be abolished. The report asserts that professionals who work with youth should have a solid understanding of homosexuality.

Police raid gay bars in Chicago and arrest twenty-three patrons even though homosexual activity conducted in private is legal in Illinois.

1970s

1970   The California Federation of Teachers prepares a resolution that condemns laws against homosexuals and that suggests schoolchildren be taught that society is made up of various sexualities. The resolution asserts: "Millions of American homosexuals are harassed and intimidated by the police. . . . The government's antihomosexual policies set the tone of homosexual oppression as national policy. . . . The self-hate caused by the system's oppression is the most hideous result thereof [for a homosexual]" ("Teachers Favor Freedom for Gays" 1970, 10).

In a piece titled "The Homosexual in America," *Time* estimates that there are nearly 4 million homosexuals living in the United States.

Three universities in Chicago host a first public gay dance.

For the first time in Harvard's history, a gay student organization is officially recognized.

Two twenty-eight-year-old men in Minnesota apply for a marriage license.

About 3,000 people gather in New York City for a gay pride parade.

A *Psychology Today* poll reveals that 78 percent of the public accepts homosexuals. Eighty-three percent of men and 95 percent of women indicate they have never had a homosexual experience.

General Mills, Pillsbury, and Dayton's Department Store announce that they do not discriminate against homosexuals.

1970,   Psychiatrist Martin Hoffman writes in *Today's Education* that
cont.   teachers should strive to accept homosexual adolescents. He
           maintains that homosexuals cannot be changed and that teach-
           ers should help parents accept their children.

1971   A school counselor in Hartford, Connecticut, is suspended from
           his job after he appears on TV describing his gay advocacy work.

           More than 2,500 people march in Albany, New York, demanding
           civil rights for homosexuals.

           Five gay and lesbian people are arrested for demonstrating at
           the New York City Board of Education. They protest the anti-
           gay hiring policies that preclude known homosexuals from
           teaching.

           An eighth-grade schoolteacher is fired from the Iowa City Com-
           munity School District because he invited a member of the Uni-
           versity of Iowa Gay Liberation Front to discuss homosexuality
           with his sex education class. The students had requested dis-
           cussions about homosexuality from a relevant perspective. Crit-
           ics believe the teacher uses a teaching strategy "that doesn't take
           strong moral stands" ("Teacher Appeals Firing" 1971, 4). A few
           months later the teacher is rehired.

           The Gay Activists Alliance of Washington surveys the candidates
           for the school board. The candidates are asked (1) "Should D.C.
           youngsters be taught that homosexuality is a healthy and natu-
           ral thing? Or that it's a disease? (2) Should gay teachers be fired
           as 'degenerates'? or should they be given respect and support?
           (3) Should gay teenagers be forced to take treatment for their
           'sickness'? Or should they be taught healthy attitudes?" ("D.C.
           School Candidates Face GAA Quiz" 1971, 5).

           Parents from a Queens, New York, community demand the ban
           of Piri Thomas's autobiography *Down These Mean Streets* from
           school libraries. The book, which describes Thomas's growing
           up in East Harlem, includes a reflection on his homosexual
           encounter.

           Two young black lesbians apply for a marriage license in
           Milwaukee.

1972   A Minnesota poll of young adults between eighteen to twenty-four finds that they support homosexuals. Seventy-four percent indicate that people should not be denied a job because of their sexual orientation, 62 percent mention that laws should allow for same-sex activity between two adults, and 50 percent believe that homosexuals should be allowed to marry.

Twenty-five gay, lesbian, and heterosexual youth gather for a meeting in Woodland Hills, California, to learn about homosexuality.

A teacher in Salem, Oregon, is fired because she is rumored to be a lesbian.

The District of Columbia Board of Education passes a resolution to abolish their own antigay hiring policy. The resolution reads: "The District of Columbia Board of Education, after discussion and consideration, hereby recognizes the right of each individual to freely choose a lifestyle, as guaranteed under the Constitution and the Bill of Rights. The board further recognizes that sexual orientation, in and of itself, does not relate to ability in job performance or service" ("D.C. School Board Bans Gay Bias" 1972, 3).

Two Chicago Gay Alliance members discuss gay life with a church youth group.

The Gay Teachers Caucus is organized within the National Education Association.

Gay youth are supported at a regional conference of the National Coalition of Gay Organizations (NCGO). Two gay youth are asked to attend the NCGO national conference. Their resolution is presented and unanimously endorsed (see the resolution's demands in Sidebar 2.1).

A New Jersey school board orders that gay teacher and newly elected president of the state's Gay Activist Alliance, John N. Gish, be given a psychiatric examination. He is banished from the school campus. He later wins a court battle against the exam but goes on a hunger strike to protest his banishment.

Sidebar 2.1 Resolution Demands of Gay Youth Rights Platform, National Coalition of Gay Organizations

An end to repression of gay youth within the school and religious systems. Compulsory education is a form of imprisonment and must end. We demand the right to form our education according to our needs. Young people must have the complete knowledge to understand and unhindered rights to experience their own choices of sexuality.

An end to parental abuse of gay youth in all forms.

The right to live in a manner where we can learn the cooperation of the community rather than the oppression of the male-dominated family and society.

Not only re-affirmation of, but action upon, the repeal of the age-of-consent laws on the local, state, and federal levels.

The immediate release of all gay juvenile sisters and brothers involuntarily incarcerated in mental institutions, due solely to their sexual preferences. We further demand that sisters and brothers desiring counseling for mental and emotional problems, as a result of oppression sickness because of society and its repressive attitudes, be given proper counseling without the attempt to 'cure' them of their sexuality.

The release of all juveniles who are imprisoned for victimless sex acts.

That juvenile authorities acknowledge gay individuals and couples as suitable foster placements.

An equal voice in all matters concerning ourselves and Gay Liberation in general. We strongly urge that from now on, all groups being invited to attend any conference or convention send at least one delegate who is under 21 and make an honest evaluation of their attitudes towards Third World Gays and women.

Therefore be it resolved that we demand an end to ageism in all forms, equal privileges and rights afforded so-called 'adults,' and fair treatment with equal respect.

Therefore be it also resolved that we demand the end of ageism as it relates to younger Gays exploiting older Gays.

Source: "Bakersfield Meet Backs Gay Youth." 1972. *The Advocate* (2 August): 9.

1972,   A California school district prevents gay and lesbian people
cont.   from speaking at a high school and reprimands two teachers
who invited the discussants. The district believes that the discussants will engage in perverted and illegal sex instruction.

1973   A New Jersey school district prevents a teacher from inviting a
speaker to discuss oppression of homosexuals in the United
States with his human relations class.

Some adults become concerned with the hustling activity of
young gay males in Atlanta and Los Angeles.

PBS airs *An American Family,* a documentary on the traditional
family. By the second episode, the Loud family and 10 million
viewers learn that the nineteen-year-old son, Lance, is gay.

An American Psychiatric Association (APA) committee considers whether homosexuality should be erased from its manual of
mental disorders.

In Philadelphia, two speakers invited by a junior high school
teacher and his civics class are asked by the school principal to
leave the premises despite the fact that the principal initially approved the speaking engagement.

Despite some parent protests in Albuquerque, New Mexico,
high school students from two sociology classes strongly support a discussion on gay liberation.

The New York City Board of Education allows two high schools,
George Washington High School in Manhattan and the Bronx
High School of Science, to have a gay student club.

The National Institute of Mental Health's *Report on Homosexuality* is published and made available to the public.

In Houston, nearly 150 Lutheran youth gather to hear a gay minister talk about homosexuality. He emphasizes that an affair between two people is solely their private business.

1974   The gay rights activist group Lambda Legal Defense and Education Fund forms.

1974, *The Journal of Homosexuality* is created and one of the first cont. large-scale surveys of public attitudes toward homosexuals is published. (The findings are presented in Sidebar 2.2.)

The APA resolves that there are insufficient data to support the notion that homosexuality is an illness. Homosexuality is re-classified as an alternative sexual expression.

1975 CBS airs a TV movie, *Cage without a Key,* which features an African American lesbian adolescent.

A city of Boston grant awards $52,371 to the Charles Street Meetinghouse to develop a gay youth advocacy program. The program will serve homosexual adolescents who hustle or pros-titute themselves; the program aims to keep them from becom-ing (re-)institutionalized.

A minister from the First Baptist Temple (in Connecticut) is out-raged that sixth-grade boys at a local school must take home economics. He charges, "By having a young boy cook or sew, wearing aprons, we're pushing a boy into homosexuality" ("Home-ec for Boys Despite Baptist" 1975, 15).

The New York City Board of Education assures that teachers will not be barred from employment or fired on the basis of their homosexuality.

A Washington judge rules that a sixteen-year-old gay youth can-not be placed in a gay foster home. The youth's father had sent him to a children's home two years prior to the ruling because of his son's feminine inclinations. The youth had been placed in several group homes, but was rejected each time because of his sexual orientation.

1977 The Advocate features a special report on gay youth. In "Gay Youth: The Lonely Young," the author shares the experiences of some youth and emphasizes that these youth have very few sources for support. The article also indicates that nearly 2 mil-lion youth are gay or lesbian, most youth have their first sexual experiences with someone their own age, the gay community rarely offers the youth assistance, and some youth turn to hus-tling to survive on the streets.

Sidebar 2.2 Public Attitudes toward Homosexuality: 1970 National Survey

In a survey of 30,018 Americans:

70.2% believe that sex between persons of the same gender is always wrong;

67.4% or more believe that homosexual men should not be allowed to work as a teacher, judge, minister, doctor, and so forth;

71.7% or more believe that homosexual men should be allowed to work as a beautician, artist, musician, or florist;

73.5% agree that homosexuals are dangerous and try to become sexually involved with children;

48.8% agree that homosexuality can cause the downfall of civilization;

83.8% agree that homosexuality is obscene and vulgar;

72.9% disagree that homosexuals should be allowed to display affection for one another in public;

43.1% disagree that there should be bars serving homosexuals;

78.4% believe that homosexuals should be allowed in churches or synagogues;

68% believe that what happens between homosexuals in their own privacy is no one else's business;

80.9% indicate they would prefer not to associate with homosexuals;

64.6% think that most homosexuals are okay but still do not like them.

Source: Adapted from "Public Attitudes toward Homosexuality: Part of the 1970 National Survey by the Institute for Sex Research," by Eugene E. Levitt and Albert D. Klassen, Jr. 1974. *Journal of Homosexuality* 1 (1): 29–43.

1977,   Forward Foundation (San Antonio), Project Lambda (Boston),
cont.   Survival House (San Francisco), Growing American Youth (Los
        Angeles), and GaYouth (Oregon) are agencies that serve gay and
        lesbian youth.

        California Republican legislator John Briggs proposes a
        statewide measure to dismiss teachers (gay or straight) who
        support homosexuality. He claims: "There are many teachers
        who have a lot of abnormalities that they keep inside and don't
        project to their students. But I'm talking about a public homo-
        sexual . . . one who will advertise to the world, 'I am a homosex-
        ual and I am proud of it.' That's when they should be re-
        moved. . . . I think it's a bunch of garbage when homosexuals
        maintain they have a right to be teachers" (Oddone 1977, 15).

1978   Over $1 million are raised to support the Briggs initiative. Carl
        Karche, owner of Carl's Jr. Burgers, contributes $5,000 toward
        the initiative.

        A Dallas superintendent initially asserts that known gay teach-
        ers will be forced to resign. He later recants, saying that teachers
        are entitled to their own private lives and that gay teachers will
        not be dismissed unless it is proven that their misconduct inter-
        fered/interrupted their teaching.

        An Alaskan (Copper River) school district votes to fire teachers
        engaging in homosexuality, lesbianism, and/or sodomy. More-
        over, any openly gay or lesbian employee will be dismissed from
        his or her duties.

        The Gay National Educational Switchboard is created to inform
        callers about gay and lesbian issues.

1979   For the first time in American history, the gay, lesbian, bisexual,
        and transgender community marches and rallies in Washing-
        ton, D.C.

        Randy Rohl, seventeen, takes a boy to his Sioux Falls, South
        Dakota, prom.

        A prom for gay youth is held in Boston.

The Gay Academic Union raises scholarship funds for gay students.

Gay and Young, a New York City social service agency, receives $40,000 to enhance its efforts and drop-in center.

The Gay Youth Community Coalition of the Bay Area begins to publish the *Gay Youth Community News,* which contains articles written by and for gay and lesbian youth.

Emery Hetrick and A. Damien Martin start the Institute for the Protection of Lesbian and Gay Youth (IPLGY) in New York City.

1980s

1980   Aaron Fricke, a Rhode Island high school youth, obtains a court order allowing him to take a male date to his prom.

Jerry Hyde, a Los Angeles teacher, starts Network—a social organization for gay and lesbian youth under twenty-one. Nearly 400 youth members partake in social, "family-like" activities.

Presidential candidate George H. W. Bush informs the Los Angeles Times: "I don't think American society should be asked to accept that homosexuality is a standard which should be held up for acceptance. . . . I just don't believe that, and I'm not going to push for it" ("Bush Comes Out Hard against Gay Rights" 1980, 7). Contender Ronald Reagan is asked for his viewpoint: "My criticism of the gay rights movement is that it isn't asking for civil rights, it is asking for a recognition and acceptance of an alternative lifestyle which I do not believe society can condone, nor can I. . . . You could find that in the Bible it says that in the eyes of the Lord, this [homosexuality] is an abomination" ("Reagan Won't 'Condone' Gays, Will Take Funds from Fundamentalists" 1980, 7).

1981   Timothy Curran sues the Boy Scouts of America for firing him on the grounds that he is gay.

The National Council of Teachers of English resolves to boycott Holiday Inn for its antigay stances. The council favors policies that ban discrimination against gay and lesbian people.

1981, Louisiana senator Joe Sevario introduces a bill that allows par-
cont. ents the right to request a heterosexual teacher for their child.
This would require teachers to disclose their sexual orientation
on districts' applications.

1982 Wisconsin is the first state to pass a gay rights law.

The Illinois Gay and Lesbian Task Force sends packets of information on how to work with gay students to Chicago–area high
school counselors. The packet includes information brochures,
a number to a gay and lesbian hotline, and poster that reads,
"Your counselor has information on gay issues."

1984 Dr. Virginia Uribe, a high school science teacher and activist on
behalf of gay and lesbian students, establishes the Los Angeles
Unified School District's PROJECT 10, a support program for
gay, lesbian, and bisexual youth. The program provides them
with counseling services and factual information on sexual orientation and health.

A federal court supports an Ohio public school district's dismissal
of a guidance counselor who announced that she was bisexual.

A National Gay Task Force finds that of 2,074 gay and lesbian
adults, one fifth indicated that they had been harassed in junior
or senior high school because they had been perceived to be gay
or lesbian.

1985 The Nevada Supreme Court rules that parental rights may be
terminated when the parent undergoes a sex change.

The Virginia Supreme Court denies a father his parental rights
to his biological daughter because he is gay. The court rules,
"Continuous exposure of the child to his immoral and illicit relationship [with his lover] renders him an unfit and improper
custodian" (Schroeder 1994, 30).

More than 70 percent of persons with AIDS have been
homosexual men. About 0.1 percent have been gay youth under
twenty.

Harvey Milk High School, a school for gay and lesbian youth,
opens in New York City.

A Philadelphia Lutheran social service agency plans for a foster care system for gay youth. Gay couples and heterosexual couples alike are encouraged to apply as foster parents.

The Bobbie Andelson Youth Home, a government-supported home for gay youth, opens in Los Angeles. The home will care for gay and lesbian youth between thirteen and seventeen years old who are homeless and on the streets prostituting themselves.

The Dallas school superintendent denies the Dallas Gay Alliance permission to adopt an elementary school located in the gay community.

1986   The Institute for Continuing Education in Adolescent Health Care, the University of Minnesota Adolescent Health Program, the Department of Pediatrics, the Alcohol and Other Drug Abuse Programs, and the Minnesota Task Force for Gay and Lesbian Youth hold the first national conference on adolescent homosexuality.

1987   The gay, lesbian, bisexual, and transgender community marches and rallies in Washington, D.C., for the second time. The crowd size is estimated at 200,000.

The New Hampshire Supreme Court approves barring gay and lesbian couples from adopting children.

There are 36,000 reported AIDS cases, 72 percent of which involved homosexual or bisexual intercourse. Nearly 1.5 million Americans are believed to be infected with HIV.

The Advocate runs an article titled "Sex Education and the Gay Issue: What Are They Teaching about Us in the Schools?" The author underscores that schools do very little to teach about gay and lesbian issues.

1988   The Los Angeles County Board of Education passes a resolution that guarantees respectful treatment to all students, including those who are gay, lesbian, bisexual, or transgender. Students who use slurs against any person are subject to disciplinary action.

1988,   Texas state judge Jack Hampton comments that two "queer"
cont.   murder victims "wouldn't have been killed if they hadn't been
cruising the street picking up teenage boys."

The Society of Adolescent Medicine devotes an issue of its *Journal of Adolescent Health Care* to gay and lesbian youth.

A study finds that one half of gay and lesbian youth seeking assistance from a New York City social service agency had been physically assaulted by their parents or siblings.

1989   Massachusetts Republican governor William Weld establishes the Governor's Commission on Gay and Lesbian Youth.

The *Report of the Secretary's Task Force on Youth Suicide, Volume 3: Prevention and Interventions in Youth Suicide* projects that gay youth are two to three times more likely to attempt suicide. Gay youth make up about 30 percent of adolescent suicides.

Leslea Newman publishes the children's book *Heather Has Two Mommies.*

1990s

1990   Michael Willhoite publishes the children's book *Daddy's Roommate.*

1991   Cracker Barrel Old Country Store fires eleven employees because they are gay or perceived to be gay.

1992   MTV launches *Real World,* a reality type soap opera designed for generation X. Norman is the first gay housemate.

The FBI begins to track crimes motivated by sexual orientation.

A study finds that in a sample of youth in seventh through twelfth grades, 1 percent mention they are gay, lesbian, or bisexual, yet 11 percent are unsure of their sexual orientation.

1991   A court convicts serial murderer Jeffrey Dahmer of killing fifteen gay men and boys.

1993   President Bill Clinton lifts the fifty-year ban on "homosexuals" in the military. Since the federal government's official sanction of discrimination against gay, lesbian, and bisexual personnel, over 80,000 people had been discharged. Nearly 13,000 had been discharged since the 1980s. The president emphasizes: "The issue is not whether there should be homosexuals in the military. Everyone concedes that there are. The issue is whether men and women who can and have served with real distinction should be excluded from military service solely on the basis of their status. And I believe that they should not" (Bull 1993a, 43). Clinton ultimately announces the "don't ask, don't tell" plan that will replace the ban.

A study finds that 73 percent of gay youth and 71 percent of lesbian youth encounter verbal and physical abuse at school.

The New York City Board of Education votes to end the tenure of school chancellor Joseph Fernandez. The decision is made after an intense battle over his support for condom distribution and a gay-friendly multicultural curriculum, Children of the Rainbow, which promotes tolerance. The 443-page curriculum is designed to promote tolerance of minority groups and enhance the self-esteem of children in first through third grades. The curriculum contains three pages on gay and lesbian families. Elements of the curriculum include passages such as, "A child being raised by adults of the same gender may not have a figure of the other gender to relate to in day-to-day experiences" (Osborne 1993, 23). The bibliography recommends children's books such as *Daddy's Roommate* and *Gloria Goes to Gay Pride*.

Members of the gay, lesbian, bisexual, and transgender community march and rally in Washington, D.C. The National Parks Service estimates that about 300,000 people gathered for the event, although rally organizers estimate a crowd size of 1.1 million. In his address to the marchers, President Clinton vocalizes: "I stand with you in the struggle for equality of all Americans. . . . In this great country, founded on the principle that all people are created equal, we must learn to put aside what divides us and focus on what we share. We all want the chance to excel in our work. We all want to be safe in our communities. We all want the support and acceptance of our friends and families" (Bull 1993b, 29). (The march's seven demands are outlined in Sidebar 2.3.)

**Sidebar 2.3 Seven Demands of the April 25, 1993,
Gay Rights March on Washington, D.C.**

- Change the 1964 Civil Rights Act to forbid antigay discrimination; repeal all sodomy laws and other laws that criminalize private sexual expression between consenting adults.
- Enact massive increases in funding for AIDS education, research, and patient care; ensure universal access to health care.
- Enact legislation to end discrimination against lesbians, gays, and bisexuals in child custody, adoption, and foster care; define family to encompass the full diversity of all family structures.
- Ensure equal inclusion of lesbians, gays, and bisexuals in the educational system and in multicultural studies programs.
- Protect the right to reproductive freedom and choice; end sexist discrimination.
- End racial and ethnic discrimination.
- End discrimination and violent oppression based on sexual orientation or identification, race, religion, age, class, or AIDS/HIV infection.

Source: "Marching Orders" insert in "A Capital Idea." 1993. *The Advocate* (1 June): 31.

1993,
cont.   The comic strip "For Better or for Worse" features adolescent Lawrence coming to grips with his sexual orientation.

A study finds that most youth realize that they are gay, lesbian, or bisexual around the age of ten.

Students elect Carlos Vizcarra as their homecoming king. He is the first openly gay homecoming king at California State University, Los Angeles.

The Massachusetts Governor's Commission on Gay and Lesbian Youth encourages high school districts to (1) include sexual orientation in their antidiscrimination policies, (2) establish support groups for gay and lesbian youth, and (3) send school representatives to be trained on the needs of gay and lesbian youth. The Massachusetts governor emphasizes: "The concept of schools as safe havens must apply to all students, including gay and lesbian students. . . . This is not about a different way of life;

it is about life itself. We can take the first step toward ending gay-youth suicide by creating an atmosphere of dignity and respect for gay youth in our schools" (Bull 1993d, 53).

Simon LeVay finds that the hypothalamus of gay men are smaller than that of heterosexual men or sometimes entirely absent.

The American Association of University Women conducts a study on sexual harassment and finds that sexual harassment is pervasive in schools. *Hostile Hallways: The AAUW Survey on Sexual Harassment in America's Schools* finds that 17 percent of the sample report they have been called gay or lesbian, and 86 percent indicate that they would become "very upset" if they were called gay or lesbian.

A National Institutes of Health study finds that homosexuality may run in families. The Human Rights Campaign, a gay activists group, asserts, "When people learn that homosexuality is not a choice, they will be more willing to treat us as equal members of society" (Bull 1993c, 32). Right-wing groups respond: "Why people are homosexual is irrelevant. We're campaigning on the fact that sexual orientation is not a legitimate criterion for special rights," and "Homosexuals want to manipulate science to support their lifestyle and gain acceptance" (Bull 1993c, 32).

A Virginia judge denies a lesbian mother her parental right to her biological son, Tyler. Sharon Bottoms loses custody of her son because her own mother, Kay Bottoms, has asserted that her daughter's sexual orientation will negatively impact Tyler's psychological development. The judge awards custody to Kay because he believes that Sharon's sexual orientation is immoral and the child will grow up confused about gender differences if she raises him.

A San Francisco survey finds that of gay men seventeen to twenty-three years of age, one third engaged in at least one instance of unprotected anal intercourse within the previous six months.

A San Francisco Health Commission report finds that nearly 4 percent of gay men between seventeen and nineteen are HIV positive.

1993, New York City schools chancellor Ramon C. Cortines supports
cont. the multicultural curriculum Children of the Rainbow. He in-
sists that school districts implement the curriculum but modify
it to meet their needs. Cortines announces: "Part of the Catholic
Church's dogma is that it doesn't condone the gay lifestyle. . . .
That's where we disagree. These are social issues that have to be
dealt with in the schools" (Lopez 1994, 28).

A Harris Poll finds that 86 percent of high school youth would be
very upset if one of their peers called them gay.

1994 After an earthquake hits Southern California, televangelist Pat
Roberts claims that God caused the earthquake because God is
unhappy with gays and lesbians, supporters of legal abortions,
and the level of perversity in society.

A lesbian couple in Ovett, Mississippi, plans to build a nonprofit
community center called Camp Sister Spirit. The 120-acre property is to be used by organizations that work toward civil and
human rights and other charitable causes. The Ovett community, however, believing that the couple wants to establish a "lesbian community," becomes outraged. Schoolchildren yell at the
camp, "Hey, faggots," prompted by their bus driver. One resi-
dent mentions, "These people can pick up our little girls and
take them to this place and do whatever they want to" (Ricks
1994, 36). And a reverend states: "I would like to see their
lifestyle abandoned and have them turn to a biblical lifestyle.
My second hope is that the camp Sister Spirit group move away
if they can't be converted" (36).

Florida and New Hampshire are the only two states that explic-
itly forbid the adoption of children by gay and lesbian couples.

IKEA, a supplier of home furnishings, televises a commercial focused on a gay couple.

Surgeon General Joycelyn Elders mentions that gay and lesbian
youth are at high risk for HIV infection and should therefore be
taught how to protect themselves when they have sex. She vocalizes: "If there are young gay men out there who are not hearing the message, then we have to step in and figure out how to
get to them. . . . The federal government has a responsibility to

all of our citizens, not just the heterosexual citizens. This country has to get over the judgmental way it makes decisions and make sure we are fair to all our citizens" (Bull 1994, 34). Elders adamantly advocates for (1) the adoption of children by gay and lesbian couples, (2) gay scoutmasters in the Boy Scouts of America, (3) more open discussions about sex, and (4) suicide prevention programs aimed at gay and lesbian youth.

The Denver Police Department announces an initiative to recruit openly gay, lesbian, and bisexual officers.

The Los Angeles Unified School District announces a high school prom for gay and lesbian students.

The ABC drama *My So-Called Life* features a gay teen.

The Virginia State Court of Appeals rules that Sharon Bottoms must maintain legal custody of her son, Tyler.

The Catholic church responds to Surgeon General Joycelyn Elders's convictions: "It is one thing to defend the human rights of homosexual men and women; it is quite another to encourage, as she does, a lifestyle which puts so-called homosexual unions on par with marriage and family and condones homosexual behavior among young people" (Bull and Gallagher 1994, 26).

New York City schools chancellor Ramon C. Cortines temporarily bars Gay Men's Health Crisis (GMHC), an AIDS service group, from schools. The GMHC inadvertently distributed explicit safe-sex material intended for adults to youth peer counselors (ages twelve to twenty-four).

More than 200,000 Americans have died of AIDS.

The Fairfax County, Virginia, library system purchases 100 copies of eleven antigay books because a conservative group believes that the current resources are progay.

MTV's *Real World* debuts a gay character who is HIV positive, Pedro. The show shadows his romantic interests and relationship with another man. *The Advocate* calls this filming a "landmark for lesbians and gays on television" (Frutkin 1994, 56).

1994, cont.   Network executives demand that a gay kiss be deleted from an episode of *Melrose Place* and *Northern Exposure*.

An openly lesbian police officer announces that she will have a sex-change operation; Stephanie Thorne becomes the first openly transsexual police officer in San Francisco.

1995   In an ABC special, openly gay Olympic gold medal diver Greg Louganis discloses to Barbara Walters that he has AIDS. The media criticize him because he knowingly risked infecting a physician following a diving accident.

A *Developmental Psychology* study suggests that boys who play with dolls and wear feminine clothes have a 75 percent chance of growing up to be gay. In the same journal, another study indicates a link between womb exposure to a synthetic estrogen and lesbianism.

Judith Vigna publishes the children's book *My Two Uncles*.

California governor Pete Wilson reverses a state policy that allows gay and lesbian couples to adopt children because it "discounts marriage."

The U.S. Supreme Court rules that organizers of the Boston St. Patrick's Day parade have the constitutional right to ban gay, lesbian, bisexual, and transgender marchers.

More than 300 gay men and lesbians protest at the New York City St. Patrick's Day parade because organizers of the parade deny the Irish Lesbian and Gay Organization the opportunity to march.

On the *Jenny Jones* talk show, openly gay man Scott Amedure confesses his secret admiration for his neighbor Jonathan Schmitz. Schmitz, a heterosexual, claims he has been humiliated on national television since he had no idea that his secret admirer was another man. Shortly after the show's taping, Schmitz shoots and kills Amedure.

The Illinois State Court of Appeals rules that gay and lesbian couples can legally adopt children as a couple.

Carol and Susan of *Friends* become the first lesbian parents in a sitcom.

The Virginia Supreme Court overturns the court of appeals decision regarding Sharon Bottoms's custody of her son, Tyler. Kay Bottoms, Sharon's mother, is again granted custody.

Seventeen-year-old Kelli Peterson of Salt Lake City, Utah, decides to start a gay-straight alliance at her high school. She later asserts, "I started this group to end the misery and isolation of being gay in high school" (Snow 1996a, 24).

The Fox drama *Party of Five* features a gay violin teacher.

The Southern Poverty Law Center's KlanWatch Project of Montgomery, Alabama, finds that the number of general hate crimes increased 25 percent from 1993 to 1994. Antigay assaults accounted for 25 percent of the hate crimes reported.

An openly gay member of the Des Moines, Iowa, school board is defeated in an election because the board earlier considered a school curriculum that included discussions of homosexuality.

Even though a district in Merrimack, New Hampshire, has no enacted policy or curriculum on homosexuality, the school board votes to ban "any activity that has the purpose or effect of promoting or supporting homosexuality" (Gallagher 1995, 18) in the schools.

High school English teacher Penny Culliton faces being fired because she uses gay-themed books in her class.

Conservative Christians boycott Disney because of its decision to extend domestic partner benefits to gay and lesbian employees.

At a congressional House subcommittee hearing titled "Parents, Schools, and Values," affiliates of the Traditional Values Coalition mention that teachers imply an approval of homosexuality when they teach about tolerance.

1996   Frederick Mangione is a victim of a hate crime after two self-

1996,
cont.
proclaimed neo-Nazis in Katy, Texas, stab him to death. They explain that they had "cut up this fag real bad" (Longcope 1996, 37).

Rudy Galindo, figure skating athlete and champion, discloses that he is gay in the book *Inside Edge: A Revealing Journey into the Secret World of Figure Skating* by Christine Brennan.

The University of Notre Dame imposes restrictions on a gay and lesbian student group. Unlike other student organizations, a faculty member must monitor the Gay and Lesbians of Notre Dame and St. Mary's College, and any material distributed by the group must first be judged for Catholic doctrine consistency. Prior to this, the group was denied the opportunity to meet on campus.

The Salt Lake City School Board votes to ban all noncurricular clubs rather than permit the Gay-Straight Alliance to meet. A few weeks thereafter, the Utah state legislature bars teachers from promoting illegal conduct (homosexuality) that threatens the American moral fiber. Thus, teachers are unable to discuss gay and lesbian issues in a positive light and later protest that they are unable to condone the actions of Rosa Parks and Harriet Tubman. A state senator later expresses, "Encouraging [gay and lesbian] students who are confused about their sexual orientation to label themselves as homosexual causes psychological and emotional harm" (Snow 1996b, 23).

South Dakota and Utah have laws that ban gay marriages.

Gay youth Jamie Nabozny sues the Ashland, Wisconsin, school district for failing to protect him from youth who tormented him.

A New Hampshire school district institutes a policy banning resources that are gay and lesbian friendly.

High school teacher Veronica Berrill places a pink triangle decal on her classroom door as a symbolic gesture of tolerance. Soon after, a student's parents accuse her of recruiting students to become homosexual.

More than 700,000 people are currently infected with HIV.

The school district in Merrimack, New Hampshire, repeals a new policy that bans activities that promote sex or sexual orientation, including discussions about homosexuality.

High school track athletes at Huntington Beach High School in California are consistently harassed because their coach is openly gay. "We had people throw a bottle at us. We had kids drive by while we were running and call us fags. We had kids in class called fags" ("Unsportsmanlike Conduct" 1996, 18). One football player severely punches a track athlete while calling him antigay names.

A *USA Today*/CNN/Gallup Poll finds that over 63 percent of Americans are against same-sex marriages.

Thirty-nine states require AIDS education programs in schools. A Centers for Disease Control and Prevention report indicates that only 31 percent of the programs' teachers have been trained to discuss the topic.

A study finds that gay and bisexual males are fourteen times more likely to attempt suicide than heterosexual males. Those at highest risk are celibate homosexual males.

1997   Andrew Cunanan is profiled a gay killer.

Just seven months after passing a policy to protect students and staff from sexual orientation discrimination, a school board in Detroit votes 6–1 to eliminate the policy.

A study finds that gay and bisexual males are seven times more likely to attempt suicide than heterosexual males.

The Gay, Lesbian, and Straight Education Network holds its first national conference.

Since 1992, thirty-one gay men have been killed in gay-bashing incidents.

The National Conference of Catholic Bishops distributes a letter titled "Always Our Children" that encourages Catholic parents to unequivocally love their children, including those who are gay.

1997,
cont.

The letter reads: "God loves every person as a unique individual. . . . God does not love someone any less simply because he or she is homosexual" ("Children before Church: Catholic Bishops Say Parents Must Love Their Children—Even the Gay Ones" 1997, 13). The letter also encourages priests to accept gay, lesbians, bisexual, and transgender people in their congregations.

In Davenport, Iowa, a school board refuses to add sexual orientation to its antidiscrimination policy.

Actor Ellen Degeneres's alter ego Ellen Morgan comes out in the sitcom *Ellen.* Degeneres is also featured in a *Time* magazine front cover with the caption "Yep, I'm Gay."

Lawrence, of the comic strip, "For Better or Worse," returns, and newspapers across the country retract the strip.

In Oak Park, Illinois, gay and lesbian couples are allowed to register as domestic partners.

A school district in Utah instructs high school teacher and volleyball coach Wendy Weaver to remain silent about her sexual orientation.

The soap opera *All My Children* features a story line about a gay teen.

1998

A New Jersey superior court rules in favor of James Dale, who sued the Boy Scouts of America because they expelled him in 1990 when they learned that he is gay. The court decision reads: "There is absolutely no evidence before us . . . supporting a conclusion that a gay scoutmaster, solely because he is a homosexual, does not possess the strength of character necessary to properly care for or impart BSA humanitarian ideals to the young boys in his charge" (Meers 1998, 46). BSA emphasizes it will appeal the decision.

A Stockton, Missouri, high school band cancels its trip to Disney World because school board members find Disney's progay policies immoral.

Five high school students in San Luis Obispo, California, submit their history project on the gay movement in their school's history competition and win first prize.

More than 7,500 adolescents attend Boston's annual Gay and Straight Youth Pride Day.

Openly gay youth Jeremie Garza of Denver is asked to withdraw from his Lutheran High School because he refuses to stop wearing "gay jewelry" and a host of other gay-themed accessories.

Matthew Shepard is killed in Laramie, Wyoming.

A *Time*/CNN Poll indicates that despite an increased acceptance of gay, lesbian, bisexual, and transgender people, one third of Americans still do not accept them. One half of the sample believes that homosexuality is morally wrong.

NBC premiers *Will & Grace*, a sitcom about the friendship between a gay man and a straight woman.

There are twenty-six gay, lesbian, and bisexual characters in the season's TV lineup.

The American Family Association encourages the Texas State School Board to sell $45 million worth of Disney stock as means of protesting the gay-friendly institution; the school board continues to hold stock in liquor and gambling firms.

The forty-two largest school districts in the nation receive a D grade average from GLSEN for their lack of support of gay, lesbian, bisexual, and transgender students. About 76 percent of the districts have no formal training for their teachers on sexual orientation issues, and one district says it has no gay students in the schools.

Thirty-nine states have ex-gay ministries that want to cure their members of homosexuality. The largest concentrations are found in California (twenty-two) and Texas (fifteen).

GLSEN estimates that there are 150 gay-straight alliances in schools throughout the country.

1999   GLSEN convinces Chicago public schools officials to train forty school employees about gay issues, and they in turn train 340 social workers.

President Clinton is the first president to mention sexual orientation in a state of the union address. He asserts: "Discrimination or violence because of race or religion, ancestry or gender, disability or sexual orientation, is wrong and ought to be illegal. Therefore I call upon Congress to make the Employment Non-Discrimination Act and the Hate Crimes Prevention Act the law of the land" ("He Said It First" 1999, 15).

The U.S. Department of Education, Office of Civil Rights distributes *Protecting Students from Harassment and Hate Crimes: A Guide for Schools* to school districts throughout the country. The guide is to assist schools in developing sexual harassment policies and recommends how to establish safe school environments.

Students at Notre Dame go on a hunger strike to impel university officials to institute policies that prohibit discrimination against gays and lesbians.

In Idaho, a conservative faction opposed to the public television airing of *It's Elementary: Talking about Gay Issues in School*—a documentary about how some teachers talk about homosexuality in the classroom—places twenty-five billboards throughout the state that read, "Should public television promote the homosexual lifestyle to your children? Think about it!"

In the youth drama *Dawson's Creek*, Jack's character explores his sexuality. The show's main characters remain supportive of Jack despite some homophobic comments from other characters.

GLSEN estimates that there are about 400 gay-straight alliances throughout the country.

Disturbed by the number of gay, lesbian, and bisexual characters on television, the Christian Action Network demands that the rating HC (for homosexual content) join the ratings S (sexual situations), L (coarse language), V (violence), and D (suggestive dialogue). These ratings allow parents to monitor the shows' content before their children watch the programs.

A Michigan court orders the *Jenny Jones* show's parent company to pay $25 million to the family of slain victim Scott Amedure. Jonathan Schmitz, a heterosexual, killed Amedure after the two appeared on a show where Amedure admitted his sexual attraction to Smith. Warner Brothers promises to appeal the court's decision.

Public broadcasting stations in Cleveland, New Jersey, Iowa, New Hampshire, Indianapolis, and Orlando refuse to air *It's Elementary: Talking about Gay Issues in Schools*. Much of the opposition believes that the film will "lure children into acceptance of homosexuality" and that children as young as five will learn "deviant sexual behavior" (Schenden 1999, 63).

An *Archives of Pediatric and Adolescent Medicine* study finds that gay, lesbian, bisexual, and questioning youth are three times more likely to attempt suicide than heterosexual youth.

A GLSEN survey of 496 gay, lesbian, bisexual, and transgender youth finds that 61 percent have experienced some form of verbal harassment in school and 28 percent have endured a physical harassment.

California joins Massachusetts, Connecticut, and Wisconsin in banning antigay harassment of public school students. Students and teachers are protected from discrimination based on their sexual orientation or gender identity.

In Antelope, California, a journalism teacher is fired when he becomes a woman. More than 200 students gather to protest the board's decision and demand her reinstatement.

THE NEW MILLENNIUM

2000   On behalf of Derek Henkle, Lambda Legal Defense and Education Fund files a lawsuit against school administrators in Reno, Nevada, for allowing other youth to verbally and physically abuse Derek.

2001   The American Medical Association (AMA) proposes a resolution that advises national youth groups to extend their memberships to gay youth. The AMA believes that a ban of gay youth has egregious repercussions. This proposal is a response to the U.S. Supreme Court's decision to allow the Boy Scouts to ban gay youth and adults from becoming scoutmasters.

The American Association of University Women conducts another study on sexual harassment in schools. *Hostile Hallways: Bullying, Teasing, and Sexual Harassment in School* finds that 36 percent of the sample had been called gay or lesbian, and 73 percent indicate they would become "very upset" if they were referred to as gay or lesbian.

U.S. Census figures indicate an increase in the number of same-sex couple households. There is a 700 percent increase in these households in Delaware and Nevada; more than 400 percent in Vermont, Indiana, Nebraska, and Louisiana; and 200 percent in Connecticut, Illinois, Massachusetts, and Montana.

A GLSEN study finds that about 81 percent of gay, lesbian, bisexual, and transgender youth have been harassed because of their sexual orientation.

A Gallup Poll finds that Americans are supportive of gay, lesbian, bisexual, and transgender people.

2002   The American Academy of Pediatrics supports the adoption of children by same-sex partners.

The teacher of the year in Fort Lauderdale, Florida, Connie Hines, discloses when she accepts her award that she is lesbian.

Talk-show host Rosie O'Donnell announces that she is lesbian and advocates for the adoption of children by gay and lesbian parents.

Patrick Guerrero, an openly gay man and former mayor of his hometown Melrose, Massachusetts, is a nominee for the state's lieutenant governor.

Marc Hall, a high school senior, sues his Oshawa, Ontario,

Sidebar 2.4 National Day of Silence Card
April 10, 2002—Day of Silence

Please understand my reasons for not speaking today. I am participating in the Day of Silence, a national youth movement protesting the silence faced by lesbian, gay, bisexual, and transgender people and their allies. My deliberate silence echoes that silence, which is caused by harassment, prejudice, and discrimination. I believe that ending the silence is the first step toward fighting these injustices. Think about the voices you are not hearing today.

What are you going to do to end the silence?

Source: GLSEN. "Day of Silence Project." 2002. *The Advocate* (2 April): 34.

---

catholic school so that he can take his boyfriend to the prom. The youth cannot attend the prom if his date is male. The school remains adamant that the Catholic Church does not condone homosexuality.

In April, students in more than 1,600 high schools participate in the National Day of Silence. Students, regardless of their sexuality, do not speak for nine hours in an attempt to convey that discrimination silences people's voices. When approached by nonparticipants, the youth hand them a card that explains their political position (see Sidebar 2.4). Some schools are open to the peaceful protest and ask teachers not to call on the participants. Other schools warn that the day should not conflict with instruction.

The governor of Washington signs a bill that requires all school districts to institute antibullying policies. Washington joins seven other states in prohibiting bullying behavior in schools.

High school students in Fairfield, California, write five articles for their school newspaper on what it is like to be gay, lesbian, or bisexual. A school board member organizes parents to counter the "homosexual agenda under the guise of tolerance."

Four teachers from Hayward, California, ask to be excused from staff development training titled "Safe Schools for All: Supporting Gay, Lesbian, Bisexual, Transgender, and Questioning Youth and

2002, "Families," citing religious convictions contrary to the training. The
cont. school board denies them and the teachers retain legal counsel.

A school superintendent in Trenton, New Jersey, allocates $1,600 for the purchase of gay- and lesbian-themed books and resources for a high school library. The collection will affirm the lives of people with diverse sexualities.

Nearly 2,000 gay-straight alliances function among the nation's 26,000 high schools.

REFERENCES

Bull, Chris. 1993a. "And the Ban Played On: Behind the Scenes with Bill Clinton, Gay Activists, and the Pentagon." *The Advocate* (9 March): 37–43.

———. 1993b. "A Capital Idea." *The Advocate* (1 June): 25–29.

———. 1993c. "Mom's Fault: A Study That Says Homosexuality May Run through Families Sparks Scientific and Political Debate." *The Advocate* (24 August): 30–33.

———. 1993d. "Safety Net: The Massachusetts State Board of Education Moves to Make High Schools Safe for Gay and Lesbian Youths." *The Advocate* (7 September): 52–53.

———. 1994. "The Condom Queen Reigns: Surgeon General Joycelyn Elders Speaks Out Where the President Fears to Tread." *The Advocate* (22 March): 33–38.

Bull, Chris, and John Gallagher. 1994. "The Surgeon General's Cardinal Sin." *The Advocate* (19 April): 26.

"Bush Comes Out Hard against Gay Rights." 1980. *The Advocate* (6 March): 7.

"Children before Church: Catholic Bishops Say Parents Must Love Their Children—Even the Gay Ones." 1997. *The Advocate Report* (11 November): 13–18.

"D.C. School Board Bans Gay Bias." 1972. *The Advocate* (21 June): 3.

"D.C. School Candidates Face GAA Quiz." 1971. *The Advocate* (27 October): 5.

Frutkin, Alan. 1994. "MTV's Real Gay World." *The Advocate* (12 July): 56–57.

Gallagher, John. 1995. "Indirect Assault: Attacks on Gay-Related School Curricula Are Providing Religious Conservatives with a Powerful Organizing Tool for the 1996 Presidential Campaign." *The Advocate* (17 October): 18–19.

"Happy Birthday to Us." 1967. *The Los Angeles Advocate* (September): 1.

"He Said It First." 1999. The Advocate (2 March): 15.

"Home-ec for Boys Despite Baptists." 1975. *The Advocate* (25 January): 15.

"Homosexual Acts Morally Neutral, Priests Say." 1968. *The Los Angeles Advocate* (February): 4.

Longcope, Katy. 1996. "Blood Sport: The Brutal Staffing of a Gay Man by Neo-Nazis in Texas Provokes an Outcry Concerning Hate-crime Laws." *The Advocate* (20 February): 37–40.

Lopez, Rob. 1994. "It's Not Over Yet: New York City's New Schools Chancellor Takes Office as the Battle over 'Children of the Rainbow' Continues." *The Advocate* (19 October): 28–29.

Meers, Erik. 1998. "The Model Boy Scout." *The Advocate* (14 April): 46–48.

Oddone, Maureen. 1977. "Of All, the Most Vulnerable: Homophobia Hits the Classroom." *The Advocate* (14 December): 15.

Osborne, Duncan. 1993. "N.Y. Changes Curriculum, but the Fight Goes On." *The Advocate* (9 March): 23.

"Reagan Won't 'Condone' Gays, Will Take Funds from Fundamentalists." 1980. *The Advocate* (17 April): 7.

Ricks, Ingrid. 1994. "Mississippi Showdown: A Lesbian Couple Plans to Build a Center Dedicated to Charitable Work, but the Good Folks of Ovett, Miss., Don't Cotton to It." *The Advocate* (8 February): 36–39.

Schenden, Laurie. 1999. "School's 'Out' for Summer." *The Advocate* (8 June): 63–64.

Schroeder, Jim. 1994. "Twenty-Five Years of Courtroom Trauma." *The Advocate* (23 August): 26–31.

Snow, Kat. 1996a. "Utah High School Students Have Galvanized the State's Gay Movement—and Set the Stage for a National Debate." *The Advocate* (2 April): 24.

———. 1996b. "Utah's New Law against Gay Clubs Is Being Examined by Gay and Antigay Activists across the Nation." *The Advocate* (28 May): 23.

"Teacher Appeals Firing." 1971. *The Advocate* (26 May–8 June): 4.

"Teachers Favor Freedom for Gays." 1970. *The Los Angeles Advocate* (March): 10.

"Unsportsmanlike Conduct." 1996. *The Advocate* (23 July): 18.

Chapter Three

➳ A Historical Perspective

Some time in the 1950s, my mother and I went to see a picture. In this one small scene a flamboyant man, I think he was a waiter, makes a "nelly" comment. My mother mentioned that there were some "soft" men around. She didn't elaborate what that meant, but I inferred that they were effeminate and gay. I had never fathomed that women could be homosexual. At seventeen, I didn't even know that I could be a lesbian. I just remember hoping to run into this one gal and hoping she could be my friend. We eventually became friends and I even kissed her once, but nothing ever became of it, and she never read anything into it; her heart was toward a fellow. We lived in a pretty sheltered environment back then, so for the longest time I thought I was the only gal that liked other gals. . . . There was nothing I could do; I had to date men. That's just the way it was. You wore white gloves, you went to secretarial school, you were home by supper, and you got married. And about three years into my marriage, I went to my neighbor's house and that's when she told me her devastating news—her sister was a lesbian. She cried and cried and asked me to pray with her. All I thought was, "Hmmmm. I wonder if I could meet this sister of yours." I never did, of course, and I stayed married to a man for twenty-one years until I met Evelyn.

—Ruth, Fifty-eight, Oak Park, Illinois

Author and actor Quentin Crisp (1968), a notoriously gay and transgender gentleman wrote in his autobiography, "Even in childhood I was mad about men in uniform" (7). In *The Naked Civil Servant,* Crisp reflects on his early life (circa 1910–1920) and the experiences he had growing up overtly effeminate in England. Crisp and Ruth in the narrative are examples of how gay, lesbian, bisexual, and transgender youth have always existed in society. Most GLBT adults recount that they knew early on that their sexual orientation was fixed; they simply did not turn into adults one day and determine their sexual orientation. Historically, however, there has been a gap in the literature devoted to these youth despite the significant literature on homosexuality. One of the first pieces of research literature on gay, lesbian, bisexual, and transgender youth was published in the 1960s; not until the 1980s did this topic gather some momentum, and by the 1990s more literature was readily available. The foundation for the literature available today is in the work of Robert Deisher, A. Damien Martin, Emery Hetrick, Richard Troiden, Gary Remafedi, Ritch Savin-Williams, Eric Rofes, and Gilbert Herdt, among other scholars. This chapter presents some of the work that has provided society with a better understanding of gay, lesbian, bisexual, and transgender youth today.

1960s: INITIAL STEPS

The social sentiment of the time toward gay and lesbian adults was exceedingly conservative; homosexuality was not tolerated. If people were caught engaging in homosexual conduct even in the privacy of their homes, they were convicted of a sexual felony. In the District of Columbia, for instance, one criminal code read: "Every person who shall be convicted of taking into his or her mouth or anus the sexual organ of any other person or animal or who shall be convicted of having carnal copulation in an opening of the body except sexual parts of another person shall be fined not more than $1,000 or be imprisoned not exceeding ten years" ("The Lays of the Land: The Price of Sex around the U.S." 1968, 20).

The American Psychiatric Association (APA) maintained that homosexuality is a mental disease that can be cured. Alcoholic drinks were not served to homosexuals in New York City, homosexuals could be fired from civil service jobs, police raided homosexual hangouts, and the armed forces dismissed homosexual personnel. Considering the social attitude of the time, it is easy to understand why very few articles on these youth were published. One of the earliest articles that discussed homosexuality and youth was titled "Effeminate Homosexuality: A Disease of Childhood" and was published in 1965 by the *American Journal of Orthopsychiatry*. Even then the focus of the article was based on adult recollections. The authors, Eugene Holeman and George Winokur, examined two groups of adult male prison inmates: an active homosexual group and a heterosexual control group. The homosexual group was further divided into "grossly" effeminate and noneffeminate groups. The researchers interviewed the men and asked questions about their childhood:

1. Did you play with dolls?
2. Play with girls rather than boys?
3. Play with guns and cars?
4. Use cosmetics?
5. Were you active in contact sports?
6. Were you involved in fights?
7. Were you considered to be a sissy by your peers? (50)

Questions about early sexual behavior followed. In their analysis, the researchers found that one half of the effeminate men had had homosexual experiences by the age of ten, and only one noneffeminate homosexual had had such an experience by that age. None of the heterosexuals had had a homosexual experience. The effeminate homosexuals were more likely to engage in heterosexual sex in their early youth than their noneffeminate counterparts. The study also revealed that 75 percent of the effeminate sample had learned about homosexuality before they were thirteen years old, and only 50 percent of the noneffeminate homosexuals had learned about it by that age. The researchers concluded that effeminate behavior preceded homosexual orientation and relations. They asserted, "It appears then that the aberration is effeminacy with homosexual lustful behavior being a secondary manifestation. Effeminate homosexuality is then a disease of childhood" (Holeman and Winokur 1965, 56).

The second article of this genre was "The Early Development of Homosexuality: A Study of Adolescent Lesbians." The *American Journal of Psychiatry* published this work by Malvina Kremer and Alfred Rifkin (1969), which investigated twenty-five lesbians between the ages of twelve and seventeen. The girls were students in New York City schools, and their teachers or counselors had referred them for psychiatric evaluations because many had exhibited psychological problems (such as aggressive personality, obsessive-compulsive personality, and schizophrenia) in addition to their homosexuality. Some of the girls were "evidently" lesbian—they had "boyish" looks and had ongoing sexual experiences with other girls. Some were ambivalent about their sexuality, and other girls denied being lesbian. The researchers found that their data contradicted the Freudian understanding that a person becomes homosexual because of an "over-intimate, close-binding" attachment to the opposite-sex parent. (At the time there was widespread belief that a girl became a lesbian because she was overly attached to her father, or a boy became gay because of his emotional bonding with his mother.) None of the twenty-five girls had close-knit ties with their fathers. In fact, their fathers were either hostile, completely detached, or absent altogether from their lives, and their mothers were critical of men, often speaking negatively about their partners or men in general. The researchers concluded that lesbianism may occur without a father figure to whom a girl can attach. Kremer and Rifkin concluded: "For the patients reported in the paper the role of the female was neither rewarding, satisfying, nor desirable, while the male was dangerous and untrustworthy. Females provided these girls with whatever modicum of security they had experienced in the past. Under the pressure of pubescent drives they followed the path of lesser (not least) resistance and sought female partners" (133).

1970s: PAUCITY OF LITERATURE

The decade was still conservative despite a riot in a New York City gay bar that launched the gay and lesbian civil right movement and despite pressure by mental health professionals for the social acceptance of homosexuals. Sentiment toward homosexuality was nevertheless changing (albeit slowly), and the APA had altered its position on homosexuality early in the decade. By 1974 the APA had resolved that homosexuality is not a psychiatric illness. Despite this paradigm shift, the literature on homosexual youth was meager. In 1970, however, in *Today's Education,* the National Education Association's journal, psychiatrist and author Martin Hoffman discussed his work with homosexuality. He elaborated on the stereotypes that society held of homosexuals and emphasized that

- gay men are not necessarily effeminate and lesbian women are not necessarily masculine
- homosexuals do not seduce children
- homosexuals do settle down and live happy and productive lives
- sexual orientation cannot be changed

Hoffman asserted that teachers of homosexual youth must be mindful that effeminate boys get teased a lot and teachers should do what they can to stop this. He added that effeminate boys do not necessarily grow up to become homosexuals. He recommended that parents accept and support their children when they learn about their sexuality, and entire families should be counseled if the need arises.

Thomas Roesler and Robert Deisher (1972) published an article, "Youthful Male Homosexuality," in the *Journal of the American Medical Association.* They interviewed twenty-five homosexual males between the ages of sixteen and twenty-two and found that the average age for their first homosexual experience had been fourteen, and that most had self-identified their sexual orientation by eighteen. The authors found that the younger the youth had engaged in sex, the more likely it was that he frequented public places (parks, theaters, restrooms, and so forth) looking for sex when he got older. But when he was old enough to socialize in gay bars, he was less likely to frequent public baths. For the youth who had not come out, eight of thirteen indicated that there was a good or fair chance they would become heterosexual. For those out for a full year, four of nine mentioned that chances were good or fair that they would become straight. And nine of the thirty-three youth who had been out for over a year believed they could become straight. The youth also expressed their greatest concerns about being gay, some of which are listed in Sidebar 3.1. Roesler and Deisher found that homosexual identity develops through a series of significant events: (a) having early sexual experiences, (b) looking for others to engage in homosexual sex, (c) being introduced to the homosexual subculture, and (d) self-declaring one's sexuality.

In 1977, Thomas McKinlay, Jeffrey Kelly, and Jud Patterson published their work with a passive gay youth. Evidently, the youth was overtly effeminate and so severely passive that he could not defend himself against his peers; moreover, he was distressed because he was repeatedly ridiculed and scorned. The authors noticed that he had poor eye contact, could not tell his tormentors to stop, and would passively comply with his tormentors' requests. The authors taught him assertiveness skills, modeled the assertive behavior, allowed for him to practice his newly acquired skills, and gave him feedback on his performance. By the end of his therapy sessions, the youth had made significant strides and his behavior became convincingly firm. The authors believed that their work would be beneficial for other gay youth (or those perceived to be) whose affect had precluded them from achieving social success.

In 1978, Arnold Gilberg discussed his perspective on the psychological treatment of homosexual youth. Ultimately, he believed that youth could not change their sexual identity at the hands of a psychiatrist or any other form of therapy. He believed that psychotherapists should involve the family in a homosexual youth's therapy, and parents should be convinced to accept their child. He also asserted that psychotherapists should help homosexual youth feel more comfortable with themselves.

The following year, R. M. Gonzalez (1979) presented a case study of a homosexual youth who turned to drugs as a means of coping with

Sidebar 3.1 What Some Homosexual or Bisexual Male Youth Consider Their Greatest Problems, Circa 1972

"Acceptance from others."

"Sometimes I fear discovery."

"Blackmail."

"Discovery."

"It has to be so hidden. If you can adjust to the fact it's not socially accepted, you've got it made."

"Lack of acceptance in the straight world. The repulsion others feel toward gay persons."

"Acceptance by people. For me it is difficult at school. I have to be so careful."

"The rejection from society in general and also the rareness of love in homosexual relationships."

"Embarrassment—not being accepted."

"Not being accepted by people and being alone."

"The lack of acceptance by heterosexual society. Homosexuals have no basis of culture in which to grow."

"Homosexuals need more understanding from other people, both straight or gay."

"The fact that it is not socially accepted. I have a guilt complex because of my moral conviction that it is wrong."

"The inability of others to accept a human being for what he is."

Source: Adapted from Table 4—Question: What Do You Consider the Greatest Problem Connected with Homosexuality? in Thomas Roesler and Robert W. Deisher, 1972, "Youthful Male Homosexuality: Homosexual Experience and the Process of Developing Homosexual Identity in Males Ages 16 to 22 Years," *Journal of the American Medical Association* 219(8): 1021.

his homosexuality. The author noted that other homosexual youth used drugs to escape their homosexual urges.

1980s: EMERGENCE OF ACADEMIC RESEARCH

Some significant events of the late 1970s impacted the 1980s. The adult gay and lesbian community started to hold gay pride events throughout the country, some national marches were held at the nation's capital, and AIDS pierced the fabric of our society. The entire nation learned that having sex could prove lethal. Gay men got the most attention initially, but by the late 1980s homosexuals and heterosexuals alike had become sexually cautious. AIDS prevention programs were taught in schools, youth learned buzzwords like safe sex, no to sex, and know to sex, and scholars noticed that gay and lesbian youth were at risk for AIDS and a host of emotional problems.

Alan Malyon (1981) wrote one of the first articles of the decade, "The Homosexual Adolescent: Developmental Issues and Social Bias." He stated that health care professionals need to understand that research suggests homosexuality is a natural development and propensity. Contrary to the belief held by some professionals that adolescents struggling with their sexuality are just in a phase, Malyon emphasized that there are homosexual adolescents. As many as 10 percent of persons with same-sex interests are likely to be youth, and he advised health care professionals that these youth are not in a phase. He indicated that youth seeking mental health are likely to be anxious and confused and that mental health professionals should be supportive and approach these youth in an unbiased manner. Such professionals were encouraged to give their clients accurate information about homosexuality (for example, that it is a natural outcome), approach the social stigma as the problem, and have attitudes that facilitate the development of a positive identity. Malyon discussed how homosexual adolescents adapt to their same-sex desires—some youth repress their sexuality, others suppress their sexuality, and some come to full self-acceptance. Despite their adaptation mode, these youth are likely to find themselves in challenging situations:

> Self-acknowledged homosexual adolescents, then, are often an alienated and neglected population. The personal, social, and institutional support systems that assist the adolescent heterosexual minor are not available to the homosexual minor. As might be expected, this situation often produces rather morbid psychological consequences. The homosexual adolescent must either try to complete the developmental process in a hostile and psychologically impoverished heterosexual social environment or must decide to seek peer support and social opportunities in the homosexual community. Neither alternative is very satisfactory. The decision to remain in the heterosexual community nearly always results in estrangement and confusion. A move into the homosexual community precipitates a separation from parents, and requires premature assumption of adult responsibilities and social roles. (328)

David Wellisch, G. G. DeAngelis, and Carl Paternite (1981) investigated the individual and group therapy provided to homosexual adolescent drug users who were in residential treatment and compared it to the therapy provided to their heterosexual counterparts. The researchers found that the treatment that the homosexual youth received was no different from that given their heterosexual counterparts. In group and individual counseling sessions, however, homosexual youth talked about sex more often than did heterosexual youth. The authors believed that this was their way of circumventing the drug issue. They noted that homosexual youth were just as defensive and anxious about discussing deeper issues as heterosexual youth were.

Martin (1982) was the first scholar to emphasize the critical issues surrounding gay, lesbian, and bisexual youth. In "Learning to Hide: The Socialization of the Gay Adolescent," Martin described how these youth are a minority group that has "conflict, guilt, and anxiety" in their lives (53). He chronicled homophobia and its effect on the esteem and identity of homosexual youth. He mentioned that these youth have no role models and no familial support. Many hide in the closet, lie about who they are, and monitor their behavior—how they walk, talk, and stand—because they do not want the homosexual stigma. Martin concluded: "The young person must have access to accurate information about homosexuality and to the possibility of maintaining one's personal, social, ethical, and professional integrity with the homosexual attribute. Greater attention should be paid in sex education curricula to discussions of homosexuality as a normal variation of sexual orientation" (63).

In 1983, the American Academy of Pediatrics drafted a position statement on homosexuality and adolescence that asserted: "Teenagers, their parents, and community organizations may look to the pediatrician, for clarification of the medical and social issues involved when the question or fact of adolescent homosexual practices arise.... The American Academy of Pediatrics recognizes the physician's responsibility to provide health care for homosexual adolescents and for those young people struggling with the problems of sexual expression" (249–250). The statement further affirms that (1) homosexual experimentation in adolescence does not necessarily lead to homosexuality in adulthood, (2) youth are often aware that they are homosexual even if they appear heterosexual and engage in heterosexual conduct, and (3) under certain circumstances (juvenile detention, military boarding, and so forth) some heterosexual youth may exhibit homosexual behavior but revert to heterosexual behavior when the circumstances change. The AAP recommended that pediatricians treat their homosexual patients in a nonjudgmental fashion. The pediatrician who feels unable to treat a homosexual should politely explain his or her point of view and refer the youth to another medical professional. The AAP cautioned that homosexual youth may have secondary emotional problems because of potential difficulties at home or school or with peers.

In 1985, pediatrician William Owen discussed the medical problems associated with homosexual adolescents. He recommended that physicians ask their patients about their sexual orientation in their annual physical exam in a nonjudgmental and nonthreatening fashion. For instance, a doctor could ask, "Are you gay or straight?" or "Have you ever had sex with guys, women, both, or neither?" (279). Owen also elaborated on sexually transmitted diseases common to sexually active homosexual adolescents. He advised physicians to acquire their patients' sexual history and treat their homosexual patients with respect and understanding. Like the AAP, Owen suggested that physicians who are uncomfortable treating homosexuals refer those patients to another physician.

Remafedi (1985) wrote about adolescent homosexuality with implications for pediatricians. He applied Troiden's (1979) work on homosexual identity to the homosexual adolescent patient. He described how a youth may feel apart or different from his or her peers, discount homosexual feelings or behaviors, come out to others, and gain self-acceptance. Remafedi explained how these youth contend with the stigma associated with homosexuality and how they are at risk for a host of emotional problems. He recommended that pediatricians

- refrain from interjecting their personal bias when treating their homosexual patients
- be mindful that homosexuality is a stigma and families may be in discord and need counseling
- engage in frank and confidential discussions with their homosexual patients to ascertain their full sexual history
- regularly examine their sexually active patients
- monitor their homosexual patients' psychosocial stability
- provide some sex education

Remafedi later presented two studies in a 1987 issue of *Pediatrics*. In the first study, Remafedi (1987a) determined the stress factors in the lives of gay and lesbian youth between ages fifteen and nineteen. The twenty-nine participants were asked questions regarding family relations, employment, education, friendships, intimate relationships, sexual victimization, physical health, substance use and abuse, mental health, and impact of age on physical and mental health. The data showed that most of the youth had experienced significant difficulties with school, substance abuse, and other psychosocial problems that warranted mental health interventions. The results also showed that the youth had high rates of school avoidance, deteriorating school achievement, and serious substance abuse. Nearly one half of the youth had had problems with the law, run away from home, and acquired sexually transmitted diseases, especially ectoparasitic infestations, gonococcal illnesses, and nonspecific urethritis. Remafedi emphasized the need to attend to these youth and monitor their behavior: "Younger gay adolescents may be at higher risk for dysfunction because of emotional and physical immaturity, unfulfilled developmental needs for identification with a peer group, lack of experience, and their dependence upon parents who may be unwilling or unable to provide emotional support around the issues of homosexuality" (336).

In the second study, Remafedi (1987b) described how the participants perceived homosexuality. Specifically, he set out to answer these questions:

- What do teenagers mean when they describe themselves as homosexual?
- What is the process whereby they acquire a gay identity?
- What is the impact of homosexuality on the various aspects of their lives? (326)

He found that most of the youth believed that homosexuality is more than a sexual preference for men; to them, homosexuality is a positive attribute that indicates an emotional and physical attraction to men. Eight of the youth had become aware of their homosexuality before the age of six, and eighteen had become aware of their homosexuality between the ages of eleven and sixteen; most of the youth self-identified their sexuality at the age of fourteen. The youth were most likely to disclose their sexuality to their mothers; only five youth discussed their sexuality with their fathers. For the most part, parents were upset with this news and responded negatively and unsupportively. Twenty-seven of the youth revealed their sexual orientation to their friends, and twenty-six had at least one gay friend. Twelve youth had a friend reject them because of the news. About one half of the youth believed that homosexuality is caused by family discord and/or environmental factors, and the remaining youth attributed homosexuality to genetics or personal choice. About ten of the youth were severely affected by their religion. They indicated they felt guilt and inner conflict because of religious messages about homosexuality. Despite whatever turmoil they may have experienced, over one half of the youth were satisfied with being gay and only six wished they were straight. Remafedi concluded that adolescent homosexuality is not a passing phase since many of the youth were homosexually stable over a period of time.

In 1987, Ronald Kourany published one of the first articles regarding suicide among homosexual adolescents. Up to this point, suicide was the third leading cause of death among adolescents fifteen to nineteen years old, and suicide had risen an astounding 300 percent in twenty years. He acknowledged that the literature on suicide and homosexual youth was very limited and set to out to determine whether there was a critical need to address this population. Sixty-six members of the American Society of Adolescent Psychiatry responded to a ten-item questionnaire regarding suicide among homosexual adolescents and adolescents in general. Thirty-nine of the respondents mentioned they had no experiences with or opinions about homosexual adolescents. The remaining qualified that homosexual youth were at higher risk for suicide. Most the respondents believed that suicidal behaviors were more serious among their homosexual patients than among their heterosexual ones. The homosexual youth considered suicide for various reasons, including

1. feelings of rejection
2. self-hate, rage, and depression
3. identity problems, dependency conflict, narcissistic vulnerability, feelings of shame, embarrassment, guilt, and humiliation
4. homophobia, feelings of being different, fear of failure, plea for help

Adolescent suicide was indeed a serious problem in 1987. Kourany reminded his readers that homosexual "adolescents who face society's negative pressures, whether from family, peers, or other groups may well experience more acutely their conflicting impulses, needs, and desires. These conflicts may generate a series of negative responses, including low self-esteem, loneliness, feelings of worthlessness, rejection, and shame, all possibly culminating into depressive symptoms and suicidal gestures" (116).

That same year, Hetrick and Martin (1987) wrote an article titled "Developmental Issues and Their Resolution for Gay and Lesbian Adolescents." The authors had founded the Institute for the Protection of Lesbian and Gay Youth (IPLGY), and much of the material in the article reflected their work with the youth they had served. (IPLGY is now known as the Hetrick-Martin Institute.) They discussed three issues with which homosexual youth contend: antilocutions, discrimination, and violence. Antilocution precedes discrimination, and the two precede violence. Antilocutions are disparaging comments and negative beliefs about a hated group, such as the derogatory remarks directed at gays and lesbians (faggot and carpet muncher). Discrimination is prejudice toward gay and lesbian people plus the power to act on it. This has been addressed elsewhere, but generally discrimination ranges from being fired from a job to losing custody of a biological child because of a person's sexual orientation. And violence is the physical and verbal abuse that youth endure from parents, siblings, peers, classmates, and others. Youth encountered this treatment because they were "noticeably" gay or lesbian (flamboyant or masculine) or when they revealed their sexual orientation. The authors also discussed isolation, suicide, and other emotional problems. Based on their sample of youth who received IPLGY services, Hetrick and Martin concluded:

- Most youth feel socially and emotionally isolated. That is, they often feel they have no one to talk to and they fear being discovered, or they feel disconnected and separated from any social network, including the family.
- Most youth feel detached from their families and live in fear of the crisis sure to erupt when the family finds out about their sexual orientation. Many times youth are overwhelmed by this stress and act out by becoming truant and/or running away.
- One quarter of the youth had attempted or considered suicide.
- Nearly 90 percent of the youth had other emotional problems, such as depression or feelings of anxiety.
- One quarter of the youth were in need of emergency shelter or needed help locating other living arrangements.

In the remainder of the article, Hetrick and Martin described the strategies that youth employed to cope with being gay or lesbian. These included hiding their identity from peers and family, denying being gay or lesbian, trying to become heterosexual, degrading themselves, and engaging in cross-dressing.

Paul Paroski (1987) studied the lives of eighty-nine gay males and thirty-two lesbians who had visited a New York City clinic for youth. He discovered that most (95.5 percent) of the boys had learned about gay

---

Sidebar 3.2 Paroski's Study: The Process by Which an Adolescent Accepts His or Her Own Homosexuality

1. The realization of one's desire to have same-sex relationships and encounters.
2. The development of guilt, shame, fear of discovery of one's homosexuality, and a sense of engaging in abnormal behavior.
3. An attempt to "change" to heterosexuality through behavior and fantasy.
4. Failure to "change" sexual orientation, and subsequent development of poor self-esteem.
5. Investigation of the homosexual lifestyle through various methods including sexual activity.
6. Acceptance and development of a positive gay/lesbian identity.

Source: Table 3—The Process by Which an Adolescent Accepts His or Her Own Homosexuality in Paul A. Paroski, Jr., 1987, "Health Care Delivery and the Concerns of Gay and Lesbian Adolescents." *Journal of Adolescent Health Care* 8(2): 190.

---

life through sexual encounters, whereas most of the girls (87.5 percent) had learned about lesbianism from TV and other media. Both groups also learned about gay and lesbian life from word of mouth. Paroski also assessed their knowledge of gay and lesbian people in general. Surprisingly, most of the youth believed that gay men tend to be effeminate and lesbians tend to be masculine. More than one half of the boys thought that homosexuals are unhappy, and more than one half of the girls indicated that gay men dislike women. The youth also revealed the process by which they accepted their sexual orientation. The results are found in Sidebar 3.2, but generally the youth progressed from a realization phase to denial and then to desire, change, and full acceptance.

The latter portion of Paroski's article was on the provision of health care. The boys mentioned the importance of receiving nonjudgmental care, whereas the girls indicated they wanted a provider who would be gentle with their physical body. Both groups desired a provider who was knowledgeable about the health care needs of gay men and lesbians. The youth wanted medical and mental health professionals who

- understood that not all youth are heterosexual
- could refer them to peer support groups
- were openly gay or lesbian
- could provide them with resources on gay and lesbian issues

Joyce Hunter and Robert Schaecher (1987), both affiliated with the Institute for the Protection of Lesbian and Gay Youth, based much of their article "Stresses on Lesbian and Gay Adolescents in Schools" on their work with gay and lesbian youth in New York City. The authors reported that these youth often feel different from their peers early in their development, and feel emotionally isolated when they realized that they did not have the same sexual interests as everyone around them. The youth often "fail to develop close trusting relationships because they cannot relate in an honest way when discussing friends, sexuality, and relationships" (182) and will do whatever it takes to make others believe that they are heterosexual. One young man dated every available girl in high school so that he would be considered a ladies man among his peers. The authors also discussed that these youth were at risk for in-school harassment, rejection by family, and suicide.

In 1988, the Society of Adolescent Medicine published a special section on adolescent homosexuality in its *Journal of Adolescent Health Care* (see Sidebar 3.3 for the table of contents of the section in that issue). These papers were the proceedings of a national conference on gay and lesbian youth held in 1986. Remafedi (1988a) underscored that the articles "comprise[d] the first multidisciplinary and comprehensive group of papers on the subject of adolescent homosexuality" (94). He introduced the issue with a brief chronicle of homosexuality in Western society and emphasized that homosexuality is a fact of life to be embraced. He asserted, "The time has come, then, for adolescent health professionals to be actively involved in the care of young gays and lesbians and to promote understanding of their experiences and needs" (94).

Savin-Williams's (1988) article was the first in the series. He reported that homosexuality is common among humans (regardless of culture) and across nonhuman mammals. He elaborated on behavioral genetics, hormonal studies, and biologic normalcy, which explain that sexual orientation is biologically determined (like eye color). He went on to discuss how homosexuality was regarded in psychoanalytic and social process theories. Savin-Williams explained, "Psychoanalytic theorists generally integrate sexuality and other aspects of personality development; deviance in one arena increases the likelihood of deviance in the other" (98). There are various psychoanalytic perspectives about homosexuality; some theorists believe that homosexuals are driven away from heterosexuality, and others assert that homosexuality develops out of conflict in the preoedipal and oedipal stages. Sigmund Freud believed that people are born bisexual, and he was therefore sympathetic toward homosexuals. In a mid-1930s letter to a mother of gay son, Freud wrote "Homosexuality is assuredly no advantage, but it is nothing

---

Sidebar 3.3 Table of Contents of Special Section on Adolescent Sexuality, 1988, *Journal of Adolescent Health Care* 9(2)

---

to be ashamed of, no vice, no degradation; it cannot be classified as an illness; we consider it to be a variation of the sexual function, produced by a certain arrest of sexual development. . . . It is a great injustice to persecute homosexuality as a crime—and a cruelty, too." (1960, cited in Savin-Williams 1988, 98).

Social process theory argues that homosexuality is a learned behavior. This theory approaches homosexuality as a behavior (not a trait or an identity) existing within a social context. Savin-Williams summarized: "My leanings are toward a biologic, ethologic perspective of human behavior and homosexuality. The major premise of ethology is that all human behaviors are biologic phenomena shaped by both genetic and environmental influences, and that all behaviors have or have had direct or indirect adaptive significance" (101).

Troiden (1988) then presented his four-stage model of homosexual identity development. The model comprises (1) sensitization, (2) identity confusion, (3) identity assumption, and (4) commitment. In the sensitization stage, youth initially fail to see the personal significance of homosexuality. At this stage youth feel different from others and marginalize their sense of self. A youth may think, "I'm just not like the others," and "I don't like the things that other children like." Rarely is sexuality attached to such statements; rarely will such a child think, "I'm gay and that's why I'm not like the other kids." Some youth may have an interest in or attachment to toys predominantly used by the other gender, and may self-label as homosexual early on. If a boy, for instance, was in the habit of playing with dolls, playing dress-up or house, and desiring

---

Sidebar 3.4 Troiden's Model: Responses to Identity Confusion (Stage 2)

1. Denial: disavow homosexual feelings or actions
2. Repair: seek counseling or a "cure"
3. Avoidance: shun situations or behaviors that confirm desires
   a. Inhibit homosexually associated interest, behaviors
   b. Limit opposite-sex exposure to avoid discovery
   c. Limit exposure to information about homosexuality
   d. Anti-homosexual attitudes and actions
   e. Heterosexual immersion as means of "cure"
   f. Escapism through drug use and abuse
4. Redefinition: behavior redefined along conventional lines
   a. Special case strategy ("I'd only do this with you")
   b. Ambisexual strategy ("I guess I'm bisexual")
   c. Temporary identity strategy ("This is only a phase")
   d. Situational strategy ("It was only experimentation")
5. Acceptance: Homoeroticism accepted, more information sought

Source: Table 1—Responses to Identity Confusion (Stage 2) in Richard R. Troiden, 1988, "Homosexual Identity Development." *Journal of Adolescent Health Care* 9(2): 108.

---

to marry a prince, he may identify himself as homosexual early in his development (especially if others tell him that he is).

In the second stage, identity confusion, youth reflect on the possibility that they may be homosexual. They may develop feelings of "confusion, inner turmoil, and anxiety" (107). For the most part, males realize they are homosexual at the average age of thirteen, and females become aware of their sexuality between fourteen and sixteen. Boys tend to have homosexual experiences by fifteen, and girls start to have these experiences at around twenty. At the identity confusion stage, some youth employ coping strategies as a means to contend with the stigma attached to homosexuality (these strategies are found in Sidebar 3.4).

At the third stage, identity assumption, youth assume their homosexual identity. They tolerate being gay or lesbian, they experiment sexually, and they explore gay and lesbian culture. Troiden found that gay males reach this stage between nineteen and twenty-one, and lesbians tend to assume their sexual identity some time between twenty-one and twenty-three. Gay males arrive at this stage from a sexual standpoint—from their experiences at gay bars, parties, men's rooms, and so forth. Lesbians, however, are more affectionate. They arrive at this stage from their emotional involvements with other women.

At the fourth stage, commitment, people commit to a homosexual life. They no longer feel the need to act heterosexual, and life as a gay, lesbian, bisexual, or transgender person is easier than masquerading as straight. They start to come out to others, generally in the order of other homosexuals first, then friends and family, coworkers, employers, and the public. On average, gay males come out to heterosexuals between twenty-three and twenty-eight, and lesbians come out by the age of twenty-eight. Gay males tend to come out to parents by the age of twenty-eight, whereas lesbians tend to come out to parents by thirty. Troiden emphasized: "Homosexual identity development is not a linear, step-by-step process, nor is developmental change a matter of either progress or regression. Instead, identity development is a horizontal spiral. . . . Progress through developmental stages occurs in a back-and-forth up-and-down fashion. Characteristics of stages may overlap and recur in different ways for different people" (105).

John Gonsiorek (1988) discussed measures to enhance the mental health of gay and lesbian youth. He first explained that these youth are negatively affected by social and internalized homophobia. Many of them learn early on that society sanctions antihomosexual bias, and consequently they develop negative feelings about themselves, often having self-doubt and self-hatred; many believe themselves to be evil, inferior, and unworthy. To cope with such challenges, many of these youth deny their sexual orientation. In addition, they may cope by becoming "perfect" youth—perfect in sports and academics, popular among their peers, and immersed in hobbies. They may tolerate others making degrading remarks about or even harassing those who are gay or lesbian. He wrote:

> The challenge for gay and lesbian individuals is to develop a sophisticated decision-making process about disclosure, responding to prejudice and ostracism, and other potentially threatening situations. When is it important to take a stand? When is it too risky? What are the consequences of action or inaction? How should a response be paced and timed? In other words, gay and lesbian persons must develop the skills to perform a complex "cost-benefit analysis" when faced with external bigotry and oppression. (117)

Gonsiorek went on to discuss the difference between gay and lesbian youth. He found that gay males tend to come out abruptly, whereas lesbians tend to be more ambiguous about coming out. This he attributed to gender roles—boys cannot have emotional or physical contact with one another, yet girls can. Thus, lesbians sometimes find their emotional and sexual attachments as extensions of their friendships. He also discovered that gay males tend to be competitive, autonomous, and independent in developing their relationships, whereas lesbians are more intimate and less autonomous. Gonsiorek concluded that these youth need support groups, family support, health care and support, roles models, advocacy and education, and AIDS education.

In her article, Mary Borhek (1988) shared her experiences as a mother of a gay son (she was the author of the 1979 book *My Son Eric*). She mentioned that gay and lesbian youth often asked her if they should come out to their parents and how to best do this. They are often fearful of the disapproval that awaits them, and many fear being disavowed or disowned by their parents. She advised that if youth may be disinherited, they should hold off breaking this news until achieving financial independence. It is not uncommon for youth to disclose their sexual orientation to their family and then their family throws them out. With nowhere to turn, these youth prostitute themselves to survive.

Borhek also recommended that youth determine their motivation for coming out to their parents. She warned that coming out may not be a good idea if they are looking for their parents' approval as a means of self-acceptance. But if the motivation is to strengthen the relationship with their parents, they may explain, "Mom and Dad, I have been wanting to share something with you because it is important to me, and I care about you" (124). According to Borhek, youth cannot avoid the pain associated with coming out. Most parents, regardless of the family constellation and dynamics, are likely to be upset with the news. She explained that youth lose certain social benefits because they are homosexual. They may lose some friends, job security, protection from harassment and violence, acceptance by their religion, and the right to marry. Therefore, youth sometimes need to grieve the loss of their heterosexual identity, and parents also grieve the loss of their heterosexual child.

In his article, Jonathan Zenilman (1988) presented current information on sexually transmitted diseases (STDs) among homosexual youth. By 1986, there were nearly 13 million cases of STDs in the United States, and over 35 percent of these were among persons less than twenty-five years old. STDs had increased to an all-time high in the 1970s because the baby boomers had become sexually active and there was a more liberal social attitude toward sexual activity. Rates of STDs, especially syphilis, gonorrhea, and venereal warts, were especially high in the gay community. Zenilman attributed this to the fact that gay men tended to have more casual or anonymous sex than ever before and their sexual techniques were riskier than before. By far, the most devastating STD was HIV, and gay men still accounted for the largest group living with AIDS. As of 1986, 18,162 gay/bisexual men had AIDS. The community of gay men was definitely impacted by AIDS—by the time the article was published, gay men had started having fewer partners and were practicing safe sex. Zenilman elaborated on specific STDs (ulcerative lesions, puplar lesions, and so forth) and stressed that youth should receive some form of preventive education by health professionals, physicians, and schools.

Remafedi (1988b) concluded the series with an article on AIDS prevention for youth. At the time, over 36,000 Americans were reported to have AIDS and another 1.5 million were infected with HIV. There were 140 adolescents with AIDS; 79 percent of these had a homosexual or bisexual connection. Empirical data seemed to indicate that (1) AIDS was transmitted primarily by homosexual and bisexual males, (2) a large number of youth had AIDS, and a larger number were infected with HIV, and (3) young adults with AIDS most likely acquired the virus in their adolescence. This evidence led Remafedi to believe that gay youth were at high risk for acquiring HIV and therefore needed AIDS prevention programs. He asserted that the programs should present the AIDS prevention message "in a manner that is acceptable, realistic, clear, and nonjudgmental, culturally sensitive, and positive" (141). Moreover, he believed these programs must emphasize that youth should use a condom when they engage in sex, and those who use drugs should refrain from sharing needles. He added that the programs would be far more beneficial if they employed messages to increase gay youth's self-esteem and enhance a positive identity. Lastly, Remafedi asserted that the programs should extend beyond the classroom and into the communities where these youth live and congregate.

That same year, Martin and Hetrick (1988) published "The Stigmatization of the Gay and Lesbian Adolescent." The authors began their article with a discussion of three types of isolation—cognitive, social, and emotional—that gay and lesbian adolescents experience. Cognitive isolation stems from the fact that these youth have very little information about homosexuality from which to draw, and the information available to them is often pejorative. Martin and Hetrick provided an analogy that has since received some recognition: African American children learn early on that they are a member of a minority group, and their parents teach them how to adapt to the majority; but gay and lesbian youth do not have this luxury and are insufficiently prepared for the dynamics of the outside world. Instead they learn that homosexuals are predators, seducers, the cause of AIDS, and so forth.

Social isolation derives from the expectations of what a homosexual youth can or cannot do—the roles that homosexuals can play.

Youth learn that homosexuals are best suited for certain roles—hairdressers, florists, and so forth—and should not be teachers, cannot be Christians, or are not patriotic members of society. Under social isolation, youth must either try to pass for straight or admit their sexual orientation, which renders them discredited or discreditable. Discredited youth are those considered "obviously" gay—a flamboyant young man or masculine young woman. Discreditable youth are those who hide from the stigma of homosexuality and can pass for straight. Discredited gay and lesbian youth risk harassment, humiliation, or violence at the hands of their heterosexual peers. Discreditable youth live in fear that they will be discovered and will be exposed to similar treatment. Some youth will exercise every means possible to appear heterosexual—some get pregnant, others get married, and others harass discredited youth.

Emotional isolation comes from having few other youth or adults with whom to interact. Many of the youth served by the IPLGY mentioned they were lonely and desired the opportunity to talk to someone else like them. Many of them also had problems at home with their parents, who were more than disappointed in their child—they were angry and sometimes violent on receiving the news their child was homosexual.

Finally, the authors elaborated on the violence that homosexual youth encounter. More than 40 percent of the IPLGY youth had experienced some form of violence because of their sexual orientation; nearly one half of these mentioned they encountered violence from their parents and/or siblings.

In 1989, Joseph Harry investigated physical abuse by parents of gay males. The premise of his work was based on studies that found that gay males were more likely to report having poor relationships with their fathers or to mention that their fathers were "cold, rejecting, indifferent, hostile, or simply distant" (251). He was convinced that parents are more likely to abuse their gay children because these children fail to meet their parents' heterosexual expectations. Harry was particularly interested in fathers: "Early cross-gender behaviors may sometimes be thought to be 'cute.' However, when they are systematic and/or persistent, they take on a more ominous significance in the eyes of parents, particularly in the eyes of fathers. Fathers are usually more gender-conventional than mothers in their approach to the behaviors of children" (252).

His sample comprised seventeen gay and sixty-seven heterosexual undergraduates. They were asked to rate the level of closeness they had with their parents; the amount of physical abuse they endured from their parents (pushing, grabbing, kicking, and so forth); and their interest in particular play, such as football, basketball, dolls, and drawing.

Harry found that the gay males were less emotionally attached to their fathers than the heterosexual males, and they seemed to report more physical abuse from their parents than the heterosexual control group. He also found that the homosexual males were less likely to exhibit childhood masculinity and more likely to engage in female-based play activities. He surmised: "A history of childhood femininity is also likely to sensitize parents to the possibility of homosexual behavior during adolescence. When this history is also accompanied by weakened attachments between parents and child, the possibility of physical abuse is heightened" (259).

That same year, Nancy Sanford (1989) provided an overview of the issues affecting gay and lesbian youth. Much of her content reflected what had been published to this point. However, she offered several recommendations for medical professionals:

- Help youth feel comfortable enough to reveal their sexual orientation
- Provide their care in a safe environment—youth should be made to feel accepted, respected, and welcomed
- Understand the emotional issues with which these youth contend—assess if the patient has thoughts of suicide, running away, dropping out, and so forth
- Assess their sexual activity level—compile a complete sexual history and test for sexually transmitted diseases, including HIV
- Teach them about AIDS
- Give them clear, factual, nonbiased information about sexuality
- Provide them sex education that is specific to the needs of gay and lesbian young people
- Have resources available—associations, books, and so forth
- Assist their parents—provide them with information about gay and lesbian youth and associations that will help them to accept their children

Savin-Williams (1989) investigated the association between the self-esteem of gay and lesbian youth and coming out to parents. In particular, he wanted to know the parents' characteristics, the type of relationship they had with their children, and how these affected their child's self-esteem. Up until now, qualitative accounts indicated that parents were often displeased, disappointed, violent, and angry when they learned of their child's sexual orientation. Many gay and lesbian people reported hesitancy and stress in revealing this aspect of their lives to their parents, and many never came out to their parents. The author shared some real-life responses from youth and their dialogue with their parents:

- "You can't be gay. . . . You must be mistaken. . . . Don't come back home until we say you can."
- "You fucking queer, you goddamn faggot . . . sissy. . . . Do you actually have sex with your lover? . . . It *is* my fucking business."
- "Your mother and I have no further reason to live. I don't know what the hell we have done to deserve the treatment we are getting. Terry, you were our only hope." (2, 3)

The coming-out literature of the time advised youth not to come out to their parents unless they had a secure and positive perspective about homosexuality and a solid relationship with their parents. The Savin-Williams sample comprised 214 gay males and 103 lesbians between fourteen and twenty-three years of age. They were asked to respond to self-esteem items and questions regarding parenting, intimate relationships, and so forth such that the variables were self-esteem, parental knowledge of a child's homosexuality, satisfaction with maternal and paternal relationship, contact with parents, parents' marital status, and age of parents. Among his findings, his data suggested:

- Lesbians had higher self-esteem than gay males
- Gay males had come out to their fathers more often than lesbians had come out to theirs
- Youth reported greater satisfaction with their mothers than with their fathers
- Fathers were less likely to know that their child was gay or lesbian than were mothers
- Younger parents were more likely to know that their child was a lesbian
- Lesbians were likely to have good relationships with their fathers if the fathers knew about their daughters' sexuality
- Gay males had better relationships with their parents if the parents were young
- Mothers (but not fathers) influenced the self-esteem of lesbians
- Mothers and fathers influenced the self-esteem of gay males

⊷ Gay males had higher self-esteem if their mothers knew about their sexuality, but this was not the case if fathers knew
⊷ Gay males had higher self-esteem if they had infrequent contact with their fathers

Even though the sample lacked diversity (few racial/ethnic minorities, few high school youth), Savin-Williams's data showed, "There is reason to believe that the parents are a significant factor in the developing sense of sexual identity for gay and lesbian youth, especially in terms of comfortableness and acceptance of one's sexual orientation and in one's general self-evaluation" (5).

Eli Coleman and Gary Remafedi (1989) wrote about the challenges that gay, lesbian, and bisexual youth present to counselors. The authors reiterated that counselors and school professionals need to understand that adolescent homosexuality is not just a phase that some youth will pass through, that homosexuality is not an illness, and that no therapy can change a sexual orientation. Counselors were advised to be aware that gay and lesbian youth have a host of psychosocial problems they may have to deal with (depression, rejection, loss of friendships, suicide ideation and attempts, exposure to AIDS). Counselors were advised to create an atmosphere that encourages their clients to discuss sexuality and to initiate conversations about homosexuality. Moreover, counselors were asked to maintain a positive attitude toward homosexuality and help youth adjust to their sexual orientation. This may be difficult given some counselors' personal convictions. The authors explained, "Although some counselors are intellectually positive, their emotional responses hinder them from conveying full acceptance and encouraging homosexual or bisexual adolescents to explore or experiment with their sexuality in the same ways that they help other adolescent clients focus on their opposite-sex feelings" (38). Coleman and Remafedi also advised counselors to provide their gay and lesbian clients with accurate, realistic, nonjudgmental, sensitive, and positive information about AIDS. The very youth who need AIDS education are often absent from the classes (they have either run away, dropped out of school, or skipped classes to avoid harassment). Lastly, counselors were advised to help the families of these youth sort through such emotions as blaming themselves for the youth's sexual orientation, fearing the stigma associated with homosexuality, and fearing the future.

Philip Nader et al. (1989) conducted a comparison study among urban, suburban, incarcerated, and gay adolescents concerning their beliefs about AIDS. The authors wanted to determine the group most at risk for acquiring AIDS and consequently provide them with AIDS prevention programs. Nader and his associates surveyed the youth in four areas: their knowledge of AIDS, their perceptions about the threat of AIDS, their perceptions about preventing the acquisition of AIDS, and their perceptions about safe sex practiced by their peers. With respect to the gay youth, the authors found that the gay males did not consider themselves threatened by AIDS (even though most cases of AIDS were among gay and bisexual males), and they were more likely to report that their peers practiced safe sex (used a condom, avoided risky sexual activity). Overall, the data indicated that the incarcerated youth were in greatest need of AIDS education. The authors recommended that AIDS education programs emphasise that adolescents (a) are vulnerable to AIDS, (b) can prevent HIV infection, and (c) can influence others to practice safe sex.

Eric Rofes (1989), an openly gay former schoolteacher, published "Opening Up the Classroom Closet: Responding to the Educational Needs of Gay and Lesbian Youth" in *Harvard Educational Review.* His study focused on what gay and lesbian youth endure, including the fact that school personnel are unresponsive to their needs, are at times homophobic, are unapologetic for not supporting these youth, and are ignorant about homosexuality in general. Many teachers, parents, and other professionals believe that these youth are simply in a rebellious phase, and do not want to discuss homosexuality for fear that youth will turn to it. Many adults do not advocate for these youth because they are fearful that they will be perceived as "recruiters."

Two innovative programs were reaching out to gay and lesbian youth: Project 10 in Los Angeles and the Harvey Milk School in New York City. Project 10, whose moniker is based on research suggesting that 10 percent of the population is homosexual, was started in the fall of 1984 in response to an incident involving a seventeen-year-old gay boy who was repeatedly harassed by his peers and teachers and completely ignored by many administrators. Fed up with his situation, teacher Virginia Uribe decided that something had to be done to alleviate it. After some critical deliberation, Uribe began Project 10 as a means to prevent gay and lesbian youth from dropping out of her high school, but the project later grew into a district-wide program offering counseling and various education services. Gay and lesbian youth could choose to participate in rap groups, peer counseling, or mental health counseling. The project adapted existing literature and resources on suicide, substance abuse, and so forth to include gay and lesbian needs. Project 10 also facilitated safe school environments—harassment was not tolerated. By the time Rofes's article was published, 200–300 youth were served annually and the majority of the clients were young gay males. Meanwhile, Harvey Milk School (discussed further in Chapter 5) was created to meet the academic and psychosocial needs of gay and lesbian youth. Students learned coping skills, such as how to deal with homophobia, and they received counseling services to help them build their self-confidence.

In concluding his article, Rofes advocated for some fundamental changes in schools:

- ◆ Schools must focus on the needs of students first and worry about the political backlash later. So often parents and community members influence schools officials against the protection of gay and lesbian youth.
- ◆ Schools must discuss sex, including those topics considered taboo. Many times youth receive AIDS education, but gay young males, for instance, do not receive the realistic information they need to protect themselves.
- ◆ Teachers need to feel more comfortable talking about homosexuality in a positive, nonjudgmental manner. Teachers are often targets of witch-hunts when they implement activities about or initiate discussions of homosexuality.
- ◆ Curricula should include the work of gay and lesbian people, and teachers should discuss this work in the context of the authors' lives.
- ◆ Teachers must fully understand that positive discussions about homosexuality do not make youth gay.

Rofes poignantly asked: "Can we continue our pattern of averting our eyes from the tremendous threats to the lives of these children, or will we find the courage and commitment to educate and serve this special group of young people?" (453).

Stephen Schneider, Norman Farberow, and Gabriel Kruks (1989) studied suicide ideation and attempt in 108 young gay men. The men, whose ages ranged between sixteen and twenty-four, were asked how seriously they had considered suicide at particular stages of their life, and they answered several demographic items (information about race, ethnicity, and so forth). Initial thoughts of committing suicide occurred at the average age of sixteen years; one respondent indicated he first attempted suicide at twelve. Twelve respondents had attempted suicide once, and ten had attempted it more than once. The sample was then divided into two groups—suicide attempters and nonattempters—and the authors found that attempters were more likely to have fathers who were alcoholics, come from families where physical abuse was evident, and come from minority families. The data also revealed that attempters were more likely to have intrapersonal than interpersonal challenges (that is, contemplate suicide as a direct result of an unsuccessful relationship). The authors wrote:

> The role of a dysfunctional family in (1) providing inadequate resources
> with which to cope with homosexuality, or (2) setting the stage for
> stressful or rejecting relationships, warrants further investigation.
> It is likely that gay youths from functional families may be more able
> to mobilize resources (familial and other) with which to cope with the
> stressors associated with their incipient homosexuality: Their personal
> relationships may be more supportive, and they may more readily
> establish intimate relationships with partners (associated in this
> study with being nonsuicidal). In gay youths from dysfunctional
> families, it is difficult to determine whether stressful (and possibly
> suicidogenic) relationships are related to or independent of the youth's
> homosexuality. (392)

As the decade drew to a close, one significant contribution to this academic discourse was a special double issue of the *Journal of Homosexuality*. Nineteen authors wrote on various topics related to gay and lesbian youth (see Sidebar 3.5; readers are referred to the compilation of these in Herdt [1989a], since not every article is addressed here). Herdt (1989b) introduced the issue and explained the need to confront the challenges associated with making life better and easier for these youth. He addressed four assumptions regarding these youth—they are heterosexual, they are inverts (different from normal, seemingly unnatural) if they are not heterosexual, they are stigmatized because they are inverts, and they are homogeneous—and elaborated on how these assumptions are fallacious. The second half of the article investigated variations in the coming-out process. Herdt reported that gay youth were coming out at earlier ages; research indicated that some youth were coming out by age nineteen in 1971 (Dank 1971), sixteen in 1980 (Troiden and Goode 1980), fifteen for males and twenty for females in 1982 (Coleman 1982), and fourteen in 1987 (Remafedi 1987b). Lastly, Herdt touched on the articles in the issues and stressed: "We have just begun to open a new discourse on understanding homosexuality and adolescence. . . . There is so much that remains unknown; we barely scratched the surface of the sensibilities and culture of these young people" (33).

**Sidebar 3.5 Table of Contents of Double Issue of
1989 Journal of Homosexuality 17(1–2)**

Gay and Lesbian Youth: Part I
Adolescent Homosexuality: Preface, *Robert W. Deisher*
Introduction: Gay and Lesbian Youth, Emergent Identities, and Cultural Scenes at Home and Abroad, *Gilbert Herdt*
The Formation of Homosexual Identities, *Richard R. Troiden*
Widening Circles: An Ethnographic Profile of a Youth Group, *Camille J. Gerstel, Andrew J. Feraios, and Gilbert Herdt*
Parental Influences on the Self-Esteem of Gay and Lesbian Youths: A Reflected Appraisals Model, *Ritch C. Savin-Williams*
Sappho Was a Right-On Adolescent: Growing Up Lesbian, *Margaret Schneider*
The Development of Male Prostitution Activity among Gay and Bisexual Adolescents, *Eli Coleman*
Male Prostitution and Homosexual Identity, *Debra Boyer*
Gay Youth and AIDS, *Douglas A. Feldman*

Gay and Lesbian Youth: Part II
Lesbian and Gay Youth in England, *Ken Plummer*
Gay Liberation and Coming Out in Mexico, *Joseph M. Carrier*
Growing Up Gay or Lesbian in a Multicultural Context, *Bob Trembl, Margaret Schneider, and Carol Appathurai*
Youth, Identity, and Homosexuality: The Changing Shape of Sexual Life in Contemporary Brazil, *Richard Parker*
To Be 20 and Homosexual in France Today, *Jean Le Bitoux*
Gay Youth in Four Cultures: A Comparative Study, *Michael W. Ross*
The Life Course of Gay and Lesbian Youth: An Immodest Proposal for the Study of Lives, *Andrew M. Boxer and Bertram J. Cohler*

Camille Gerstel, Andrew Feraios, and Gilbert Herdt (1989) discussed their work with the Chicago Gay and Lesbian Youth Project. The project was based in a larger gay and lesbian community/social service center where youth were encouraged to create friendships with one another and develop self-help skills. The authors wrote, "The Youth Group thus shows itself to be not a counseling agency, but an avenue for teenage self-affirmation and development, generating leadership skills and peer networks within a future adult cohort" (84). Unsatisfied with the literature on young lesbians, Margaret Schneider (1989) interviewed twenty-five self-identified lesbians between the ages of fifteen and twenty. The women were asked questions about their coming out: how they knew they were lesbians, how they reacted to the self-revelation, and how they felt since then about being a lesbian. Schneider found that some of the respondents had initially acted according to the masculine stereotype, but were now more interested in the "femme" look. Some believed that the feminist movement was passé, others were indifferent to it, but overall the movement was a source of pride. The women indicated they did not have role models, and many questioned their future—"I can't imagine being sixty-five and still with the same person," one woman remarked, and another asked" "What happens when you get old? What happens to old lesbians?" (121). They all had positive self-identities credited to internal (strong sense of self) and external (friends) supports. One youth mentioned, "I guess I trusted my own feelings not to believe anybody else's negative one" (121). Another asserted, "All the things that made me feel different were also the things that made me feel good" (122). They all indicted that gay bars were inappropriate for them and expressed the need for a hangout of their own. In all, Schneider found that the youth had varied responses to what it means to be lesbians. Some of their responses included:

- ➡ "It's a real love and trust of women, and respect. It's something inside me that I can't explain."
- ➡ "It's just realizing something about yourself that's different. You're not going to get married and live the way your parents want you to."
- ➡ "It's not that important. Like, it's the most important unimportant issue. It's not a way of life. It's just a part of my life. You have to sneak around. It's difficult that way." (123)

Coleman (1989) discussed the events that led gay and bisexual youth to become male prostitutes. Essentially, he wanted to know why they became prostitutes, why they continue to hustle, and what impact this had on their current and future well-being. In his review of the literature, he found that there were seven categories of hustlers arranged in a caste-type system (street hustlers were the lowest ranking and the "kept boy" held the highest). Most of the youth studied were about seventeen or eighteen, although most began hustling around fourteen. Most of the youth were from working- or lower-class backgrounds, often having run away from "chaotic and disorganized" families. Many of them had been thrown out of their homes because their families could not tolerate homosexuality. Most of the youth engaged in prostitution for the money, had been exposed to alcohol or drug use in their families, and were themselves alcoholics and drug users.

Likewise, Debra Boyer (1989) added to the body of literature on young gay male hustlers. She interviewed forty-seven adolescent male prostitutes, and fifty adolescents served as a control group. The average age of the hustlers was sixteen years old, and most first became involved in prostitution at fourteen. Most of the youth were white (70.2 percent), came from homes where the parents had no more education than high school, had parents who were divorced (83 percent), and were not in school (87.2 percent). As was expected, the hustlers came from homes where physical, sexual, and psychological abuse was prevalent.

The remaining articles in the issue discussed how various cultures (English, Mexican, Canadian, French, and so forth) perceive and treat gay and lesbian youth.

1990s: PROLIFERATION OF THE LITERATURE

Things began to change for the gay and lesbian community in the1990s. The advent of AIDS brought the gay, lesbian, bisexual, and transgender community to social consciousness, and a more liberal attitude held sway in the White House. Moreover, the media coverage of the issues surrounding the community—adoption of children by gay and lesbian people, gay men and lesbians in the military, the biological source of homosexuality, and so forth—was controversial and widespread. The combination of these led to increased attention on gay and lesbian youth, and more scholars took notice.

Remafedi (1990) wrote one of the first articles of the decade in *Medical Clinics of North America*. "Fundamental Issues in the Care of Homosexual Youth" encompassed discussions about the meaning of adolescent homosexuality, the development of the homosexual identity, and some of the psychosocial problems these youth endure. Remafedi asserted that health care providers should work toward providing the following:

- Gay and lesbian youth with social support groups
- Support for their families (through organizations such as Parents, Friends, and Families of Lesbians and Gays [PFLAG])
- Accurate, reliable, factual information about being gay or lesbian (health information, ways to protect themselves from violence, how to maintain healthy relationships with other gay and lesbian people, and so forth)
- Resources to sustain support (information about the gay and lesbian community, where to find social services, accepting religious congregations, and so forth)

•• Quality medical care with periodic testing of sexually transmitted diseases

In 1991, Remafedi, Farrow, and Deisher published "Risk Factors
for Attempted Suicide in Gay and Bisexual Youth" in *Pediatrics*. The
scholars surveyed 137 young males between fourteen and twenty-one
years of age; 88 percent considered themselves gay and 12 percent identified themselves as bisexual. The results revealed that 30 percent had
attempted suicide at least once and almost 50 percent repeated similar
attempts. Eighty percent of these attempted to overdose on medication
or had self-inflicted wounds. Nearly 44 percent indicated familial problems as the source for a suicide attempt. The data also indicated that
youth who attempted suicide were more likely to be feminine, had come
out to others at younger ages, had had homosexual and heterosexual experiences at younger ages, and were more likely to have used illicit
drugs than those gay males who had not attempted suicide. The authors
underscored: "One third of all suicide attempts were attributed to personal or interpersonal turmoil about homosexuality. One third of first
attempts occurred in the same year that subjects identified their bisexuality or homosexuality, and most other attempts happened soon thereafter. The apparent connection between sexual milestones and attempts may be a clue to the appropriate timing of the suicide
prevention efforts" (873).

That year, Kruks (1991) discussed his experiences in operating a
youth center for gay and lesbian homeless youth of Los Angeles. His
center served nearly 2,500 youth annually, and of these he found that
the majority were gay (65–70 percent) and most of them were males (88
percent) between the ages of eighteen and twenty-three; 17 percent
were between thirteen and seventeen years old. Many of these youth
had left their homes to escape familial discord and/or peer torment and
had expected to live in urban communities that were more accepting.
Once they arrived in Los Angeles, however, many found themselves
homeless, exploited, and involved in survival sex. Unsurprisingly, more
than one half of the gay street youth had attempted suicide. Kruks noted
that many of the youth had low self-esteem and believed that the best
they deserved was life on the street as prostitutes. Many of them were
vulnerable, easily exploited, and often trapped in a cycle where they believed they would be cared for by a "sugar daddy."

In 1991, the *Journal of Homosexuality* devoted another issue to
gay and lesbian youth but the focus this time was on the school. Eleven
articles appeared in this issue, appropriately titled "Coming Out of the
Classroom Closet: Gay and Lesbian Students, Teachers, and Curricula"

**Sidebar 3.6 Table of Contents of 1991 Double Issue
of *Journal of Homosexuality* 22(3–4)**

Introduction, Karen M. Harbeck

Addressing the Needs of Lesbian, Gay, and Bisexual Youth: The Origins of PROJECT 10 and School-Based Intervention, *Virginia Uribe and Karen M. Harbeck*

Educators, Homosexuality, and Homosexual Students: Are Personal Feelings Related to Professional Beliefs? *James T. Sears*

Liberal Attitudes and Homophobic Acts: The Paradoxes of Homosexual Experience in a Liberal Institution, *William P. Norris*

Gay and Lesbian Educators: Past History/Future Prospects, *Karen M. Harbeck*

Living in Two Worlds: The Identity Management Strategies Used by Lesbian Physical Educators, *Sherry E. Woods and Karen M. Harbeck*

From Hiding Out to Coming Out: Empowering Lesbian and Gay Educators, *Pat Griffin*

Images of Gays and Lesbians in Sexuality and Health Textbooks, *Marianne H. Whatley*

Teaching Lesbian/Gay Development: From Oppression to Exceptionality, *Anthony R. D'Augelli*

Educating Mental Health Professionals about Gay and Lesbian Issues, *Bianca Cody Murphy*

HIV Education for Gay, Lesbian, and Bisexual Youth: Personal Risk, Personal Power, and the Community of Conscience, *Kevin Cranston*

(see Sidebar 3.6; since not the articles are addressed here, readers are referred to the compilation of these in Harbeck 1992). The first article discussed PROJECT 10 of the Los Angeles School Unified School District. Virginia Uribe and Karen Harbeck (1991) wrote:

> PROJECT 10 . . .was originally envisioned as an in-school counseling program providing emotional support, information, resources, and referrals to young people who identified themselves as lesbian, gay, or bisexual or who wanted accurate information on the subject of sexual orientation. A second goal of the program was to heighten the school community's acceptance of and sensitivity to gay, lesbian, and bisexual issues. Subsequently, PROJECT 10 had become a district-wide and nationwide forum for the articulation of the needs of lesbian, gay, and bisexual teenagers. (11)

By the 1997–1998 school year, PROJECT 10 was available district-wide. Between 1984 and 1987, the authors collected data on two groups of youth—one was a group of 50 gay, lesbian, and bisexual youth, and the other was 342 randomly selected youth. The results from the former sample indicated that gay, lesbian, and bisexual youth were physically and verbally harassed at school and the frequency and intensity of the harassment increased as the students got older. Many of the students noted that some youth had dropped out of school because their experiences were too distressing; to escape the torment, many emphasized that they had to act heterosexual. The results from the latter sample were very supportive of PROJECT 10. In fact, much of the data suggested that teachers and students engaged in discussions about the project and about homosexuality in general, and many students felt that the project was worthwhile and critical for the needs of gay, lesbian, and bisexual youth.

James Sears (1991) began his article with student narratives that suggested that teachers were detached from and seemingly unconcerned with the issues surrounding gay and lesbian youth. One student wrote "I would think that a student would be quicker to want to talk to teachers if they had been kind to them. If they had just started talking to me on a personal basis. Just to talk about interest, 'Well, how's the rest of school? What do you like to do? I hear you're in chorus.' I might have more easily been able to bring it up" (34).

Sears then assessed prospective teachers' attitudes and feelings toward gay and lesbian people. The prospective teachers were given two scales to complete: the Index of Homophobia and Attitudes toward Homosexuality. The results found that eight out of ten prospective teachers had negative feelings toward gays and lesbians, and one third were considered "high-grade homophobics" (40). In particular, future elementary education teachers were more likely to express negative feelings and attitudes toward gay and lesbian people than were future secondary education teachers, and African American future teachers were more likely to hold negative attitudes and feelings toward gays and lesbians than were their white counterparts. The study found that one out of five future teachers had been friends with someone who was gay or lesbian and were consequently more likely to hold less negative feelings toward GLBT people in general.

The respondents were also surveyed on their knowledge of homosexuality. The results indicated that most of the future teachers had adequate knowledge about homosexuality, although many of them were unaware that most people engage in homosexual behaviors sometime in their life and that same-sex behaviors occur in many animal species. In all, white future teachers were more knowledgeable about homosexuality than their African American counterparts, secondary education respondents were more knowledgeable than elementary education respondents, and males were more knowledgeable than females. Unsurprisingly, the more knowledge a respondent had about homosexuality, the less likely he or she was to have negative attitudes and feelings toward gay and lesbian people. Sears also assessed high school counselors and found that two thirds of the sample held negative attitudes and feelings toward gay and lesbian people. Counselors whose duties were more administratively focused were found to have more negative feelings and attitudes than their counterparts who were therapy focused, and counselors who were white, male, or had more education were more likely to have a positive attitude toward gay and lesbian persons. Sears was disturbed by the negativism reflected in the data and recommended that educators receive professional development that deals with teachers' emotions about homosexuality.

The last article in the series was on HIV/AIDS education/prevention for gay, lesbian, and bisexual youth. Kevin Cranston (1991) emphasized that even though AIDS/HIV education was widespread in schools, much of the content failed to address the needs of gay, lesbian, and bisexual youth. In fact, he alleged that the content assumed that all youth are heterosexual. He recommended that these youth needed a comprehensive health education program that simultaneously enhanced their self-esteem and taught them decisionmaking, relationship-building, and negotiating skills. In all, Cranston wanted to empower these youth with the skills, information, and resources to sustain healthy sexual lives.

James Price and Susan Telljohann (1991) conducted a study of 289 high school counselors' perceptions of adolescent homosexuals. The authors understood that these youth were at risk for a host of problems and that the school counselor was the likely source of support given that peers, parents, teachers, and others often held antihomosexual attitudes. Prior research (Rudolph 1988) had found that nearly one third of counselors in a graduate program were concerned about homosexuality, so the authors set forth to answer these questions:

- ⇢ Have school counselors assisted adolescent homosexuals?
- ⇢ How did they find out about these students?
- ⇢ How were the students assisted?
- ⇢ How competent do school counselors feel they are in assisting adolescent homosexuals?
- ⇢ What do they perceive as their role in dealing with this population?
- ⇢ Where have school counselors received most of their information regarding homosexuality?
- ⇢ What are the perceptions of school counselors regarding adolescent homosexuality?

> ➼ Do the perceptions of school counselors vary by age, gender, and number of years as a counselor? (436)

The counselors answered demographic questions and twenty items regarding adolescent homosexuality. The results found that of the respondents:

> ➼ Nearly 67 percent estimated that 1 to 5 percent of students were gay
> ➼ More than 15 percent of counselors thought there were no gay students in their school
> ➼ 71 percent had counseled a homosexual student
> ➼ They were more likely to counsel a gay male than a lesbian student
> ➼ 25 percent thought they were competent in their counseling ability, whereas 20 percent thought they were not very competent
> ➼ 20 percent did not find counseling homosexual students gratifying
> ➼ 41 percent thought that schools were not doing enough for homosexual adolescents

The authors were concerned with the data and indicated: "When working with this population, school counselors and other school personnel should be open minded and competent in dealing with homosexual issues. The first step toward this goal involves admitting the presence of homosexuals attending high school" (436). They made some recommendations, among them (1) graduate preparation programs should address adolescent homosexuality, (2) districts should provide training on gay and lesbian adolescent issues for counselors, (3) professional literature should be made available to counselors, (4) schools should offer group support for these youth, and (5) counselors should collaborate with other school professionals to ensure that students receive accurate information about homosexuality.

In 1992, Gary Remafedi, Michael Resnick, Robert Blum, and Linda Harris conducted a large-scale empirical study of sexual orientation among adolescents in a Minnesota public school system. The authors surveyed 36,714 youth in seventh through twelfth grades to ascertain their sexual orientation self-identification, sexual attractions/ behavioral intent, sexual experiences, and sexual fantasies. Most of the youth (88.2 percent) in the study identified themselves as heterosexual and a small percentage (0.4 percent) reported themselves as homosexual; 10.7 percent indicated they were "unsure" of their sexual orientation. The data indicated that as youth got older, the percentage of "unsure" reports decreased (from 25.9 percent of twelve-year-olds to 5 percent of eighteen-year-olds). Youth who were "unsure" were more likely to be male, nonwhite, and from a lower socioeconomic status. Despite the age of the youth, the rates of self-identified homosexuals were low (from 0.2 percent to 0.5 percent). The rate of homosexual attractions, however, increased as the youth got older; overall, 4.5 percent of the youth reported homosexual attractions, but the group of eighteen-year-olds reported a higher figure of 6.4 percent. About 1 percent of the sample indicated they had had some homosexual experience, and about 3 percent of the sample reported having bisexual or homosexual fantasies. Religion and gender played a factor to some degree. More than 50 percent of the homosexual boys and 25 percent of the bisexual boys indicated they were not very religious, and the same held true for boys who had homosexual or bisexual attractions. Boys who had not had homosexual experiences or homosexual attractions were more likely to consider themselves religious. In terms of gender, boys were more likely to label themselves as predominantly homosexual, girls were more likely to report having homosexual attractions, and girls were more likely to report having bisexual or homosexual fantasies.

That same year, Leo Treadway and John Yoakam (1992) discussed how schools could enhance their environments to make academic life better for gay and lesbian youth. The authors, like Rofes (1989) before them, found that teachers were often unaware of who was gay or lesbian. Many youth intentionally hid this information from their teachers and peers, but teachers and counselors were often unaware that these youth might be in their school. When asked if any students had revealed that they were gay or lesbian, one school professional exclaimed, "We don't have that problem in this school" (353). The authors emphasized that school personnel should

- ➥ promote respect for individual differences and teach youth to appreciate diversity
- ➥ teach counselors how to support youth who are questioning their sexuality
- ➥ train counselors that if they are uncomfortable with discussing homosexuality or their personal convictions are contrary to lending support to gay and lesbian youth they should refer such youth to someone who is more objective and supportive

- provide pamphlets that let youth know that counseling is available
- display posters that inform youth how to support or maintain a supportive friendship with someone who is gay or lesbian
- create environments where disparaging remarks about gay and lesbian people are not tolerated

In 1993 the Massachusetts Governor's Commission on Gay and Lesbian Youth issued an education report titled, "Making Schools Safe for Gay and Lesbian Youth: Breaking the Silence in Schools and in Families." Disturbed by the statistics on gay and lesbian adolescent suicide, Governor William F. Weld established the commission to ensure that Massachusetts schools would be safe for and supportive of these youth. The commission sought to abolish the prejudice, isolation, and harassment these youth faced and support them in realizing their academic and social potential. The commission sponsored five public hearings where youth, parents, family members, teachers, health professionals, and others were able to vocalize the injustices visited on them. The hearings revealed that these youth encountered enormous social and emotional obstacles because they were rejected by their peers and subjected to severe hostility. Some of the testimonies captured in the report are chilling. One youth mentioned: "Last year at my high school, there was an incident which shocked everyone. Two female students were standing in the hall with their arms around each other. Students began to encircle them and yell profanities, until a group of about thirty kids surrounded them" (8). Almost every youth who testified emphasized the need for change at their school. The report had several findings:

- One high school found that 97.5 percent of the respondents heard homophobic remarks at school
- Teachers could be just as hostile toward these youth
- Schools lacked support groups for these youth
- These youth often had low self-esteem and negative self-perceptions
- One high school found that 60 percent of the sample indicated they would become afraid or upset if others thought they might be gay
- Gay and lesbian youth felt alienated from some school activities (such as gym class)
- These youth often dropped out of school to avoid hostility at school

The report provided a series of recommendations for schools, state agencies, and the Massachusetts legislature (see Sidebar 3.7).

That same year, Bernie Sue Newman and Peter Gerard Muzzonigro (1993) asked twenty-seven gay males between the ages of seventeen and twenty to reflect on their boyhood and how they felt about being gay. The study found the majority (73 percent) of the boys felt different from the others; they had a mixture of friends; 41 percent felt they were a little less masculine than other boys; most boys had had their first crush at nearly thirteen years old; the length of their sexual confusion had lasted from a few months to three years; 50 percent of them had denied being gay; and 85 percent had pretended to be straight. More than 60 percent had accepted they were gay and expressed such sentiment as "I feel like it's one of the best things that ever happened to me" and "I'm proud of who and what I am and what being gay represents for gay people" (220). The authors found that the boys had generally realized they were gay before they had had a crush on another boy. "This supports the view that sexual orientation is a more integral part of identity than sexual behavior alone" (223). There were differences between boys from the traditional two-parent families and boys from nontraditional families. Boys from traditional families reported feeling different to a greater degree than boys from nontraditional families. Boys from traditional families had had crushes on other boys earlier than boys from nontraditional families, and traditional families were more disapproving of homosexuality than nontraditional families.

William Marsiglio (1993) surveyed self-identified fifteen-to-nineteen-year-old heterosexual males to determine their attitudes toward homosexuality and having gay friends—1,463 respondents were rated on how distasteful they found homosexuality and the degree to which they could befriend a gay male. The respondents harbored negative attitudes toward homosexuality and gay men in general. Nearly 89 percent agreed with the item "the thought of men having sex with each other is disgusting" (15), and 59 percent of the sample were opposed to the notion of befriending a gay male. Only 12 percent were found to agree "a lot" with the idea of having a gay male friend, with Hispanic males more likely to befriend a gay male than their white counterparts. In all, if a youth had a traditional perception of the male role, considered himself religious, and had parents with fewer years of education, he was not receptive to creating friendships with gay males.

Telljohann and Price (1993) conducted a qualitative study about the life experiences of 120 gay and lesbian youth between the ages of fourteen and twenty-one. They were asked twenty-eight open-ended questions. To a question about when they first realized that they were ho-

**Sidebar 3.7 The Massachusetts Governor's Commission
on Gay and Lesbian Youth, Recommendations to Schools,
State Agencies, and the Legislature**

The Commission urges Governor Weld, the Department of Education, and the Executive Office of Education to endorse these recommendations and to devise a plan for their implementation throughout the Commonwealth.

Five specific recommendations to schools are in the following areas:

- School policies protecting gay and lesbian students from harassment, violence, and discrimination.
- Training teachers, counselors, and school staff in crisis intervention and violence prevention.
- School-based support groups for gay and straight students.
- Information in school libraries for gay and lesbian adolescents.
- Curriculum which includes gay and lesbian issues.

The Commission makes three recommendations for helping families of gay and lesbian youth:

- School-based counseling for family members of gay and lesbian youth and community-based peer support in the PFLAG (Parents and Friends of Lesbians and Gays) model.
- Education of families through information in public libraries.
- Parent speakers bureaus to advocate for fair treatment of gay and lesbian youth in schools.

To facilitate both implementation of its recommendations in local schools and to educate teachers, school personnel, families, and students about the problems of gay and lesbian teenagers, the Commission makes recommendations to three state agencies: the Department of Education, the Executive Office of Education, and Massachusetts Commission Against Discrimination. The Commission also endorses legislation for the Massachusetts Legislation to enact.

The Commission's three recommendation to the Department of Education are:

- Sponsor training for teachers, families, and students to learn about the problems of gay and lesbian youth.
- Make presentations to school committee associations concerning the problems faced by gay and lesbian youth.
- Develop and disseminate a yellow pages resource book about gay and lesbian youth, one version each for students, teachers, and families.

The Commission's three recommendations to the Executive Office of Education focus on policies and research:

- ⟶ Develop and promote anti-harassment policies and guidelines for protecting gay and lesbian students in school across the curriculum.
- ⟶ Develop school policies that will guarantee gay and lesbian students equal rights to an education and equal access to school activities.
- ⟶ Research the problems of gay and lesbian students, and the needs of teachers and families of gay and lesbian youth.

The state's leading civil rights agency, the Massachusetts Commission Against Discrimination (MCAD), is urged to do the following three things:

- ⟶ Conduct outreach to teachers and school personnel to inform them of their rights under the state's Gay and Lesbian Civil Rights Law, which was enacted in 1989.
- ⟶ Sponsor anti-discrimination awareness programs in schools for all students to learn about the gay and lesbian civil rights law.
- ⟶ Sponsor legislation to extend MCAD's jurisdiction to include complaints of education discrimination.

Finally, the Massachusetts Legislature is urged to enact, and Governor Weld urged to prioritize passage of, legislation protecting gay and lesbian students in public schools against discrimination in admission to schools or access to school activities and courses of study.

Source: The Governor's Commission on Gay and Lesbian Youth, February 25, 1993, *Making Schools Safe for Gay and Lesbian Youth: Breaking the Silence in Schools and in Families,* pp. 2–3. Reprinted with permission.

mosexual, the age range for the lesbians was from four to seventeen and from four to ten for the gay males. No particular age group was significant, although one in three youth knew between four and ten years old.

To questions about whether their peers and parents knew about their sexual orientation and how they responded to the news, 73 percent of the males and 87 percent of the females had friends who knew about their sexual orientation. Thirty-three percent of the females mentioned they received positive responses, and most of the responses for the males were favorable. Eighty-four percent of the lesbians' families and 74 percent of the gay males' families knew they were gay and 35 percent of both groups indicated their parents reacted positively and supportively. Gay males were eight times more likely than lesbian females to report that the family reacted negatively to the news.

When questioned regarding how responsive school personnel were, about 25 percent of the youth reported being able to talk to their counselor about their sexual orientation and the majority were satisfied with their counselor. Sixty-eight percent of the females and 41 percent of the males said their teachers knew of their sexual orientation. Most mentioned that their teachers reacted favorably to the news.

To a question about whether homosexuality was addressed in their school curriculum, about 50 percent mentioned that homosexuality was discussed in class. However, 50 percent of the lesbians and 37 percent of the gay males indicated that the topic was addressed poorly or negatively.

When asked whether they would like to share anything else, the lesbians responded that youth need resources to prevent others from committing suicide, more information to curtail homophobia, and more educational programs that discuss sexual orientation. The gay males mentioned the need for programs to support gay youth, a social outlet, and training for teachers and counselors.

Telljohann and Price concluded that to reduce the stress for these youth (1) human sexuality should be required coursework for teachers and counselors, (2) schools need to take a strong stand against homophobia, and (3) sexual orientation should be addressed in the academic curriculum.

Anthony D'Augelli and Scott Hershberger (1993) studied the personal challenges and mental health problems of 194 gay, lesbian, and bisexual youth. The data revealed that 13 percent of the youth knew their sexual orientation before the age of five, and most (91 percent) knew they were gay or lesbian before the age of fifteen. Males were more likely to be aware of their same-sex attractions earlier than females were, and both groups self-labeled their sexual orientation about four years following their initial awareness. Most of the youth came out to someone by the age of fifteen, and a year later 75 percent of the sample had come out to a parent. Nearly 67 percent of the sample had had heterosexual experiences. Twenty-five percent of the youth were completely out, but all mentioned that several barriers (fear of losing a job, fear of losing friendships, fear of verbal harassment, and so forth) kept them from coming out completely. About 50 percent of the sample had had a friend reject them after the news was disclosed. About 75 percent had told someone about their sexual orientation, and only 19 percent mentioned that they were in the closet to their family. Most (63 percent) of the youth who had come out to their parents had come out to their mothers only, and of these mothers more than 50 percent were accepting of their child's sexual orientation.

The respondents had some deep concerns, too. At least 50 percent of the sample worried about "disclosure to family, coworkers, and friends; dissatisfaction with sex life; problems in a close relationship; depression and anxiety; and worry about HIV" (435). Eight percent indicated they contemplated suicide often, and 42 percent had made a suicide attempt. The predictors of suicide attempt included low self-esteem, alcohol abuse, depression, loss of friendships, and parental reactions.

Later that year the *High School Journal* published an issue with twenty articles focused on gay and lesbian youth (see Sidebar 3.8; not all of them are addressed here). Andi O'Conor (1993) reflected on the testimonies from a gay and a lesbian adolescent and concluded that gay and lesbian youth

- ➡ often have problems at home that stem from being gay or lesbian. The young man was called faggot by his mother, who did not want a queer in her house, and his brother called him a sick fag. The young woman's parents refused to believe that she could be lesbian, and her father seemed unaffected by and clueless about the situation.
- ➡ are subject to hostility at school. Their teachers often did not care whether lesbian and gay students were safe from other youth, and they were forced to act straight to avoid being harassed.
- ➡ feel ostracized and isolated. The youth said that even gay and lesbian teachers never extended themselves, and the gay and lesbian community excluded adolescents. The young man stressed, "Our parents hate us, our teachers hate us, straight kids hate us, adults hate us" (11).

Rofes (1993) began his article by reflecting on his childhood and adolescence as a sissy. His early life was difficult for him, as it is for many feminine boys, because of torture from bullies. Bullies often do bodily harm, but the emotional damage is irreparable and severe. He wrote: "I know a lot about bullies. I know they have a specific social function: they define the limits of acceptable conduct, appearance and activities for children. They enforce rigid expectations. They are masters of the art of humiliation and technicians of the science of terrorism. They wreaked havoc on my entire childhood. To this day, their handprints, like a slap on the face, remain stark and defined in my soul" (37).

Rofes recommended that school administrators and teachers

Sidebar 3.8 Table of Contents of the 1993–1994
High School Journal 77(1–2)

Thinking about the Homosexual Adolescent, *Gerald Unks*
Who Gets Called Queer in School? Lesbian, Gay, and Bisexual
Teenagers: Homophobia and High School, *Andi O'Conor*
Lesbian and Gay Adolescents: Social and Developmental Considera-
tions, *Dennis A. Anderson*
African American Gay Youth: One Form of Manhood, *Kenneth P.
Moteiro and Vincent Fuqua*
Making Our Schools Safe for Sissies, *Eric E. Rofes*
The Elusive "Gay" Teenagers of Classical Antiquity, *Cecil W. Wooten*
Gay Teens in Literature, *Jim Brogan*
Silence, Difference, and Annihilation: Understanding the Impact of
Mediated Heterosexism on High School Students, *Alfred P. Kielwasser and
Michelle A. Wolf*
Homophobia in Sports: Addressing the Needs of Lesbian and Gay
High School Athletes, *Pat Griffin*
Lesbian, Gay, and Bisexual Teens and the School Counselor: Building
Alliances, *Amy L. Reynolds and Michael J. Koski*
The Case for a Gay and Lesbian Curriculum, *Arthur Lipkin*
Project 10: A School-Based Outreach to Gay and Lesbian Youth,
Virginia Uribe
"Gay/Straight" Alliances: Transforming Pain to Pride, *Warren J.
Blumenfeld*
Learning Gay Culture in "A Desert of Nothing": Language as a
Resource in Gender Socialization, *William L. Leap*
OutRight: Reflections on an Out-of-School Gay Youth Group,
Hugh Singerline
Challenges for Educators: Lesbian, Gay, and Bisexual Families,
James T. Sears
Moral Panic, Schooling, and Gay Identity: Critical Pedagogy and the
Politics of Resistance, *Peter McLaren*
Invisible No More: Addressing the Needs of Gay, Lesbian, and
Bisexual Youth and Their Advocates, *Karen M. Harbeck*
Homophobia in the High School: A Problem in Need of a Resolution,
John P. Elia
Politics of Adolescent Sexual Identity and Queer Responses,
Glorianne Leck

---

make a concerted effort to ensure that schools are bully free, and that
boys should not be forced to participate in gender-conforming activities. He remarked that one of the most frightening and detested aspects
of school for the sissy is gym class. He elaborated: "Traditional team
sports and individual athletic prowess are fraught with opportunities for
humiliation and public degradation for sissy boys. The situation is exac-

erbated when gym teachers themselves participate in the harassment by using sexist taunts to encourage better participation or higher achievement" (40). He encouraged school officials and teachers to re-think gym class altogether.

Warren Blumenfeld (1993) discussed gay/straight alliances in sev-eral high schools throughout the Boston area. Many of the alliances were driven to eliminate homophobia in their schools, raise their peers' awareness about homosexuality, and deal with some of their members' personal problems. One high school's goals included "to promote ac-ceptance, support, and celebration of all sexual orientations, and discus-sions about homophobia," and "to provide a safe place for Brookline High School students and staff to talk about sexuality, and anti-homo-phobia programs in the community" (114). The alliances, which identi-fied themselves with clever acronyms such as GASP! (Gay and Straight People) and LeSGaB (Lesbian, Straight, Gay, and Bisexual), met regularly, participated in school events, and marched in local and national pa-rades. Many of the clubs were well supported by their peers and schools.

John Anderson (1994), a gay high school teacher, made recom-mendations to schools based on his observations. He believed that schools were simply ignorant and remained silent about the needs of gay and lesbian youth, thereby limiting their emotional, social, and aca-demic development. One administrator went so far as to say that he had never heard the word faggot in his building before, and a principal told Anderson that gay and lesbian youth had all the support they needed, al-though a teacher received death threats after he wrote an article on ho-mophobia in the school paper. Andersen suggested that schools

- •◦ have teachers learn how to enhance the educational experi-ences of gay and lesbian youth
- •◦ have specially trained support staff (counselors, nurses, and so on) to contend with gay and lesbian situations or homo-phobia
- •◦ investigate how sexuality is addressed in the health curricu-lum and ensure that gay and lesbian people are included in a positive manner
- •◦ increase the quality and quantity of books and resources on homosexuality in the school library
- •◦ address gay and lesbian issues in the academic curriculum

Uribe (1994), founder of PROJECT 10, recommended strategies to alleviate the challenges presented to gay and lesbian youth. She be-lieved that teachers and youth should have complete, accurate, and unbiased information and open discussions about homosexuality. If everyone understood that homosexuality was "not a choice, not a sickness, and not a developmental flaw," then students and faculty members would become more accepting and supportive of gay and lesbian youth (170).

The project had grown by the 1993–1994 academic year to thirty-six senior high schools. More than one half of the youth involved in the project were boys, and most of the participants were Latino. Although there was some dissension about implementing the project, participants, school officials, and teachers generally found it valuable enough to institute. Other school districts inquired about PROJECT 10 and were eager to implement similar models in their schools.

That same year, Curtis Proctor and Victor Groze (1994) published an article on suicide attempts and ideation among gay, lesbian, and bisexual youth. Their sample consisted of 221 participants whose average age was eighteen and a half; most of the respondents were males. The youth were assessed with the Adolescent Health Questionnaire (White 1987), which measures perceptions of family, social environment, and self. The results found that 40.3 percent had attempted suicide, 25.8 percent had thought about it at least once, and 33 percent reported neither attempting suicide nor thinking about it. Youth who had considered suicide scored the lowest on their family, social, and self-perceptions. Those with no thoughts of suicide scored the highest on all three areas. Proctor and Groze maintained: "The youths that neither considered nor attempted suicide possessed internal and external qualities that enabled them to cope well in the face of discrimination, loneliness, and isolation" (509). These findings led the scholars to recommend that support groups should be made available to these youth and their families and that intervention service personnel thoroughly understand what leads many of these youth to attempt suicide.

By the mid-1990s, discussion on gay and lesbian youth had gathered momentum and academic literature was readily available. By the end of the decade, articles were appearing in journals from a variety of disciplines. *Adolescence, Educational Leadership, Family Medicine, Independent Schools*, the *Journal of Gay and Lesbian Social Services*, the *Journal of Sex Research*, the *Journal of Teacher Education, Professional School Counseling, Reaching Today's Youth*, and *Reclaiming Children and Youth*, among others, have all featured work on gay and lesbian youth. Some journals continue to devote entire issues to the topic. The *Journal of Gay and Lesbian Social Services*, for instance, assigned "School Experiences of Gay and Lesbian Youth: The Invisible Minority" as the rubric for a series of articles appearing in a 1997 issue. Moreover, these youth have been the topic of various books (Bass and Kaufman 1996; Due 1994; Kay, Estepa, Desetta 1996; Lipkin 1999; and Owens 1998). In the latter part of the decade and in the new millennium, research broadened from gay and lesbian youth to gay, lesbian, bisexual, transgender, and questioning youth. We continue to learn about these populations, and as society becomes more tolerant of diverse sexualities, emerging research will transform the way we attend to them.

SUMMARY

The academic discourse on gay and lesbian youth has come a long way. Until very recently, society simply could and did not embrace the fact that adolescents could be gay, lesbian, or bisexual, let alone transgender. Homosexuality was perceived as a diabolical sickness that affected only adult men and women. Times have changed, and the research outlined in this chapter (as well as documented throughout the text) has shown that youth can be gay, lesbian, and bisexual. Because of the work of dedicated scholars who know that these youth live in relatively hostile environments, society is far more aware of the issues central to the lives of gay and lesbian youth. Empirical research and qualitative data have validated that these youth are often alienated from or harassed by their peers, are at risk for a host of problems, and describe themselves as isolated and desirous of a more accepting school community. With this valuable information, advocates have demanded that schools take notice of these youth and attempt to better understand their unique needs and challenges.

REFERENCES

American Academy of Pediatrics. 1983. "Committee on Adolescence: Homosexuality and Adolescence." *Pediatrics* 72(2): 249–250.

Anderson, John D. 1994. "School Climate for Gay and Lesbian Students and Staff Members." *Phi Delta Kappan* 76(2): 151–154.

Bass, Ellen, and Kate Kaufman. 1996. *Free Your Mind: The Book for Gay, Lesbian, and Bisexual Youth—and Their Allies.* New York: HarperPerennial.

Blumenfeld, Warren J. 1993. "'Gay/Straight' Alliances: Transforming Pain to Pride." *High School Journal* 77(1–2): 113–121.

Borhek, Mary V. 1988. "Helping Gay and Lesbian Adolescents and Their Families: A Mother's Perspective." *Journal of Adolescent Health Care* 9(2): 123–128.

Boyer, Debra. 1989. "Male Prostitution and Homosexual Identity." *Journal of Homosexuality* 17(1–2): 151–184.

Coleman, Eli. 1982. "Developmental Stages in the Coming Out Process." *Journal of Homosexuality* 7(2–3): 31–43.

———. 1989. "The Development of Male Prostitution Activity Among Gay and Bisexual Adolescents." *Journal of Homosexuality* 17(1–2): 131–150.

Coleman, Eli, and Gary Remafedi. 1989. "Gay, Lesbian, and Bisexual Adolescents: A Critical Challenge to Counselors." *Journal of Counseling and Development* 68: 36–40.

Cranston, Kevin. 1991. "HIV Education for Gay, Lesbian, and Bisexual Youth: Personal Risk, Personal Power, and the Community of Conscience." *Journal of Homosexuality* 22(3–4): 247–260.

Crisp, Quentin. 1968. *The Naked Civil Servant.* New York: Penguin Books.

Dank, B. 1971. "Coming Out in the Gay World." *Psychiatry* 34: 180–197.

D'Augelli, Anthony R., and Scott L. Hershberger. 1993. "Lesbian, Gay, and Bisexual Youth in Community Settings: Personal Challenges and Mental Health Problems." *American Journal of Community Psychology* 21(4): 421–448.

Due, L. 1994. *Joining the Tribe: Growing Up Gay and Lesbian in the 90s.* New York: Anchor Books.

Freud, Sigmund. 1960. "Letter No. 277 (Anonymous), April 9, 1935." In *Letters of Sigmund Freud.* New York: Basic Books.

Gerstel, Camille J., Andrew J. Feraios, and Gilbert Herdt. 1989. "Widening Circles: An Ethnographic Profile of a Youth Group." *Journal of Homosexuality* 17(1–2): 75–92.

Gilberg, Arnold L. 1978. "Psychosocial Considerations in Treating Homosexual Adolescents." *American Journal of Psychoanalysis* 38: 355–358.

Gonsiorek, John C. 1988. "Mental Health Issues of Gay and Lesbian Adolescents." *Journal of Adolescent Health Care* 9(2): 114–122.

Gonzalez, R. M. 1979. "Hallucinogenic Dependency during Adolescence as a Defense Against Homosexual Fantasies: A Reenactment of the First Separation-Individuation Phase in the Course of Treatment." *Journal of Youth and Adolescence* 8(1): 63–71.

Governor's Commission on Gay and Lesbian Youth. 1993. *Making Schools Safe for Gay and Lesbian Youth: Breaking the Silence in Schools and in Families.* Boston: Author.

Harbeck, Karen M. 1992. *Coming out of the Classroom Closet: Gay and Lesbian Students, Teachers, and Curricula.* Binghamton, NY: Harrington Park Press.

Harry, Joseph. 1989. "Parental Physical Abuse and Sexual Orientation in Males." *Archives of Sexual Behaviors* 18(3): 251–261.

Herdt, Gilbert. 1989a. *Gay and Lesbian Youth.* Binghamton, NY: Harrington Park Press.

———. 1989b. "Introduction: Gay and Lesbian Youth, Emergent Identities, and Cultural Scenes at Home and Abroad." *Journal of Homosexuality* 17(1–2): 1–42.

Hetrick, Emery S., and A. Damien Martin. 1987. "Developmental Issues and Their Resolution for Gay and Lesbian Adolescents." *Journal of Homosexuality* 14(1–2): 25–43.

Hoffman, Martin. 1970. "The Searching Mind: Homosexuality." *Today's Education* 59(8): 46–48.

Holeman, R. Eugene, and George Winokur. 1965. "Effeminate Homosexuality: A Disease of Childhood." *American Journal of Orthopsychiatry* 35: 48–56.

Hunter, Joyce, and Robert Schaecher. 1987. "Stresses on Lesbian and Gay Adolescents in Schools." *Social Work in Education* 9(3): 180–190.

Kay, Philip, Andrea Estepa, and Al Desetta. 1996. *Out with It: Gay and Straight Teens Write about Homosexuality.* New York: Youth Communication.

Kourany, Ronald F.C. 1987. "Suicide among Homosexual Adolescents." *Journal of Homosexuality* 13(4): 111–117.

Kremer, Malvina, and Alfred H. Rifkin. 1969. "The Early Development of Homosexuality: A Study of Adolescent Lesbians." *American Journal of Psychiatry* 126(1): 129–134.

Kruks, Gabe. 1991. "Gay and Lesbian Homeless/Street Youth: Special Issues and Concerns." *Journal of Adolescent Health* 12(7): 515–518.

"The Lays of the Land: The Price of Sex around the U.S." 1968. *The Advocate* (December): 20.

Lipkin, Arthur. 1999. *Understanding Homosexuality: Changing Schools.* Boulder, CO: Westview Press.

Malyon, Alan K. 1981. "The Homosexual Adolescent: Developmental Issues and Social Bias." *Child Welfare* 60(5): 321–330.

Marsiglio, William. 1993. "Attitudes toward Homosexual Activity and Gays as Friends: A National Survey of Heterosexual 15- to 19-Year-Old Males." *Journal of Sex Research* 30(1): 12–17.

Martin, A. Damien. 1982. "Learning to Hide: The Socialization of the Gay Adolescent." *Adolescent Psychiatry* 10: 53–65.

Martin, A. Damien, and Emery S. Hetrick. 1988. "The Stigmatization of the Gay and Lesbian Adolescent." *Journal of Homosexuality* 15(1–2): 163–183.

McKinlay, Thomas, Jeffrey A. Kelly, and Jud Patterson. 1977. "Teaching Assertive Skills to a Passive Homosexual Adolescent: An Illustrative Case Study." *Journal of Homosexuality* 3(2): 163–170.

Nader, Philip, David B. Wexler, Thomas L. Patterson, Leon McKusick, and Thomas Coates. 1989. "Comparison of Beliefs about AIDS among Urban, Suburban, Incarcerated, and Gay Adolescents." *Journal of Adolescent Health Care* 10(5): 413–418.

Newman, Bernie Sue, and Peter Gerard Muzzonigro. 1993. "The Effects of Traditional Family Values on the Coming Out Process of Gay Male Adolescents." *Adolescence* 28(10): 213–226.

O'Conor, Andi. 1993. "Who Gets Called Queer in School? Lesbian, Gay, and Bisexual Teenagers: Homophobia and High School." *High School Journal* 77(1–2): 7–12.

Owen, William F. 1985. "Medical Problems of the Homosexual Adolescent." *Journal of Adolescent Health Care* 6 (4): 278–285.

Owens, Robert E. 1998. *Queer Kids: The Challenges and Promise for Lesbian, Gay, and Bisexual Youth*. Binghamton, NY: Harrington Park Press.

Paroski, Paul A., Jr. 1987. "Health Care Delivery and the Concerns of Gay and Lesbian Adolescents." *Journal of Adolescent Health Care* 8(2): 188–192.

Price, James H., and Susan K. Telljohann. 1991. "School Counselors' Perceptions of Adolescent Homosexuals." *Journal of School Health* 61(10): 433–439.

Proctor, Curtis D., and Victor K. Groze. 1994. "Risk Factors for Suicide among Gay, Lesbian, and Bisexual Youth." *Social Work* 39(5): 504–513.

Remafedi, Gary J. 1985. "Adolescent Homosexuality: Issues for Pediatricians." *Clinical Pediatrics* 24(9): 481–485.

———. 1987a. "Adolescent Homosexuality: Psychosocial and Medical Implications." *Pediatrics* 79 (3): 331–337.

———. 1987b. "Male Homosexuality: The Adolescent's Perspective." *Pediatrics* 79 (3): 326–330.

———. 1988a. "Preface." *Journal of Adolescent Health Care* 9(2): 93–94.

———. 1988b. "Preventing the Sexual Transmission of AIDS during Adolescence." *Journal of Adolescent Health Care* 9(2): 139–143.

———. 1990. "Fundamental Issues in the Care of Homosexual Youth." *Medical Clinics of North America* 74(5): 1169–1179.

Remafedi, Gary, James A. Farrow, and Robert W. Deisher. 1991. "Risk Factors for Attempted Suicide in Gay and Bisexual Youth." *Pediatrics* 87: 869–875.

Remafedi, Gary, Michael Resnick, Robert Blum, and Linda Harris. 1992. "Demography of Sexual Orientation in Adolescents." *Pediatrics* 89: 714–721.

Roesler, Thomas, and Robert W. Deisher. 1972. "Youthful Male Homosexuality: Homosexual Experience and the Process of Developing Homosexual Identity in Males Aged 16 to 22 Years." *Journal of the American Medical Association* 219(8): 1018–1023.

Rofes, Eric. 1989. "Opening Up the Classroom Closet: Responding to the Educational Needs of Gay and Lesbian Youth." *Harvard Educational Review* 59(4): 444–453.

———. 1993. "Making Our Schools Safe for Sissies." *High School Journal* 77(1–2): 37–40.

Rudolph, J. 1988. "Counselors' Attitudes towad Homosexuality: A Selective Review of the Literature." *Journal of Counseling and Development* 67(3: 165–168.

Sanford, Nancy D. 1989. "Providing Sensitive Health Care to Gay and Lesbian Youth." *Nurse Practitioner* 14(5): 30–47.

Savin-Williams, Ritch C. 1988. "Theoretical Perspectives Accounting for Adolescent Homosexuality." *Journal of Adolescent Health Care* 9(2): 95–104.

———. 1989. "Coming Out to Parents and Self-Esteem among Gay and Lesbian Youths." *Journal of Homosexuality* 18(1–2): 1–35.

Schneider, Margaret. 1989. "Sappho Was a Right-On Adolescent: Growing Up Lesbian." *Journal of Homosexuality* 17(1–2): 111–123.

Schneider, Stephen G., Norman L. Farberow, and Gabriel Kruks. 1989. "Suicidal Behavior in Adolescent and Young Gay Men." *Suicide and Life Threatening Behavior* 19(4): 381–394.

Sears, James T. 1991. "Educators, Homosexuality, and Homosexual Students: Are Personal Feelings Related to Professional Beliefs?" *Journal of Homosexuality* 22(3–4): 29–80.

Telljohann, Susan K., and James H. Price. 1993. "A Qualitative Examination of Adolescent Homosexuals' Life Experiences: Ramifications for Secondary School Personnel." *Journal of Homosexuality* 26(1): 41–56.

Treadway, Leo, and John Yoakam. 1992. "Creating a Safer School Environment for Lesbian and Gay Students." *Journal of School Health* 62(7): 352–357.

Troiden, Richard R. 1979. "Becoming Homosexual: A Model of Gay Identity Acquisition." *Psychiatry* 42: 362–373.

———. 1988. "Homosexual Identity Development." *Journal of Adolescent Health Care* 9(2): 105–113.

Troiden, Richard R., and E. Goode. 1980. "Variables Related to Acquisition of Gay Identity." *Journal of Homosexuality* 5: 383–392.

Uribe, Virginia. 1994. "The Silent Minority: Rethinking Our Commitment to Gay and Lesbian Youth." *Theory into Practice* 33(3): 167–172.

Uribe, Virginia, and Karen M. Harbeck. 1991. "Addressing the Needs of Lesbian, Gay, and Bisexual Youth: The Origins of PROJECT 10 and School-Based Intervention." *Journal of Homosexuality* 22(3–4): 9–28.

Wellisch, David K., G. G. DeAngelis, and Carl Paternite. 1981. "A Study of Therapy of Homosexual Adolescent Drug Users in a Residential Treatment Setting." *Adolescence* 16(63): 689–700.

White, George Lovelle. 1987. "Evaluation of Suicidal Risk Factors in Suburban/Urban Utah Teenagers." Ph.D. diss., University of Utah, Salt Lake City.

Zenilman, Jonathan. 1988. "Sexually Transmitted Diseases in Homosexual Adolescents." *Journal of Adolescent Health Care* 9(2): 129–138.

Chapter Four

•❖ Stories of Five Contemporary Youth

I hate it this way. I never know what to think. I'm scared to talk about this and sometimes I just wish it would go away. . . . I have to sneak off to watch *Will & Grace* or *Real World*. "Those shows are for girls or fags." Sometimes I pretend that me, Will, Jack, Grace, and Karen are friends or that Chris is my boyfriend. You know, I could go shopping with them, or just hang around at their apartment. . . . I just wish I could go somewhere where everyone there was like me and I wouldn't have to pretend or keep my mouth shut. . . . A guy in PE once called me fag when I didn't make the basket, and one time my friend Emilio told me I was gay because I wanted to be an architect. . . . I don't want it to be that way. I just wish it could be like it is on TV.

—Jake, Fifteen, Austin, Texas

I don't understand what the big deal is. I'm a big dyke. That's it. Get over it. You know, tough titties. . . . I can be in your face about it, but that's not all that I am. I'm an artist. I'm a singer. I'm a lot of things. . . . If anyone wants to mess with me, I'm like, "let's get it on." But I'm not going to go around kicking dust. I know there are gay kids out there, and I always say: "Be strong. Don't give a fuck about what others think. Just be yourself. And if they do go around messing with you, tell them to call me." . . . I have girlfriends, but sometimes I think that I'm never going to meet the right girl and that I'll have to marry a man so that I'm not alone and I can have kids.

—Alejandra, Sixteen, Austin, Texas

Life has not been easy for some gay, lesbian, bisexual, and transgender youth. Jake in the vignette was closeted, sexually inexperienced, fearful of his peers finding out about his sexuality, hoping for a more accepting society, and eager to socialize with others like him. He had no relationship with his father, his mother was promiscuous, and he and his mother were living in a small apartment inhabited by her parents, her sister, and two young children. His life was one hardship after another. Alejandra had similar hardships. She lived on welfare with her mother and two sisters, her father was serving a twenty-year jail sentence, she had been physically abused by her mother's former boyfriend, and she often found solace in alcohol and marijuana. Nevertheless, Alejandra was a proud lesbian. Jake and Alejandra may have attended the same school, lived on the same street, and been of the same socioeconomic background and ethnicity, but they were strikingly different.

What is evident in the life histories of some gay, lesbian, bisexual, and transgender youth is that as different as they may be, they all have to assign their stigmatized sexual orientation a permanent place in their world. For some that may mean accepting their sexual orientation early on, for others that may mean denial until adulthood, and for others that may mean living in an isolated world. Most of these youth, however, learn to adapt to their situations and are resilient. One young man emphasized: "Being gay has definitely made me tougher, made me more resistant to mental abuse or physical abuse than most people. I have a tougher skin than most. I can tune [social censure] out." In this chapter, youth from varied backgrounds and interests share their stories. Angel, William, Jericka, Jeremy, and Samantha discuss their setbacks and challenges and how they live as a transgender, bisexual, gay, or lesbian youth today.

ANGEL, SIXTEEN, FEMALE-TO-MALE TRANSGENDER

Angel is from North Carolina and now attends a school for GLBT youth. Angel was born a girl but is confident that she wants to be a boy. Early in her life she found herself in the company of boys, with strong interests in activities traditionally assigned to boys.

"I was always boyish. I was always a boy. In school I always played with the boys until eighth grade, when my teacher told me that I wasn't allowed to anymore. The girls hated me because I was so aggressive. I was the only girl on the guys' football team at my middle school; I was starting defensive end. Then I came out, 'I'm a lesbian, blah, blah, blah, and whatever.'"

She was actively involved in a youth organization sponsored by her state's network for gay and lesbian adolescents. Through the network, she was able to attend a summer youth leadership seminar where she learned more about transgender issues and began to form her gender identity.

"It was really an eye-opening experience. Just hearing them talk about what it is to be transgender—I can't even talk about that experience. They just put the words to what I had been feeling. I thought I was a boy, so I was out there playing with the boys. You know. I never wanted to play with dolls. I never had a desire to be in dance. I never wanted to do those girl things. And my mom would drive by the Tae Kwon Do place, and I would always stare and be so mesmerized. I would be like, 'Can we drive by the Tae Kwon Do, can we?' I look back and I know that it was my gender identity coming out. It's who I really was."

She is sure that she wants to transform her physical body and is well informed about the process. "One day when I get to be eighteen, I plan to take testosterone, which will make my voice drop, make me grow facial hair, make the shape of my face change to a slightly more masculine version, even make my fat shift from my hips to my stomach. It will stop my menstruation process. If I quit [testosterone] most of it will come back. Some stuff isn't reversible—like your voice dropping. If you stop taking testosterone after you've been on it, you do lose some of the muscle. Most transgender people describe taking testosterone as being a twelve-year-old boy and going through puberty. It's like you're hitting puberty and all of your testosterone is pumping and you're starting to develop. As far as surgery goes, I don't want the bottom surgery. It's not the fact that they have to take skin from my arm and it's ugly, but a lot of transgender people don't have it because it's not perfected. If they knew more about it and could reconstruct it. . . ."

Angel does not have a relationship with her father, and her mother is hesitantly supportive. "My mom knows. I told her I wanted chest surgery and to take testosterone, and she was like, 'Why do you want to look like a freak like that?' and 'Why do you want to cut your tits off?' She thinks my body modification [tattoos and piercings] has a lot to do with it. She thinks I want it for the body modification. She doesn't understand that me being a transperson is how I see myself in my head and that my body physically doesn't represent that. So my piercings and my tattoos a lot of times are about me making me love my body more because I do hate it so much. Because it's not who I really am. . . . *Boys Don't Cry* was a very good movie in the sense that my mom watched it and saw what was happening to people who were just being who they were. And that really woke her up to what happens to transpeople. And she loves me, and she doesn't like how I get treated in the outside world. She felt she didn't want to add to that. And that was part of what helped her change."

No other family members seem perturbed with Angel's sexual orientation. One uncle is starting to accept her and her girlfriend, Erin, but remains perplexed about transgender people. "My uncle is super-Christian, and he's somewhat coming around to gays and lesbians, but he has no clue about the whole trans thing. Like my girlfriend came home for Christmas and he was so confused he was asking all these questions, and it was so funny. He was respectful. He wasn't in my face."

She is open about her sexual orientation and has been for a few years, but she is respectful of those around her and will not flaunt her convictions in front of those threatened by her visible appearance. "Everyone knows that I'm gay. I'm not sure that everyone knows about my gender. I've really only known about my gender for about two years, and I've been out for three or four. I've been gay for three. . . . If they don't like it, they can 'whatever.' I don't deny being transgender; I just won't be like so queer. I won't wear all my queer shirts and all my rainbows just to respect the people I am around. Like I've done it for my grandmother before. I can't cover it up too much because I have a huge rainbow tattoo on my arm. And I have a gay Christian [tattoo] on my neck because I am gay and Christian. I go to MCC. I have another gay sign on my back. I have 'I am a boy' right here. And I have my girlfriend's name right there."

She attributes her openness to the support she has found in an organization called True Spirit. "This generation of transgender youth is more out than it used to be. It used to be: 'Hide and don't tell anyone. Just pass so no one knows.' But people like me and a lot of my friends are like: 'We're going to take T [testosterone] and we're going to get our tits cut off. We're boys, damn it!' We're going to let everyone know it. It's just that kind of thing. Every year I go to a conference called True Spirit. It takes place in Washington, D.C., and it's a conference for people born female but digress from that gender. It doesn't mean that everyone is transgender yet. . . . There are people all over the gender spectrum. . . . It's an amazing community. I know that when I go to True Spirit, I get so pumped up. I go every February, and when I come back, I am able to call people up and say, 'I'm a boy, damn it!' When people call me girl, I'm able to say, 'This is who I really am, don't blah, blah, blah.' . . . After you leave [the conference], it fades away because you don't have the community. You kind of go back in the closet, and you can be afraid again."

Angel derives much of her support from the True Spirit community. Erin, her twenty-three-year-old girlfriend, is also a source of support and has contemplated her own gender identity. "My girlfriend has played around with gender, but she's more in a questioning kind of phase, but this could be the fact that we've been home from True Spirit for a few months now. . . . I've always had a good support as far as friends go like maybe in my old school. But every now and then I feel like the only F [female] to M [male] in Dallas. Ever since I've been here, I think I have only seen two F to Ms. There's a lot of Ms [males] to Fs [females]. . . . I met Erin when I was maybe thirteen when I went to a tattoo shop with a safety pin in my tongue and she was a piercer. I kept going back, and I got my ears, and I got my belly button. She has done all of my piercings. And she moved here for me. She's twenty-three. We have been dating for a year in June. My mother likes Erin."

Books and a film on the subject also give her some support and encouragement. "There are a lot of good books out there that I've used. There's Kate Bernstein, who does the *Gender Workbook* and *Gender Outlaw*. There's Leslie Feinberg, who wrote the books *Transgender Warrior* and *Transgender Liberation*. There's this guy Juan Cameron, who's F to M. He did a book called *Body Alchemy: Transsexual Portraits*. . . . There's also a movie. It's a documentary kind of thing about transgender people. It's called *You Don't Know Dick*."

She is well aware of the hurdles that she has to overcome to transform her physical body, but remains hopeful of the day when she will be a man. "The hardest part about being transgender right now is the fact that people are telling me that I can't transition. That my mom isn't helping me because I am underage, so I just can't go do it. The cost is a big factor. Even if I get chest surgery, it will be $6,000, and I have to take testosterone and a shot every two weeks. That's very costly. The hardest part is now having to live in this body and people always see me as female and people always associate me with female. People always assume that I am female. They're like, 'There's a girl' or 'she' or 'her.' It's really hard. . . . Knowing there's the possibility that I can change my gender to align with who I am makes me not feel so weird; it makes me feel a lot more comfortable with myself. Like right now I don't feel like I am who I am in my head but I know that one day I will."

Until then, she prefers to be called a he. "I do prefer *he*. Angel is my born name, and I get that from a lot of transgender persons. They are like: 'Cool. Is that your real name or your chosen name?' I tell them it's my birth name, and they are like, 'That's so cool.' Some of their names are like Michelle, Angela, or Rebecca. I've heard some of the girliest names. At one time I was thinking of Andre, but my name is so androgynous, and I like it that way."

She is frustrated by gay and lesbian organizations that do little advocacy work for transgender people and some of the stereotypes perpetuated by society. "A lot of gay and lesbian organizations actually have the letters GLBT but the T is actually tagged on. Some don't do very much about it. Even here they don't call me he all the time. . . . I hate it that people think all of us have been sexually abused. I hate the most how people cannot realize that gender and sexuality are two different things. Gender has nothing to do with sexuality at all. It's just frustrating when people are like combining the two and thinking they are the same thing. I really don't know how to describe it or give you an example. People just don't get it when you say you're transgender and when you say, 'I'm female to male.' . . . Gender and sexuality are two different things. The whole 'There's a boy trapped inside of me' drives me nuts. It's not a boy trapped inside of me. It's who I am. I'm not a girl anywhere."

School was not a pleasant experience for Angel. "School was horrible for me. The only people who were gay or lesbians actually were feminine lesbians. They did not get beyond half as much as me. Gender got played into it so much just because I was so masculine. It was like: 'Why do you want to be a boy? Why do you want to do that to your self? Why do you have to be so butch? Why do you have to look like such a freak?' I was constantly harassed. I would tell the teachers, and they would do nothing about it. They would say, 'You're bringing it on yourself.' They just outlawed piercing at my school back in North Carolina. It's horrible. . . . Some of the guys were like, 'I want to watch.' And that would be annoying. . . . The girls would be like, 'Ooh,' and they would not want to hang around with me. They were afraid that I was going to hit on them."

The teachers were of little help to her as she struggled with her sexuality. "They were horrible. They kept saying that I was bringing everything on myself. They were conservative Christians, and they were like, 'The classroom is not the place to talk about your relationships.' They would be talking about their husbands, and I was like, 'If you're talking about your husbands, then why can't I talk about my girlfriends?' . . . It was one of those schools where the section on homosexuality had been ripped out of the health books. I talked about [my sexuality] every chance I got. I would say something very out, very in your face. . . . It was just really, really hard. People were so mean. I went back after I left, and people acted like they missed me and they were my best friends. But the way they treated me while I was there was ridiculous."

One teacher wanted to help Angel but feared losing her job, and another wanted to assist her in forming a gay-straight alliance at school. Even though the club never formed, Angel believes that she made a difference. "There was an art teacher who was a straight ally. She was going to help me with the gay-straight alliance, but she was afraid of what would happen to her because it's a very small town. Her job would not have been very secure if she had been the one to step up and do the GSA. I did have one teacher who was going to help me do a diversity club. It was going to start out as a 'Don't-pick-on-people-because-of-their-religion-or-their-color,' and I was going to work my way into making it a GSA. I never got a chance to do it, and I really didn't give a shit about it. I heard that I changed a lot of stuff there. It's a lot different now. Two girls came out after I came out, and I feel like I started something. Other people can pick [the GSA] up. I feel like I've done my duty there. I did a lot there. I sacrificed a lot. I had a lot of bad days there. It's time for other people to step up. I'm done. That's how I feel about it. Some people ask me, 'Do you feel bad for leaving them?' But I don't. I worked hard while I was there."

She lost some friends because of her sexuality and still remains hurt by this. "I was hurt most by the people who been my friends and who were my friends and wouldn't talk to me anymore or would talk to me but not around certain people—people who started out to be my friends and people would pick on them and they wouldn't want to be my friend anymore. I had one girlfriend that when I kissed her, people started finding out and she acted like she had never been with me. She started to hate gay people, and she became very homophobic."

Based on these experiences, Angel wants society to be more accepting of transgender youth. "I wish people understood that it's not bringing this on ourselves; it's who we are. And that we have just as much right as anyone else to be here and that they have no say-so. They need to leave their opinions outside of the classroom. If their opinion got left out more, there would be a lot less of my opinion. If I didn't feel I had to defend myself in the classroom, I wouldn't be defending myself."

Angel's outlook on life has changed, and members of her current school community have been instrumental in enhancing her life. "I have changed. I feel a lot more secure in who I am. I've been in my relationship a long time, and we work at it a lot. [My current teacher] helps me work on a lot of our issues. It's a lot more personal here. More one-to-one and everyone here is friends—teachers and students. I've been able to let go of a lot of it. [This school] is an amazing place, and I know a lot of people who would die to be where I am, but they just can't because most people can't move across the country. . . . If it wasn't for [this school], I probably would have quit high school."

Like all youth, Angel has dreams and plans for a fulfilled future. "I want to be a piercer and own my shop one day. I want chest surgery, testosterone, I want to take T, I want to have implants, I want to be tattooed and pierced. And I want to be a famous piercer in the community. Someone who knows a lot of stuff and is good, where people say, 'He isn't afraid to try new stuff,' and 'He isn't afraid of trying again.'"

WILLIAM, EIGHTEEN, BISEXUAL,
AND JERICKA, EIGHTEEN, LESBIAN

William and Jericka are married and have a two-year-old daughter. They met at their neighborhood high school before enrolling in a school for gay, lesbian, bisexual, and transgender youth. They considered themselves heterosexual when they first met, although they had questioned their sexuality before. They were initially attracted to each other, and neither disclosed any homosexual tendencies.

"We admitted later that we were curious, but we never explored it. . . . She liked my brother and my other brother liked her. I didn't know who she was because I had never seen her. Finally one day she needed a favor, and they needed someone with a driver's license, so they asked me. I was like, 'Okay, I'll go do the favor,' and I went to her house, and that's how I met her. That was on December 31, 1999. I did the favor, I went home, and afterwards she started calling. We started talking on the phone. I was trying to hook her up with my brother, but in the end me and her ended up staying together."

They fell in love and were married shortly thereafter. "A week later we got together, and right away we got married. I fell in love with her and she fell in love with me. . . . We got married a month later. On February 18 we did the civil, and on February 28 we did the actual Catholic thing. It was love at first sight. . . . We went all the way to Las Vegas to get married. We didn't get married for the wrong reasons. We got married for the right reasons: love."

In the short time they were together, they were desperate to start a family, even though their relationship was falling apart. "I wanted a baby and she didn't really want a family, but in the end she said yes. So afterwards we tried and tried and tried to have a baby, but couldn't. So we stopped trying, and we went back to school; we went to get jobs and get our lives together to try and have the baby again. Two months later she got pregnant, and then we had the baby. We lasted two years, and then we wound up breaking up."

Their family members coaxed them to reunite for the child's sake. They rekindled the relationship, but in a fit of rage Jericka left William and their baby and headed for Miami. "My family likes her a lot, and her family likes me a lot. They would try to get me mad and jealous and tell me that she was with her ex-boyfriends. . . . We broke up so many times. It was a lot. She would make me break up with so many girls that it was cruel. Her mom came to my job, and she convinced me to go back to her. . . . Later on we got an apartment. I was working and she was a housewife. Basically that was it. Everything was okay. . . . Life there was nice. . . . She ended up leaving for Miami because we broke up. She wanted to move to Miami so that way we could forget about each other."

Jericka was in Miami for a month before William joined her. He was determined to make the relationship work, so he headed for Miami with their baby in tow. "We were talking for like a whole month. And then we got back together again. I just quit my job and packed everything up and got my daughter, and bam that's it, I went to Miami."

Their life in Miami was cumbersome, and two months later they returned to Los Angeles. On their return, they decided to have their baby baptized. Jericka's friend would serve as one of the godparents, and she introduced the couple to a bisexual youth. This young man enticed William. "So we were going to get the baby baptized. [The godmother] introduced me to her best friend, who ended up being bisexual. She brought him home and introduced us, and he ended up telling her sister that he thought I was cute. I was like, 'Excuse me, straight guys don't tell straight guys that they're cute.' At that time [Jericka and I] liked having sex and we were sleeping together. . . . We were drinking in our house and we ended up going out with another friend of mine that is also bisexual, and all of them wanted to have a little orgy party. They asked me if I was down to mess around with them. I was curious at the time, so I thought here is my chance to experiment. . . . A couple of days later he brought us PCP. . . . We smoked it and everything, and we were playing a game called sexual truth or dare, and they dared me to go down on him, which I did and I liked it. That's when I was like, 'Okay.' We experimented for a week, and she started experimenting with her friend and stuff. We did a lot of sexual stuff with different people, but we were mainly together."

Since his childhood, William had been curious about men so experimenting with the young man seemed natural. "Me and my brothers all messed around with one guy when my brother was five, my other brother was six, I was seven, and this guy was nine or ten years old. . . . Since then I was like, 'It's not the norm; it's not the norm.' I just pushed that experience aside. And from time to time I would like girls, but I would always look at guys. You know how on TV a girl and guy are having sex, and I would always look at the guy. That's what I would do. But I never tried nothing. Everybody thought I was going to grow up to be gay, but then when I got married to her, they were like, 'He's not.'"

William began a relationship with the young man, while Jericka explored her own sexuality. Jericka always believed that she could be a lesbian since many of her family members are lesbian. "My two sisters are lesbian. One is older and one is younger. My mom used to be bisexual and my aunt is gay. My cousin is lesbian, and my aunt and my cousin are together and they have a baby. . . . My sister's girlfriend was my first crush with a girl. I had a big old crush on her. . . . I thought I could be with a woman when I kissed a girl playing the truth or dare. I liked her. I liked her when I kissed her. I was like, 'Wow.' . . . After that I noticed that I was attracted to girls because I liked it. I was like, 'Uh oh,' and I was like, 'It's just not right,' even though my aunt was gay and my cousin was gay. . . . Since then I liked girls. . . . I feel attracted to women and I like women more. . . . I will never go back to a man. [William and I] will never get back together. We act like we are a married couple; we just don't do the sexual thing. That's why people trip out on us—that we keep doing this without having sex."

Jericka eventually became serious with a young woman, and the two became legally committed. Several months later Jericka began to lose interest and ended the relationship. They are civil with each other because her ex-girlfriend is still a good friend of William's. "I just ended my relationship with my girlfriend. . . . Me and her had tried to get together again. We just broke up. It just didn't work out. . . . We did the relationship right where you sign the paper and everything. It's like a marriage certificate, so that if something happens to her everything comes to me. You know, like when you're married. . . . I don't talk to her really. It's like, 'Hi' and 'Bye.' We both go to the same school, I see her in class, I see her in parties, we are in the same crew. That's our gay scene. . . . She's a good person. She's real nice. She's not a bad person, but I changed completely from the person I was. . . . I changed. I really, totally changed from the way I was. In the beginning if she wanted something, I was like, 'What do you want?' I used to give her *caricias* [a gesture of affection] and after a while I started to treat her really bad. I became the man in the relationship, and I became a bitch. I really regret it because she took a lot from me."

Even though Jericka's mother was bisexual and now considers herself heterosexual, she believes that Jericka is going through a phase. "My mom used to be bi. She thinks that I'm confused. . . . I'm afraid to be with a guy. I'm scared I'll feel uncomfortable. I haven't had sex with a guy in two years. My mom is like: 'I know that you are just confused. This is just a little phase that you are going through.'"

Her father resides in Guatemala and remains supportive of her life choices. Her maternal grandmother was devastated with the news but appreciates William and their daughter. "[My dad] lives in Central America, but he knows [that I'm lesbian]. I called to let him know, and he was like, 'I like the way you are and if that makes you happy, then okay.' I didn't tell my grandma; I just came home with a girl. She used to talk about my sisters, and I would defend them: 'That's the way they are.

Let them be.' And I was like, 'I'm the same way, too, Grandma.' She cried with shock."

William is accepting of Jericka's relationships and remains her confidant. They plan to have another baby. "[Women] give her something that I can't. She was dating guys before she turned full lesbian, and I was like, 'I'm the husband regardless, no matter what.' She's still my wife. She ain't getting no divorce. . . . We want to have another baby, and I want to be the father. We don't believe in having kids spread out. We're like, 'No, it's only one set of parents.' We're talking about next year. I feel sorry for [our daughter] because she's lonely. She's always playing by herself, and she doesn't know how to interact with other kids. All she interacts with are people our age, so she doesn't really know how to be with other kids. Now she's barely learning how to be around another kid. . . . I want [Jericka] to get pregnant next year so that they can play together."

William finds men more attractive these days but nonetheless dates women. "I'm more towards guys. There are certain types of girls that I will go with. Guys appeal to me more. When I started coming out of the closet, I started messing around with people to see who I was. And finally I made it with a guy that I was with for a year and half."

He is very open with his family, often introducing his boy- or girl-friends to his family. His last boyfriend was well received by the family. "When I start dating somebody, I always introduce them to the family. I introduce them to everybody, and then I introduce them to my daughter. And then my daughter does the choosing for me. She chooses the guys for me. My daughter is a very picky little girl. If she doesn't like you, she doesn't go to you. And my ex-, the guy I was with for a year and half, she really didn't like him, but in the end she accepted him. He was fifteen when I was with him. And it was like having two little kids. They would fight. They would argue. They would fight for my attention and stuff like that."

William's mother knows that he is bisexual. They have a close relationship, and she suspected when he was a child that he was gay. "Me and my mom have a very close relationship. She's like, 'I'm your mother, but at the same time I want to be your friend.' That's the way we are. She knows everything. Everything I've done. It's like talking to one of my friends. She's very outgoing like me. . . . One day my stepdad came home drunk, and me and my brother were in the living room, and he came in saying: '*Eres masochista. Eres masochista*'—a person who likes to experiment sexually. He started bothering me about it. He was like, 'You like fags and this and that,' and I said, 'Why do you care?' 'If I would have known that you like fags, I would have never gotten married to your mother.' And I was like, 'What does that have to do with anything?' and then he wanted to hit me, but my brother got in the way. He pushed my brother, and he pushed me into the bedroom. So they pushed me away from him, and that was it. And then my mother came in and me and my mom talked. I asked her, 'Why do they always say that they know about me and things like that?' I told her I liked guys, and she said, 'I've known this since you were small.' They said that since I was small I had *las manitas* [limp wrists] and things like that. But this is me. This is who I am. She was like, *'Si te gusta que den por atras, que te den por atras'*—if you like it from the back, then get it from the back. And I was like, 'Okay, Mom.' And that was it. The one I couldn't tell was my grandmother. I just couldn't because she was the one who raised me."

His grandmother knows about his sexual orientation and is seemingly supportive of him. But she fears that he will get AIDS from his homosexual relations. "Now she knows. She accepts it, but not really, because, well you know how old people are. She hears so many things, like how gay people are going to get AIDS and this and that. One time I had a scare. When I was coming out, I ended up messing around with a gay guy who had AIDS, but I didn't know it at the time. I found out later on, and I was like, 'Oh, my God, what if I have it?' So I kept getting tested, and I was scared for my life, and she kept telling me that we would get a place together and she would take care of me if I had it. My family went through a hard time at that time. They didn't know what to do, and that's why my grandmother is more afraid of me being with guys. She tries to get me back together with [Jericka]."

William is very close to his family, and his brothers are supportive of his bisexual relations. His extended family at one time believed that he was gay, but now think that he is heterosexual because of his relationship with Jericka. "I've always been like this, like the way I act, but they know that I am married to her. My family went to our wedding and everything. And it so happens that every time the family comes over she ends up being at the house. . . . I have a cousin who came out to me after I came out to her. But when she told me, she was like: 'Don't tell nobody. That's our secret.' My uncle would die if he knew. He used to talk so much shit that I was going to grow up to be gay and stuff like that, and now I'm like: 'Don't even start with me. Your only daughter is gay.' . . . My immediate family is my two brothers, my mom, and our daughter. We're very close. We're a very close family. My brothers know [that I'm bisexual]. My middle brother accepted it. We used to play like we were a couple before I came out. But my younger brother, he's like the thug in the family. He wasn't okay about it, but in the end he accepted it. He told me he was my brother and that he loved me and that made me cry. They accept me. All my friends go over to the house, and I tell them my brothers are very gay-friendly. I've taken them to gay clubs. They're very open. They don't let anybody mess with me."

William's family unfailingly encourages him to pursue a sexual relationship with Jericka, even though he is adamant that their relationship is strictly platonic. "When I had a girlfriend, they were like, 'She's the only woman for you.' I go along with it to make them happy. And they always have to bother me. Like when she's in the bedroom watching TV or something, they'll call me to her bedroom and they'll be like, 'Why don't you try something with her?' I'm like, 'No, we have that respect for each other,' and they're like, 'Try it.' And I'm like, 'We're friends and that's all that we are.' They think we act too much like a couple."

He loves Jericka and is philosophical about the repercussions of his relationships with men. "My feelings for her haven't died. She knows that for a fact. I told myself and her that I'm always going to love her. My love for her is always going to stay here. Until this day it's still there. Not sexually. I'm attracted to her, but she knows that I could go without sex. I love her for who she is. . . . When I was with my boyfriend, it made it difficult for me. Loving her at the same time and falling in love with him made my heart 'Oh, my God.' He managed to pull me away from her. He did. . . . He caused me so much stress. He managed to keep me away from my daughter because I started spending less time with her."

His ex-boyfriend got him addicted to drugs, and he introduced these to Jericka. "But the bad thing was that he got me into drugs. For the whole time I was with him I was on drugs. At that time I had a car, a good-paying job, I had everything going for me. . . . I lost it all. I even lost the little bond that me and my daughter had. . . . The thing with me is that when I was with my ex, he would bring them to me. And I was like, 'Okay, I'll do it.' . . . He would go off when I was asleep, and I was so worried, like, 'What happened to him and this and that.' So I started buying it. At that time I had a good-paying job. So I would spend like $100 a day so that he would stay home and he wouldn't be out in the streets. But by doing that, I got myself into drugs. . . . He got me into crystal—glass, ice, methane. I had been doing it for a whole week. I hadn't slept for a whole week. One day I picked [Jericka] up at my friends, and we went to a gay club and she tried it. . . . I had a $60 bag. Each little bag is $20 worth. We did a 20 on the way over there in the car, and then we were dancing the whole night nonstop. That drug keeps you like this [snap, snap, snap] and keeps you alert. We were so gone on the drug that we were dancing nonstop. After a week the drug wasn't hitting no more. After that I was like, 'Here.' I gave her two bags' worth, I gave her the pipes and I fell asleep. I finally knocked out, and she spent the whole night doing it."

He knows that taking illegal drugs is unwise, but rationalizes his propensity to take them. "I'm the kind of person who's always hyper and alert. I'm always busy doing something. And when I'm on it, I get busier. I start cleaning. I start rearranging. I start doing things, but very fast. That's what it does. I like that. I like to be active. And one of the good things is that you lose weight. You don't think about eating. You see food and you're like, 'Oh, no.' That's how I ended up in the hospital and needed surgery. I had ulcers and needed gallbladder surgery. I had gallstones."

When he and his boyfriend broke up, William thought that he would be drug free. But a day before this interview he was high again. "I stopped. . . . Honestly, I won't lie. I love it. I love it. It feels good. I don't do it because of my problems. I just like it. I like the way it feels, but thanks to her, she's the one who keeps me away from it. But I caved in yesterday. I caved in. I did it. I'm only human."

Jericka had an unpleasant experience with the drugs and now refrains from using them. "She went crazy. The thing that happens when you're on this drug is that you're supposed to be with somebody. Not alone. This drug is not for somebody who's weak-minded. And she's weak-minded. So she was by herself, she ended up burning her tongue, she had blisters on her fingers because she didn't know how to do the lighter. When you do a certain amount, you start seeing things. A weak-minded person would be like, 'Oh no, it's real.' A person who's strong knows that he's hallucinating and he goes along with it. She ended up in my closet, and the thing is me and her believe in ghosts and stuff like that—the supernatural—and as it so happens there's a spirit in the closet. So she ended up in the closet going crazy hearing voices. She was hearing voices and hitting her head, saying, 'No, no.' She was just really gone. She was pale and really sick. For like a whole week she was like really sick. Because she doesn't do drugs, it was too much for her."

William and Jericka find that gay and lesbian people tend to have far more crises in their lives than heterosexuals. Both seem frustrated with the drama, and William believes that his troubles began when he entered the gay and lesbian social network. They call this network "gay world." "I don't like gay life. My life was so good when I was not gay. I turned gay and I went down. One thing about gay people is that they envy you. They envy you. If you're a little better than them, they talk so much about you. Gay men only. . . . I'm a very outgoing person and everyone looks to me. The gay people that I meet don't like that about me. They're like, 'Why do they look to you?' They're jealous of the fact that people always look to me. I'm not making this up. She can vouch for that. . . . I'm Guatemalan but most of the gay guys that I know are Mexican, and Mexican gay guys, all they like to do is fight. They try to be better than everybody else. Me, I could care less. I'm me; I go to parties to have fun. That's it. That's my thing. I don't go looking for drama. They look for drama. I don't. I go to dance, to party, to everything. I don't care. I'm being me. I hate the straight world, too. Most of my friends are girls, and guys get jealous that girls are kicking it with me. It's not my fault that they wind up falling for me."

Jericka seems more satisfied with the gay world, but is bothered by the protective role that many lesbians take in her life. "I noticed that gay relationships have more drama than straight relationships and lesbians are worse. Lesbian relationships have more drama. This is the way it is. Girls try to act so manly that they actually have to show their power. My ex-girlfriends cannot see me with another dyke. They can't stand that. So when she sees me with another girl, she asks everyone, 'Who's that?' 'Who's she dancing with?' 'Who's she talking to?' 'Do you know who she is?' And they want to pick the girl that I can be with. It's like, 'No, I don't want you to be with her.' They want to tell me what girl to be with. It's that they're very protective of me."

She is nonetheless proud to be lesbian. "I'm out there. It's not hard for me. . . . I tell people: 'Yeah, I'm gay. I'm lesbian.' I'm very open and I'm really proud of it. I wear rainbow shoelaces, my bag has little rainbows, and I wear my rainbow chain because I'm gay and I'm proud."

Much of her pride is derived from her aunt, who overcame familial battles to be with her lover. "I have my aunt who has gone through a lot. Back then she couldn't come out. She was the only one who came out to the family. A lot of the family was saying: 'No! No! No!' And it was a lot of drama and shit, and I saw that she was taking a lot from them. I don't remember what they told her because I was really small. . . . She's like thirty-one or thirty-two, but she looks a lot older because she's had such a rough life. She's with my cousin, her niece. The niece is twenty-two and [someone] just had a baby for them. The aunt and the niece are lovers. The family is not very happy about it, but they don't have a choice. The whole time [the family has] wanted to separate them and they managed to do it. But they would still see each other because in the end they got back together again."

William believes that Jericka can be proud because society is more accepting of lesbians. "But you know it's easier for lesbians than it is for gay guys. You can see two lesbians kissing on the bus, but if you see two guys kissing on the bus, you'll get fucked up or something. When I was a little kid, I was told, 'That's not right; that's not right.' My grandmother would throw away my Barbies. I would play with Barbies, and she would take them from me and throw them away even though she taught me how to be a woman, how to be a housewife."

He believes he has to adapt his mannerisms to meet social expectations whether he is in heterosexual or homosexual circles. "When I'm around a lot of girls and they don't know about me, I hate having to play the part that I'm straight. I have a lot of [feminine] hand movements, but I can play them off. But sometimes I have to be like, 'Hold on; play the masculine part.' But when I'm in the gay world, I don't have to. I hate the gay world, though. . . . In the gay world, most guys will not date bisexuals because they're afraid that they will go back to girls, and the same thing is true in the lesbian world. In the straight world, you can't be bi; you're either gay or straight. So when I'm in the straight world, I don't talk about the fact that I'm bi. And in the gay world I don't talk about the fact that I'm bi."

He also finds that heterosexuals misunderstand gay and lesbian people. "Most straight people are like: 'Oh, my God. What if they want to touch me?' and 'What if they want to do this to me or that to me? Oh, my God.' That's the way straight people think. 'What if they're checking me out?' Gay people know their boundaries with straight people. Seriously, when I look at a straight guy, it's just a look. That's the farthest it will go. Most straight people think, 'What if they try to grab my ass?'"

He limits his sexual experiences, even though he believes that gay men are notoriously promiscuous. "People think that gay guys are hos— that they sleep around. And it's true. The majority of gay guys sleep around. They have one partner, then another partner, then another partner. I don't believe in doing that at all. Believe me, the parties that we go to everybody's been with this one and that one. . . . Gay guys are hos. This is as far as I will go [he points to his mouth]. Unless I'm with that person, it's beyond that."

Neither of the two ever felt isolated or alone. They both had a network of friends and close ties to their siblings. William, however, contemplated suicide in his early adolescence. "When I was younger, I thought about suicide, but for other reasons. When I was twelve, I was molested by my uncle. And he had told me that if I told anyone, he was going to molest my brothers. . . . So I let him do what he wanted so that he wouldn't molest my brothers."

School life was not difficult for William and Jericka. William was a feminine boy but was able to defend himself from bullies. He was flamboyant in high school, but his brothers protected him from harm. "In elementary school, I always played with girls, jump rope, all those girl things, and there was one guy who was saying that I was gay. One day when I was in the bathroom, he pushed me and said that I was gay, and I was like: 'What? No.' And then I socked him one. And from that day on they never bothered me again. . . . I've always been liked. People have always liked me, and so I've never been bothered. In elementary through high school I was a nerd. I was always into my schoolwork. I was in the library. I've always studied. I never went out. . . . It was school, school, school, study, study, study. And then it was straight to my married life. I never enjoyed my childhood or nothing. . . . In high school, some guys started to bother me, saying that I was gay. But my brothers were around, and so they stopped talking shit about me. I really didn't have any problems with it in high school. They were always spreading rumors about me, but my brothers were always around to shut people up. So my high school was very normal, but then I started ditching."

Jericka had a normal school life. She was never harassed even though she was a tomboy, but she was a victim of a gay-bashing while she and a friend were on their way to a party. "I used to go to private school. I was a little tomboy—I used to play sports, I was tough, I used to kick guys' asses, and I was like: 'Don't touch me. You only touch me when I tell you to touch me.' I'd kick their asses and that's about it. In junior high I found out this girl was gay and I was like, 'What?' She was really out there. And I was like, 'Wow.' And in high school I was just into my own thing; I was into my ROTC military thing. . . . No one ever picked on me or harassed me. None of that. No one ever spread a rumor about me. I was never bullied or harassed in high school. But I have been gay-bashed. I was going to a party in South Central. I was going up a hill, and we couldn't find the party, and I was like, 'Aww man.' . . . It just so happens that they were gay-bashing in South Central that day. I was walking with one of our friends, this girl I used to like, when they started shooting. I was like, 'Oh, my God; oh, my God.' They were shooting, they turned around, and they started getting off the car. And they took the gun and put it to my friend's head. They kept saying they hated gays and things like that. And they took my jewelry and everything. I freaked out and I had a seizure. And my girl was like trying to calm me down, like, 'Calm down, Jericka; it's okay.' That was the first time I had ever been gay-bashed."

Jericka and William were eager to get their diplomas, so they enrolled at a school for gay, lesbian, bisexual, and transgender youth. William was hesitant about going back to school, but Jericka encouraged him to return to school. "She was always telling me go back to school. . . . She was always pushing me because she knew that I could do something better. So finally she dragged me, and I enrolled and I started the school. . . . She knows what I'm capable of because she's always pushing me for the best."

Jericka learned about the school from an ex-girlfriend, and after she was accepted into the program, she had her current girlfriend attend the school. "I wanted to get my high school diploma, and my ex-girl-friend told me I could finish high school there. And I was like, 'Oh, please,' because I wanted to go. So I got enrolled and everything. I took [my girlfriend] too. They're giving me that opportunity to get a high school diploma."

Jericka believes that there should be other schools for gay, lesbian, bisexual, and transgender youth, but William believes that this population of youth is further isolated when they attend such schools. He thinks that these youth must attend their neighborhood schools and learn to deal with heterosexuals. "This school is good, but I also see it as bad because it isolates us from straight people. I'm perfectly fine surrounded by straight people. She just told me that she doesn't like to party with straight people. This is what they're teaching them. . . . All those kids are surrounded by their own people, and they don't bring them with straight people. They're learning to keep to themselves, they're own kind. . . . Why do you want to isolate the gay kids from everybody else? They have to learn to get along with everybody else. I don't like the fact that she told me that she doesn't like to be around straight people. That's so wrong."

He emphasizes that public schools can do little for these youth and that they must contend with the social stigma. "Honestly, there's nothing they can do because they do get hated. When you're a little kid, you get taught that gay life is not right. You put all that stuff in your head since you're a little kid, especially if you have old-fashioned parents. That's the way it is. The high school years are the worst years. It's live and learn, and being gay, you have to go through it. . . . Most students will not come out of the closet because they're afraid. The ones that do come out are either gay-bashed or they will be accepted. They take a big chance right there. It's a part of life and they can't do nothing about it. And the groups that they have for support, 'Oh, yes, I'm there for you' and 'Yeah, you're gay,' oh whoop-tee-do. But you still go through your head, 'Oh, my God, this is wrong.'"

William graduated in June 2002, and he is unsure of what his immediate future holds. "I'm talented in so many things. I've had so many opportunities, so many career opportunities, honestly I do not know what I want to do. I'm not a money person. I don't crave money. I just want to be happy."

Jericka hopes that William becomes a designer or a comic book illustrator. She hopes to pursue a career in the performing arts. "I want to go to college. I want to go to CAL Arts. It's a performing arts school. I want to study photography. Long term, I have a lot of things that I want to do, but that's what most interests me and that's what I want to do. If I don't get to, I'll be happy being a receptionist or a secretary."

Regardless of what careers or relationships may come their way, William and Jericka intend to remain friends for a lifetime. "I always watch out for her, and she always watches out for me. We're there for each other no matter what. I feel like when we got married, we made a bond 'until death do us part.' I got married one time, and I'm not going to get married again. We're not going to get divorced, no matter what. Her ex wanted her to get a divorce from me, and my ex wanted me to get a divorce from her. No. No. We don't come in a two-pack, we come in a three-pack."

JEREMY, SIXTEEN, GAY

Jeremy lives in a conservative Midwest suburb and was apprehensive about sharing his story. The quiet and shy adolescent had attempted suicide nine months prior to this interview and was struggling with his sexuality. He is in the closet, and although his parents know that he might be gay, they wish he would change. His mother admitted him into a psychiatric hospital, where he has received therapy. He believes that he was born gay. "I've always known that I liked boys. I just never said anything to anyone. I just liked boys. I remember looking through my dad's magazines and thinking, 'He's cute, he's cute, he's cute.' . . . When I was like five or six, this boy, he was my age, too, came to spend the night at my house. He was like the son of my mom's friend. I had never seen or played with him before, but I liked him and wanted to hug and kiss him so bad. Before he left the next day, I hid his jacket, and I remember just holding it and smelling it and sleeping with it. Everybody was like: 'Where's the coat? Where is it?' but I hid it."

Jeremy was raised in a sheltered home where homosexuality was never discussed, yet he believed that being gay was wrong. "It's funny because when I was little no one ever said gay is bad, gay is bad. No one ever said anything about it, I guess. No one ever told me not to be gay. I didn't even know what that was. But it's funny because all of my coloring books showed boys and girls holding hands or girl ducks with boy ducks. I never said anything to anyone, but I knew that liking guys was wrong. . . . This girl I used to play with had a little house in her backyard. She used to say that she was going to marry her uncle Bobby. He was so gorgeous and I wanted to marry him, too, but I knew I couldn't say it. . . . And I wanted girl things for Christmas, but I knew not to ask for them."

He was always interested in play objects commonly associated with girls, and when some boys accused him of being gay, he tried to take an interest in traditional boy activities. "I always liked the girl things. I wanted to play house. I wanted to play with Barbie. I wanted the Barbie dream house and the Barbie swimming pool. I liked playing with girls. They were fun. I used to have a stuffed animal, a dog with long ears, and I remember rolling his ears up and putting a bobby pin on them to make it look like I had worked on his hair. . . . I know I was a big sissy. But you know something, I liked playing all the girl things, but I hated it when boys would say, 'You play with girls,' or 'You big sissy.' When I got a little older, they got meaner and told me that I was a fag. I didn't like that. I still don't and I hate being gay. My life would be so much easier if I were like the other guys. . . . And when I was about eleven, some kids at school kept calling me gay. They used to ask me if I was related to RuPaul. I felt so bad, so sad. That's not normal for a kid to feel depressed. But I was. I really tried to force myself to do boy things. But my father never wanted to do anything with me, and no one ever taught me football or baseball or those kinds of things. And the boys just wanted to wrestle or roll around in the grass. I didn't like that. I don't want to be all sweaty, and I hate the way grass feels. I've never played football. I don't even know how to throw the ball. . . . And other boys would go to the ponds to catch frogs, and I would scream when they would show me."

Most of his closest friends are girls, but one is a boy. Jeremy is not romantically interested in his friend Billy, but he is possessive of him. "Most of my friends have been girls. And you know something, they never ask me if I like a girl. But Billy was my first real boy friend that I met in junior high. I like him, but not that way. I don't even think he knows about this. But Billy's cool because he isn't like the other guys. He just likes to do things that I can do. Like we listen to CDs, he likes to read, we can talk about our trips, and we used to pretend that we owned a Porsche dealership. He got me turned on to Porsches. I made checks on my computer, and we used to pretend that movie stars would come to buy them from us. That's the other thing: we like movie stars. We like to see who's doing what, and we go to the movies a lot. . . . I'm not in love with Billy, but in a crazy way I don't want to share him with other guys or girls. Does that make sense? I get jealous when I find out that some girls like him. And I never want to do anything [with him] if he's going to do something with Tommy. I know that Billy's not gay."

Jeremy has had no sexual experiences. "I've never done anything with a guy. Ever. I've never kissed a girl or a guy. I'm the last American virgin. But I always think about what it would be like. I stole pictures of cute guys from the yearbook office. This one senior is way cute, like all the girls like him and stuff. And when no one is around, I put his picture on my stand and I imagine that he's my boyfriend."

Jeremy has been depressed for nearly two years. He is not sure that being gay is the cause of his depression because he now knows that he has a chemical imbalance. In his early teens he became introverted, spent most his time on the computer, and would not converse with his parents. He is an only child, and his parents thought that he was behaving like a typical adolescent. Jeremy attempted suicide after his father found him in a closet masturbating. At first the father was taken aback, but he became enraged when he found the material that Jeremy had with him. He began to yell, ridicule him, and a few hours later attacked him. He told him that if he knew that his son could be gay, he would have aborted him. His mother was upset with the situation and called Jeremy evil and asked why he had to be so weird. The humiliation led Jeremy to attempt suicide. "My mother thinks I'm going to try again. I won't. My father is weird toward me. My therapist says [my family has] got to talk about this, but we don't. We probably never will. My mom tries, but I can't. I tell her, 'Let's just move on.' I think my father hates me. He doesn't talk to me or my mom. I really don't care. If they get divorced, I don't care."

Jeremy is a high achiever involved in the school band and in honors programs. He has been teased but recognizes that his school climate could be much worse. "I always liked school. I'm quiet. I do my work. I keep to myself. I have friends, but I'm not like in some popular clique, you know. . . . Some guys used to harass me, but it was teasing. They used to make me feel like shit. If I think about being gay or faggy or someone saying that I am, I get this weird feeling in the pit of my stomach, and then it gets in my mind and I can't let go of it. . . . Kids at this high school could be much worse. I know because I've read some stuff on the Internet. . . . You hear lots of fag and queer, but that's just the way it is at my school. . . . Some kids may not be gay, but if a guy wears light blue or any pastel color, it's faggot this and faggot that. . . . One time I heard that the swim teacher was gay and that the guys on the swim team were gay, too. But that's crazy. I can only imagine what they say about me."

His school has little support for gay and lesbian youth, and discussions about homosexuality are limited. "One time in history we talked about Eleanor Roosevelt being a lesbian. All I thought was: 'Please, let's not talk about this. Let's move on. Don't even go there, Mr. F.' I felt like everyone was looking at me. . . . I don't know if there are any gay kids at my school. I'm almost sure that I'm the only one. My therapist says I should think about starting a gay-straight alliance, but there's no way. I don't want people to know that I'm gay. . . . I just don't."

He is not thrilled with the idea of a support group for gay and lesbian students but nevertheless emphasizes that society should adjust its attitude toward gays and lesbians. "I don't want a support group. I don't want a GSA. I just want people to be nice about it. I don't watch a lot of TV but it just seems to me that on *Will & Grace* people are cool with the guys being gay and they never have to explain anything. They just are."

Jeremy wishes that he was not gay or feminine. "I don't like being gay. I don't like being so faggy. I don't want people to try to help me with it. I don't want to be bothered. My therapist says that she wants to help me, and she's like, 'Just give me a chance.' I'm like, 'Okay, just to make you happy.' . . . I know that I'm making progress not because she tells me but because a year ago I couldn't even say the words gay, fag, faggot, or anything like that. Everything I've told you was all in my head. I never told anyone. But after [the psychiatric hospital] I told her and now I can tell you. . . . I just wish I was a normal guy."

Jeremy wants to go to college and pursue music or computers. He hopes to have a companion. "I want to graduate and go to a good school. I'm either going to go into piano or something related to computers. . . . And I hope I meet a nice guy when I'm there."

SAMANTHA, EIGHTEEN, LESBIAN

Samantha is a senior at Harvey Milk School in New York City. She has suffered a number of hardships—losing her mother at a young age, being physically separated from her biological sister, and moving from one foster home to another. These hardships had a definite impact on her academic success, and she started attending school less and less. All the while Samantha was coming to terms with her sexuality.

Her school counselor believed that Samantha would benefit from the attention and services provided by the school for gay, lesbian, bisexual, and transgender youth, and Samantha subsequently enrolled at Harvey Milk when she was fifteen. She had same-sex attractions at a relatively young age. "When I was seven years old, I had a crush on Cindy Crawford. I didn't know what it meant to be a lesbian. I just know that I liked Cindy Crawford. Plus everyone was calling me a little tomboy and telling me that I was going to grow up to like girls anyway. And everybody in my family knew that."

It was not until seven years later that Samantha understood that she was lesbian. "I knew I was a lesbian when I was like fourteen. I came out to a friend of mine, but I didn't officially come out until I was like sixteen. It was nothing really. And between fourteen and sixteen I just tried to act like everybody else, but not sharing it with everybody else. I was always an outcast anyway. I used to dress gothic and all that other stuff, and I was outcast. . . . I came out to all my friends when I was like six-teen and then everybody else started coming out, which scared me."

She does not have a hard time being a lesbian, but finds some people's reactions annoying. "I hate being mistaken because of the way I dress, being mistaken for a boy. . . . I don't care, but it's just annoying because like girls will be coming up to me, and especially when I'm sit-ting on the train and they'll be like, 'Ahhh, that's a cute guy.' I'm like, 'Yuck.' They blow me a kiss. I'm like, 'You figure it out.'"

Samantha lives in a foster home, and her foster mother is be-coming more accepting of her sexuality. Her seven foster siblings have been receptive to Samantha's sexual orientation but nonetheless inun-date her with naïve questions. "My mother gets on my nerves. She asks stupid questions. Ever since I've been going out with my girlfriend, she's like, 'Is there a special law about being a lesbian that will make you go to jail?' or sometimes she'll be like, 'Oh, if you don't pray, you'll go to hell.' It's like the whole redemption thing. . . . At first she was like, 'Well, you're going to hell, but you're living with me and I'll support you.' . . . My fos-ter siblings, they're just like cool. They ask me stupid questions, too. 'What's it like with a girl?' 'Is it like kissing a guy?' 'When you plan on having sex; how is that going to go?'"

Her peers in the community and extended family were just as re-ceptive, and her biological sister was not surprised with her news. "They didn't care. They were just like, 'She's still acting herself.' . . . They knew since I was little. They were not even shocked when I told them. They said they knew since I was little and that I used to talk about my best friend and living with her and being with her. I was like, 'I don't remem-ber that stuff.' . . . We're so close. We hang out every day. We hang out be-fore school, after school. We go to each other's houses. We go to parties together. . . . It was weird coming out to [my sister]. It was like, 'I already know.' Like: 'Excuse me? You took the fun out of the surprise.' She does-n't talk about it. She's like, 'When are you going to stop being a virgin?' because she lost her virginity before me. But I decided to wait."

At one time Samantha felt isolated and alone. She had so many events unfolding in her life that she did not want to contend with being lesbian. She almost got herself killed. "I always felt like I didn't think any-one understood because I had heard that it's just a phase. 'You'll get over it.' I felt I had no one to help me. I was scared to tell my therapist. I thought she would probably commit me or something. . . . [I contem-plated suicide], but it was for different reasons, though. My mom died and me and my sister got separated—we weren't getting along; we were always fighting. I only tried it once. It was kind of retarded, though. I was really down and I hated being gay and I was walking in the middle of the street and I wasn't thinking and I almost got hit by a bus. At that point I hated being gay. I didn't want to be bothered. I didn't want to be gay. I didn't want to be anything."

Now she has a network of gay, lesbian, and bisexual friends, and she knows she is emotionally supported by the school's director of educational and recreational services and her therapist. "Well Deborah's really cool. When I first got here, she welcomed me, and they helped me fit into the school and the setting and stuff like that. I really connect with Deborah."

She is comfortable being lesbian but wishes that society would be more understanding. "I never have denied being a lesbian. If I see someone on the train and they'll ask if I'm a boy or a girl, I'll say, 'I'm a girl.' And they'll be like, 'Do you like girls?' I'm like, 'Yeah.' . . . Since I've come out, it means a lot to me. I've been able to comfort myself sometimes knowing that I'm loved. Like I'm getting experience just like any other person. It's very good being who I am. . . . I envy straight people because I'm a lesbian. I can't get that acceptance that straight people get walking down the street. Like if me and my girlfriend were walking, holding hands and stuff, people would stare and talk. Which I don't care. . . . I'm not jealous, but envious."

She adamantly denounces the stereotypes. "'Why do I have to dress like a guy?' or 'Oh, you just met the wrong guy.' I've been out with plenty of guys before, and I just don't like them. And there'll be guys that say, 'I can fix that for you.' Ooooh. I have no problems speaking my mind to people. . . . It's just the way I feel. Geeeez. If you don't like it, tough titties."

Her school life before Harvey Milk was not an easy one. She was often truant, and when she attended school, she was harassed by her peers. School personnel did very little to support her. "I hardly ever went to school. I would go into the building, go through the front door, check in, and I was out the basement. . . . I never fit in. I never fit in. All my life I never fit in with the crowd. And my friends who related to me . . . we were always ridiculed by everybody else. So you know what? I stopped going after my sophomore year. . . . Because they made rumors that I was a lesbian, the girls would go to different parts of the locker room to get dressed. One year I was sitting on the basketball team and I was jumped by the girls, but they didn't do too much to me. They were just like mushing me and hitting me, you know little girl sissy stuff. . . . If I did go to school, I would stay in one or two classrooms throughout the whole day. Maybe go to lunch. I would stay with my Spanish teacher because she understood. She wasn't gay or anything. She knew what I was going through. I used to be in this program called the SPARKS program;

it's a peer mediation group. I would stay there for like half a day and not go to class because I was hiding. It wasn't that I was scared to go to class; it was the fact that when I was young, I used to take a lot of martial arts and I was afraid of hurting somebody. So I would always let them hit me and not hit back because of the discipline and stuff."

Samantha remembered one teacher vividly. "Besides the girls on the basketball team, one of my teachers was a bitch. She was my biology teacher, and I was sitting in class and I had my chain on—my gay chain—and she was telling me to take it off. I was like, 'I'm sorry, this is a symbol for who I am and what I do. If someone was wearing a yarmulka and they had it on, would you tell them to take it off?' . . . She told me that there was a new rule that all kids who have any offensive and derogatory symbols around their neck or on their head have to take them off. So I got really mad. . . . She kicked me out the classroom and suspended me from her class for the rest of the year. . . . I told the principal, but me and the principal didn't get along either. I don't like her. Never have, never will. . . . [The teacher and I] made an agreement. Because it wasn't a religious thing, I had to take it off. I took it off, but she had to stop being really rude to me. . . . So what she started doing was that there were some kids who were wearing marijuana leaves and stuff. She told them to take them off. If I had to take my thing off, they had to take their things off."

Some friends were helpful and supportive of her. "My friends helped me a lot—the ones who actually stuck by me after I came out to them. There were like sixty of us. It was kind of like our own club. We kind of made our own club called the Outsiders, but some of us graduated, some of us moved, and we kind of shrank. And the ones I did come out to were the ones I was really close-knit with. They really stuck by me. Maybe one or two of them would not bother with me. I don't care. I always had the 'I-don't-care' attitude. I think I do care, but I'm going to act nonchalant."

Ironically, when Samantha transferred to Harvey Milk, more youth started to come out at her previous school. She knows that gay, lesbian, bisexual, and transgender youth exist in schools today and strongly encourages schools to have clubs for these youth. "I realized that there were a lot of gay people at my school. . . . And [the other students] decided to pick on me because I was one of the strong ones and came out. . . . As soon as I left, my sister told me a lot of gay people came out. . . . There's a lot of gay and lesbian people who are in fear of being outed and stuff, and we needed that support. We need that stability."

She was thrilled to be a student at the Harvey Milk School. The students at the school validated that she was not the only lesbian youth in New York City, and she found everyone accommodating. "I decided to come here because I needed a place to see other gay people, to see other people like me. It was shocking. I was like, 'Oh, my God.' I had never seen gay people before. This is going to sound funny, but I expected them to look different. I had heard the stereotypes, like gay people have limp wrists, like lesbians wear baggy pants like I used to, like I do, and stuff like that, so I was expecting that. . . . I thought, 'There is no way that this is a gay organization. This place is full of straight people.' I was like, 'Oh, my God, they are gay.' I was actually seeing girls kissing girls and guys holding hands with other guys. And I was like, 'Wow.' It was weird because they were all so happy, especially when I first got here. The staff was like happy. It was like when you go to a fancy restaurant and the people are like: 'Hi. Welcome. Can I take your order?' That's the way they were all the time. The staff is so happy."

She enjoys the school community and credits the school with turning her life around. "I have fun. I have friends now who I guess like me. I'm going to graduate because I didn't think that I was going to graduate school. I'm now motivated to stay in school. . . . I used to be very bad. I used to be in trouble all the time. . . . I got arrested a couple of times. I've changed for the better. I wouldn't go to class, I would fail the school miserably, and now I'm on the verge of graduating, which I never thought that I would see. I'm happy. That's a first. It's just—I have a feeling that I've never had before. Satisfied. There you go. [Schools like this] allow the opportunity for some kids to get the education they need to graduate."

Samantha believes that the students are motivated to learn more about gay and lesbian issues, and students integrate gay and lesbian issues into many of their assignments. "It's really different here. Like when we do reports, everybody aspires to look for gay people—famous gay people. We had an English report last marking period, and we had to write a report on poets, and everybody did their report on gay or lesbian poets or on a scandalous poet. It was weird. I've never seen so many gay people intrigued by gay people before."

She and her girlfriend have been together for eight months, a record for Samantha. They met through the services provided by the social agency that runs the school. "On June 4, it will be eight months. I didn't think I could stay in a relationship that long. . . . We talk a lot. We fight a lot. We have some moments. . . . She wants to have kids. I don't. I tell her, 'How are we going to do this? I don't have sperm to give you.' I will pay for the in vitro fertilization. I'll pay for it. I'd rather have that than for some guy stabbing her. . . . Not even a good friend of mine. I don't care. Nobody's touching my girlfriend. She told me she was bi but she's more toward me. So I'm like, 'No because that may trigger your bi side.' "

Even though she is a member of a safe school community, she still encounters some harassment. On her hour-and-a-half train ride home from school one day, she overheard some youth making snide remarks about gays and lesbians. This incident almost caused a brawl. "Yesterday I was on the train, and I was sitting right across from a bunch of school kids. I didn't want to be sitting next to them because I didn't want to be affiliated with them or anything because I know how some of these people talk. And I was sitting there minding my own business, and this boy was talking to the girl about a girl and how her and her friends have a girlfriend and this girl was like: 'Oh, my God. I can't believe it.' And he was like, 'Well, what are you going to do?' 'Well, I'm not going to talk to her because I don't talk to faggots.' And I looked at her like really evil. I wanted to go up to her and smack the shit out of her, but I didn't. The guy caught on that I was looking at him, and he was like, 'Yo, yo, chill, chill, chill.' And she was like, 'I don't like dykes. I don't like gay people.' I looked at her. I grilled her so hard that she realized that I was looking at her and she stopped. She just stopped talking. Then when I got off the train, she said really loud: 'Oh, that dyke wouldn't have done nothing to me. I would have smacked the shit out of her.' I wanted to get back on that train and beat her."

Samantha believes that some people, such as the one on the train, simply do not understand lesbians. To that end she emphasizes that lesbians are no different from anyone else. "We're not coming after you. We're not trying to take over the world. If we wanted to rape you, we would have done it already. We're not to be feared. We are human beings just like everybody else. The only thing is we like the same sex. I wish they would stop looking at me like if I were from some other planet. I am still from planet Earth, even though sometimes I wish I wasn't. Basically, we're not going to attack you like you attack us. We are not monsters. You're not going to get AIDS by touching us."

She aspires to be self-employed and is considering higher education, but generally prefers to take each day for what it is worth. "I actually want to study astronomy but it's too many years of school and I really don't want to spend my life in school. So I'll just take a culinary course and an art course and double major. I'll probably take an entrepreneurial course or something. . . . I just want to live to see the next day. I just want to get a nice job, a nice apartment, be happy with my girl, and maybe one day we'll have a baby."

She encourages other gay, lesbian, bisexual, and transgender youth to be strong and hopes that through her story other young lesbians will learn that they are not alone. "Don't be scared of who you are. There are times when you feel like you are alone in this world, but there

Chapter Five

❧ Profiles of Three Schools

Well, I was about five, but I didn't have a word for it. I liked girls or whatever. When I was twelve, I was in sixth grade, and I was taking a shower and I started thinking about this girl that I had a crush on, but I didn't tell her I had a crush on her. "Oh, my God, I'm taking a shower and thinking about a girl. Oh my god, I'm gay." I just kind of laughed and I didn't think anything much of it. When I was thirteen, I had my first girlfriend. She considered herself bisexual. . . . I always felt different in the sense that I didn't have a boyfriend, but I always thought it was because I wasn't of the popular crowd. I was very self-conscious. I thought, "Well, I must not be pretty enough for boys to like me." I just didn't go after any boys. I didn't like them anyway. I didn't feel a very big difference. . . . I told my mom. When I first came out, I was bisexual; I was fourteen. She didn't care. She just took it in. No big deal. . . . My dad was like: "People will discriminate against you. It's going to be hard for you." And I was like: "I don't care. I can deal with it." My mom was like: "I'll never have a grandchild." "Mom, I'm going to have kids whether they are adopted or I teach or I have them. Kids are going to be in my life. I can feel it, you know." She eventually got over that. That was the only two people that I had to deal with. . . . When I was fifteen, I moved out and I started going to Walt Whitman. There's lots of acceptance there. Even the church I go to is very accepting of my sexuality. I work at CiCi's and they joke about it and it's no big deal at all. There's some people that you will meet randomly, I guess they'll just be kind of gross. . . . I'm surrounded by supportive and loving people and friends, even family. Had it not been for my friends taking me in when I was fifteen, I would have never gone to this school, I would have never gotten involved in the church.

—Amber, Sixteen, Dallas, Texas

Amber and other gay, lesbian, bisexual, and transgender youth are fortunate that there are schools devoted specifically to this population. The schools were created for youth whose neighborhood schools were unable

159

to safeguard them or lacked the resources to support them in their sexual orientation. Youth-serving professionals had observed that this population was often tormented, harassed, neglected, and needed school communities that were safe and supportive. With energy and initiative these professionals decided to create schools where these youth could experience a safe high school community, validate their sexual orientation, develop a social support network, earn their diploma or GED, and learn collaborative skills necessary for navigating situations dominated by heterosexuals. Without these schools, the future for some youth would be bleak, dismal, and unsuccessful. The three schools profiled in this chapter are Harvey Milk School in New York City, OASIS and EAGLES in Los Angeles, and Walt Whitman Community School in Dallas.

HARVEY MILK SCHOOL:
THE FIRST SCHOOL OF ITS KIND

Harvey Milk School was the first school to open its doors to openly gay, lesbian, bisexual, and transgender youth. The school's namesake was the politician and gay rights activist elected to the San Francisco Board of Supervisors (Hogan and Hudson 1998). Milk had been in office one year—during which he worked to pass a city ordinance protecting gay and lesbian peoples from discrimination—when political opponent Dan White assassinated him on November 27, 1978. The school opened seven years later.

School's History

Discussions about Harvey Milk School begin with the social agency known as the Hetrick-Martin Institute. Emery Hetrick and A. Damien Martin founded the institute, initially called the Institute for the Protection of Lesbian and Gay Youth, in 1979 to:

(1) promote and monitor appropriate services to gay and lesbian youth; (2) foster coordination of existing services; (3) retain youth in their biological, foster, or adoptive families; (4) prevent delinquency; (5) educate the general public, youth-serving agencies, and other concerned groups about the needs of lesbian and gay youth; and (6) identify the specific needs of this population and encourage research about lesbian and gay youth. (Hetrick-Martin Institute 1987, 33)

They had been tracking issues regarding these youth in the New

York City human services community when they encountered a case of a fifteen-year-old boy living in a group home. The young man had been brutally raped and assaulted in the home, yet his providers and the court system blamed him for the incident because he was openly gay. Realizing that these youth were under- and ill-served and shut out from social services, Hetrick and Martin established the institute to advocate on behalf of this population.

A short time after the institute was founded and services were available, the providers noticed that their clients were at the institute during school hours. The youth revealed that they were truant from school because they were afraid to attend classes and did not feel supported by school personnel. This initial survey was the impetus for the collaboration that ensued with the New York City Board of Education to develop a school program. The board was quite receptive to the idea of a school program for these youth, but was nonetheless concerned and fearful of the implications. Some years later, the institute and the board decided that the most strategic way to meet the needs of these youth was to establish an alternative high school program.

On April 15, 1985, Harvey Milk School opened in donated church space with one teacher, Fred Goldhaber, and twenty-two students (Woog 1995). A lack of resources forced the institute to implement a half-day school program and maintain a small enrollment, but in 1994 the institute and school moved to a larger location. (After the untimely deaths of the founders, the institute was renamed the Hetrick-Martin Institute in their honor.) This physical expansion and additional resources made room for more students (fifty-five) and a full-day program. The school and the agency have expanded, yet despite the institute's twenty-four-year tenure, many of the same emotional, social, and physical issues exist. In fact, the service provision needs are as great as they were in the 1980s and 1990s.

The school provides students the opportunity to earn a high school diploma (including a GED) in a safe and supportive environment, to learn how to live independently, to have goals and objectives for themselves, to work as adults comfortably, and not to be afraid of who they are. To this end, the institute offers an array of comprehensive services. Sidebar 5.1 outlines the clinical, recreational, and case management services available at the Hetrick-Martin Institute, and Sidebar 5.2 describes the services in a brochure created for youth.

Collaborative Relationships

The New York City Board of Education and the Hetrick-Martin Institute

---

**Sidebar 5.1 Clinical, Recreational, and Case-Management
Services Available at the Hetrick-Martin Institute**

Department of Counseling Services
Individual counseling
Family counseling
Intake services
Group counseling

Department of Housing and Homeless Services
Project First Step
    Street outreach
    Case management
    Café HMI

Department of Policy and Public Information
Training and resources
Youth initiatives
Youth initiative programming
    Peer orientation workers (POWers)
    Café HMI/street outreach
    Peer educators
    Peers in partnership
    Peers outreaching to peers
    Linking lives
    Internal and external internships
    Youth council
    Youth board members

Department of Education and Recreation Services
Harvey Milk School
General equivalency diploma (GED) program
Computer learning center
After-School Drop-in Center

---

cosponsor Harvey Milk School through the board's Career Education Center, which is the alternative high school center. The center, which has nearly fifty different sites throughout the city, furnishes four teachers, a site supervisor of teachers and educational programming, two paraprofessionals, and a food service person. The institute supplies a director of education and recreation services who works with the site supervisor to ensure that the programming meets the chancellor's education standards, the Board of Education's regulations, and clients' needs. The institute and board professionals collaborate to ensure that the students are being supported in every aspect of their lives. The director of

Sidebar 5.2 Brochure on the Hetrick-Martin Institute

Recreation Arts and Special Events
Gives all of you divas a time and place to strut your talent or discover a new one. Open from 3:00–6:30 P.M. The After-School Drop-In Center offers you a place to chill, listen to music, eat some snacks and make new friends. Drop-In Center activities are numerous. Find your favorites and check them out. They offer American Sign Language classes, art, photography, video production as part of our famous BENT TV SHOW, theatre and more. Every month a few trips are planned and there are some kicking celebrations throughout the year. Christmas and Thanksgiving are favorites. So check it out and see what you've been missing.

Educational Services
Let me put it this way, the name is Harvey Milk School, the idea is graduation. This department offers a full time Board of Education certified high school and GED program. This school is truly unique. Not only do you get to work individually at your own pace for some classes, but you also have some classes that you work together in as a group. Let's say you're having trouble, this is one place that will always offer you one on one tutoring when you need the extra help. If the pressure in your life is finding its way into the classroom then check out community class where everyone gets a chance to vent as well as plan events for the school. Lastly, there are some awesome electives. Everything from law, art, theatre, current events, photography, creative writing and more. So get ready because this school is intense.

Youth Initiative and Training & Resources
Looking for a job? Well, this department, focusing on peer education, job training and internships, employs over 100 youth a year in various programs.

POWers (Peer Orientation Workers)—As a POWer you meet, greet and give tours to new youth who are interested in becoming an HMI member.

Peer Education—As a peer educator you are trained in issues related to homophobia, HIV/AIDS prevention, human sexuality and body image. Then you go to schools, youth organizations, foster care agencies and share the knowledge you've attained through peer education.

Summer Internship Program—SIP offers you paid internships in a variety of employment fields.

Linking Lives—Is a three part program where you first go through an intensive HIV/AIDS training, then work at an AIDS related organization, and lastly, create educational materials and HIV/AIDS curriculum from your experiences.

Peers in Partnerships—is a program that works to build a bridge between LGBT and questioning youth and heterosexual youth through trainings in all five boroughs and in communities where youth services have been cut.

Sidebar 5.2, continued

Training and Resources—T&R offers training and technical assistance to guidance counselors, social workers, teachers, students and community groups on LGBT and questioning youth, HIV/AIDS prevention, and other concerns affecting youth.

Café HIM (Project First Step)
So you like soft lighting, mellow music and being served waiter style? Welcome to Café HMI, one of the only places known to provide meals for youth in an atmosphere that feels like you wanted to treat yourself to something a little special. Whether it's taco, pizza, or hamburger night this is a great place to fill your empty stomach and relax with other members. Café HMI (Project First Step) offers a number of services to homeless youth as well. In addition to meals, showers and clothing are available. Information and referrals for housing, health care and legal matters are provided both here and on the streets through out reach workers.

Counseling
This is serious. Whether you're lesbian, gay, bisexual, transgendered or questioning (or let's say labels just ain't your thang), counseling is available and free. Believe me, we all go through it sometimes and having someone there you can talk to can really help get you through the day. Counseling is completely confidential and if you ever want to bring your family you're more than welcome.
Now that's a mouthful.

Source: "Hetrick-Martin Institute" brochure. New York: Hetrick-Martin Institute. Reprinted with permission.

---

education and recreation services, Debra Smock, discusses the importance of collaboration:

> It's important for me to be able to handle a lot of those day-to-day conflicts so I can make sure that [the students] are referred and supported by all the other programs in the institute. And that's where counseling comes in really big and strong. If a young person is coming in off the elevator for school and is already bringing something in with them, because it's such a small school the staff is able to spot almost immediately that something's up with this child, to keep on eye on them to try to see how their day is progressing because most likely they will take it out on whoever or whatever looks at them wrong or wicked. And then you'll have conflict. It's up to me to try to work alongside the site supervisor and try to pull them in as much as possible because it is still a Board of Education site. (Campos 2002c)

All Career Education Center students follow the core curriculum as designated by the New York City Board of Education. Harvey Milk students are no exception—they must adhere to the same policies and regulations established by the chancellor's office, meet graduation requirements, earn the same number of credits for a diploma, and so forth. The core curriculum has been enriched and transformed to meet the needs of the students, and often faculty, volunteers, and interns work with the students to refine the curriculum so that it reflects their issues and interests. Gay and lesbian issues are integrated throughout the curriculum and in the after-school programs. The students have everything that is expected of any New York City high school. The assistant director of the Hetrick-Martin Institute, Christopher Rodriguez, emphasizes:

> When we were planning the move from our location on West Street to Astor Place, I did a lot of work with the young people that were in Harvey Milk School. And I said, "What do you want? What do you want this to be? We have an opportunity here to fix up the place and expand the program." "We want what everybody else has. We want a school bell, that's the most important thing of all. We want to get report cards. We want physical education. We don't want to be treated any differently." They want normalizing experiences; they want a normal experience. And they have it. So now they come to school like other teens. They hate math. They're bored to death with history. They fall in love once a day, have crushes on teachers, skip school when the day is nice, talk too much. (Campos 2002b)

Student Body

Students come from all five boroughs, and some come from Long Island and New Jersey. Because of the limited enrollment, the school is compelled to work with youth who have the greatest need and are at greatest risk. In most cases, sexual orientation is the least of their challenges. They do get referred to Harvey Milk School because of the sexual orientation/identity issue, but the biggest issue these youth face is poverty. Each year the institute offers services to more than 8,000 youth (known as members) and their families in New York City. The majority come from working-class or working-poor families of diverse backgrounds. Many of them have trust issues, depression, and internal conflict. Of that number, Harvey Milk School works with members who have the biggest challenges. It is not uncommon to find students in foster care, runaway situations, or family crises. Faculty and staff alike recognize that the students have profound challenges that cannot be reduced to a sexual orientation problem. Sexual orientation is a locus of many issues—rarely do students complain about sexual orientation or coming out; they worry about family crises and poverty. A student may say: "I don't have a problem. Being gay is not my problem. It's that they're beating me up at school when I wear my lipstick." Or "My mother won't let me in the house because she's afraid that she's going to go to hell if she lets me live with her. She's a God-fearing Catholic, and she won't let me in the house unless I have some money." Until their referral, most of the students have been unsuccessful in their neighborhood school. Rodriguez espouses:

> This is really the last stop. This is the end of the rope for a lot of these kids. This is their last opportunity. So we're talking about foster care children who have been placed fifteen times or Board of Ed children who have been in ten different school settings. They come with many, many experiences and a lot of healing to do.
>
> Each student is expected to have clinical support, whether that be group, individual, or family counseling; or case management support to assist with housing, public assistance, green card training, or job readiness training. (Campos 2002b)

Adolescents attend Harvey Milk School largely because they have experienced verbal or physical threats, harassment, or abuse in their home school. Even though many gay, lesbian, bisexual, and transgender youth in New York City are well supported in their neighborhood schools, some would nevertheless be attacked or threatened if they continued at those schools. Most youth learn about the Hetrick-Martin Institute and Harvey Milk School from their peers, or they are referred by their school or social service providers. In recent years, however, parents, neighbors, or adult friends have recommended youth to the programs.

The waiting list to attend the school is long, and inquiries and referrals are a daily routine. Potential students are ranked, and those considered at greatest risk are given priority and a seat when it becomes available; vacancies are immediately filled. Prior to seating, however, the youth are interviewed and invited to attend the institute's weekly orientation, where they are then eligible to access the comprehensive services at no cost. For some students, these services may meet their needs, but for others Harvey Milk School may be the only opportunity to earn a high school diploma. In these cases, parents or legal guardians must enroll the student. At this time, the youth and the parents/guardians are interviewed. Smock elaborates:

When they come into the interview with their guardian, they'll interview together in the same room. I'll direct questions to both of them. "So what's going on in your school right now? What are some of the things that are happening?" And then I'll direct questions to the parent and say: "You've read about the institute. You've read about the school. What reservations are you having, or what questions and concerns do you have?" Then I'll also go into: "How are you getting through this? What support systems do you as a parent have in place? Is the administration at the school being supportive of you? How are you handling it when you contact them?" Same thing with the kids: "Are there any teachers that have been supportive of you? What has happened to these other youth that have victimized you? What has happened to them?"

I try to get a whole picture of what that experience has been for them and for the parent/guardian because it's very, very important not only to have the parent approve of the child being enrolled in this school, but also to know that that parent is supported and is going to be there—not only academically but emotionally for that child. And during the interview process you get that. I'll have the young person fill out paperwork and go outside my office while I have a one-on-one with the parent. I usually get a lot more from the parent when the kid isn't in the room, and it's usually: "I'm really concerned about his safety. I'm worried to death. I'm not sleeping. No, I don't have a support system, he just told me he came out and I'm having issues with that. I don't know what to do with that information."

So I'm able to get a lot of information about where that parent or guardian is coming from and how that parent or guardian will provide support to that youth, how they've been providing for that youth emotionally, and how they're providing it for themselves. And also being able to let them know that we have family workers here; that even if their child doesn't get enrolled at Harvey Milk School, that parent can still contact us for support and assistance. (Campos 2002c)

Most parents/guardians are comforted after the interview and relieved that the school operates as a Board of Education–approved, diploma-awarding program. Smock, however, observes that parents still fear sending their children to a school designed for this population:

There's always the hope for some parent and guardian that whatever their adolescent is going through, it's part of adolescence. That they will grow out of it and what influence would it have by putting them in a school where they will be surrounded by gay, lesbian, bisexual, transgender young people?

Some parents are reluctant about and against enrolling the youth into the school. In such cases, the parent and youth are referred to schools that are gay-friendly and/or have gay alliances in their schools—schools where they would be supported. (Campos 2002c)

Sometimes, youth have run away to New York City hoping to be taken in by the institute. Many of them believe that their sole option is to leave their home and community. The youth are attended to and provided resources in their community, but nonetheless directed to return home. Rodriguez describes the process:

[If a kid came from Boston] we would do our best to find services in Boston so that young person could stay at home or in their community because there are many supports there that are important and necessary to get these kids through adolescence successfully. It's not strategic to bring teenagers, particularly preadolescents, across the nation, although many want to come to receive services. Even if we had beds, it wouldn't be strategic to take them out of their communities where there are really important resources as support that they need to activate. . . . But always if they show up, we try to put them on a bus or a plane and send them home with adequate support and a lot of preparation. (Campos 2002b)

Most students arrive lacking stable housing, adult support and supervision, adequate nutrition, education, educational opportunities, resources, and so forth. In fact, some youth have had such transient lives that they refuse to believe their school placement is a permanent one. They do not look beyond a semester, they do not want to establish satisfying relationships with teachers or classmates, and they do not allow themselves to like their surroundings, teachers, classmates, or subjects. Smock adds: "So then you're dealing with those issues with them and trying to show them that nobody can predict the future, and 'Yes all the things have happened to you, and yes, we validate that, but let's take it one day at a time. Let's work on getting your guard down a little at least'" (Campos 2002c).

Most youth come to Harvey Milk School on the defensive. They have had horrific experiences and need support to release some of the preconceptions they have about adults or schools. Because of this, they are engulfed with resources and support. Their proximity to the institute allows them to access comprehensive services five days a week. Smock explains: "I always say, 'Just because you're coming to a gay school, it doesn't mean that all of your questions are going to get answered. . . . It doesn't happen that way. . . . Conflict happens. It's an everyday part of life. It's okay. But because there are so many support systems in place here, we're going to try to catch the conflicts as they happen or before they happen so that they don't grow into something more'" (Campos 2002c).

Most of the students who come to the institute and Harvey Milk School have never had an opportunity to know other youth like themselves, nor have they been in situations where they could consistently find others like themselves. They have struggled with isolation for many years, and for the first time they are able to leave that isolation behind. Rodriguez continues:

> They really begin to work with all of their identities kind of explicitly and openly and let go of all of the defenses that they have developed over years of hiding all of their identities. Again, it turns out to be a bigger issue than just sexual orientation and sexual identity. It's about coming to terms with being a foster child or an abused child, or a runaway, or poor, or black, or whatever the things are that they are holding on to. There's a liberation. A freedom. A relief. So young people who stand in the Drop-In Center for weeks silently become the loudest, most social kids you've ever met in your entire life. (Campos 2002b)

Moreover, they are no longer afraid of getting harassed. In many instances, students may have been harassed at the neighborhood school to the point of withdrawing and losing all self-confidence and earning poor grades. But at Harvey Milk School, the students are able to regain their confidence and experience academic and social achievement. Smock emphasizes: "One of the most rewarding things is when you have that youth and you've enrolled that youth and they come in that way, and then a semester later they're surrounded by their friends. They're on the yearbook committee, and they're smiling and they're talking, they're participating, and they are sometimes becoming popular when they have never had that before" (Campos 2002c).

For the first time in their lives, the students have experiences expected of all adolescents—wanting to be popular, wanting to be in the popular clique, wanting to be on all of the student committees and have everyone like them. They are, however, still strategic about displaying their sexuality in public and will alter their behavior so that they are not victimized. Rodriguez explains:

> Meeting a young person on the street is a whole different experience compared to meeting them in the agency when they are kind of present

in all of their multiple identities. On the street they are very, very different. I've had the experience of seeing them and passing them on the
street, and they can't see me. They are so different in public, which is a
strategy that they have to use to survive on the streets. They call it passing. Passing for straight, passing for a thug, passing for a girl, they pass
so that they are not targeted or victimized. Many of them do not have
that luxury and many do. . . . They know the spaces where they're safe,
and they're really defined physically. They find them and use them.
(Campos 2002b)

Academic Programming

When enrolled in the school, students take a placement test that indicates their level of performance in all academic fields. They are then
placed in their classrooms according to their need and academic ability.
A sixteen-year-old youth who has been delinquent from school for more
than a year could be placed in the same classroom as a youth who is
transitioning directly from junior high school if they tested at the same
level. There are no ninth, tenth, eleventh, and twelfth grades per se; students are in divisions that best support and challenge them. Faculty
know which students are freshman, sophomores, and so forth by the
number of credits the students have earned toward graduation. The
school also has a GED program for young adults between the ages of
eighteen and twenty-one, and sometimes they join the high school students for specific courses. A first-period math class, for instance, could
be designated the beginner math class and comprise thirteen or fourteen high school and GED students. Then second period could be a
geometry class with a different group of students. Seniors could then be
in the next period if they needed algebra in order to graduate, and so
forth. By grouping the students by ability, the teacher ensures that all of
the students know the subject area and can adapt the curriculum according to their needs. Because there are only three teachers, the faculty
and staff must decide which courses are critical for graduation. At times
when the school is unable to offer a course to some students, the teach-
ers/staff will find a comparable class offered at one of the Career Education Center sites. The school relies on college interns to teach some of
the electives, such as physical education, dance, and music.

Occasionally, youth with a special education label (such as learning disability, emotional disturbance) are referred to the school. But
when Harvey Milk School cannot meet their needs, teachers/staff collaborate with the Board of Education to find a placement that can fully

support these students. The board has a number of sites that can accommodate gay, lesbian, bisexual, and transgender youth identified as special education candidates; prior to this, however, the teachers/staff will review and reassess a student's diagnosis because some cases have revealed that youth were placed in special education to get them out of the regular classroom. None of the professionals assume that a youth with a special education diagnosis is in fact a youth with special needs; he or she may just be gay, lesbian, bisexual, or transgender.

Students have access to comprehensive services throughout the school day. A student, for instance, can visit the case manager between classes to resolve a housing issue or see a social worker for medical follow-up. At the end of the school day, students are then able to join the Hetrick-Martin Institute members (other high school youth) at the after-school program known as the Drop-In Center. The majority of the students take advantage of this recreational opportunity. Up to 150 youth from other schools and Harvey Milk frequent the Drop-In Center daily. (Since the September 11, 2001, tragedy, nonprofit organizations have been unable to sustain their operations, and consequently more youth are using the center.) The center allows students to socialize in one area (furnished with a TV, light refreshments, and reading material associated with the population) or participate in a variety of educational and creative workshops or clinical support groups. In these after-school programs, youth develop a support network, acquire information about critical issues, and hone their creative ability. On a given afternoon, adolescents can:

- join a photography workshop
- enroll in a leadership program where they prepare to become HIV and/or human sexuality facilitators and eventually lead a workshop for other members
- join a support group (such as a coming-out group, men's group, or women's group) that is cofacilitated by a clinician
- participate in art therapy

These programs are equally beneficial for the staff as they allow them to work one-on-one with the youth and better ascertain their needs. Additionally, students help monitor one another's behaviors. Smock explains:

> We have art projects that go on. Like right now we're getting ready for gay pride. So we're doing the float. But we use those opportunities to be able to get to the issues and concerns that the kids are bringing into the

space so that we can then formulate workshops that can address them. So even if you are doing an art workshop and you're making butterflies out of cardboard, you're always listening and assessing. And they're talking: "I had sex with six different guys in the last four weeks." The conversation can turn into a sexual discussion. "Are you doing safe sex? Well, were you using a condom?" "Sometimes." "Sometimes? What's up with that?" . . . It's a great opportunity to be able to get the information out there, kind of gauge where they're at, and try to give them correct information while they're doing an art project. (Campos 2002c)

For many of the members, this is the first time that they are able to be themselves. The Drop-In Center allows them to come and be who they want to be and ask the questions they want to ask. Smock adds, "Trying to create a safe and supportive environment for these young people so that they can feel comfortable enough to give the information, ask for the information, participate in the other programs, is the task" (Campos 2002c).

Between 90 and 95 percent of the students will graduate from Harvey Milk School. A graduation ceremony (complete with cap and gown) is held every June for all the students who earned their diploma or GED in the academic year. About fifteen students graduate each year (including high school and GED students), and in 2002 eighteen students walked the stage. According to Rodriguez and Smock, the youth are undoubtedly proud of their achievements, confident in their futures, and fully equipped to work in the world. The institute encourages the youth to pursue higher education and offers them college and career advising and assistance with admissions applications, SATs, college visits, and so forth. About 30 percent of the students immediately go on to higher education, another 50 percent pursue college after a short sabbatical, and the remaining start a career.

Challenges

The Hetrick-Martin Institute and Harvey Milk School face some inherent challenges. For one, there is a much greater need to attend to this youth population, and they do not have the resources to do so. The city has a population of 1.2 million school-aged children, and if even a small percentage of them is gay, lesbian, bisexual, or transgender, that suggests a greater number of youth than can be accommodated at the school and institute. Rodriguez acknowledges: "We can never begin to address the need that's out there. So we're really working with the tip of the iceberg" (Campos 2002b). Even though the institute averages a staff of forty, the number of youth using the services is beginning to skew the student-staff ratio. Smock comments: "We don't have enough staff for the amount of young people coming in. It's a sad reality for staff sometimes to realize that we can't save them all. If they keep coming in these record numbers and we're not able to hire new staff to help out, we may have to put a cap or find out how to limit some of the numbers that are coming through. It becomes a safety issue after a while" (Campos 2002c).

Teachers also find themselves encumbered with the students' multiple needs. Teaching these youth involves far more than just meeting the academic standards. Youth come to school with a range of emotional issues, primarily because they have been bullied or abused, or they are suicidal, depressed, or infected with HIV. Imagine the extent of their experiences:

> We have youth who have gone through the foster care system since they were very, very young due to a parent with drug abuse and being taken away from their house. Or biological parents dying and being forced into the system, being taken away because a biological parent is not psychologically able to or equipped to take care of the young person. And you have those young people that have run away, have been cut off entirely by their guardian, have been voluntarily placed into the system. They just don't want to take care of them anymore. Or youth that have—because of their identity, or questioning their identity, or in confusion—acted out in school and have become a delinquent. And because of that have been taken out of the household and put through the system. . . . That's why a lot of these young people are hustling, are doing what they need to do to put food on their table. That's what they need to do to have clothing, a roof over their head. When you speak to these youth, they are survivors, and not just because they are here in New York City. They are survivors. They do what they need to do in order to survive. They are street smart for the most part at a very, very young age. They put themselves at risk at a very young age. Sometimes it's the only way to put food in their mouth. (Campos 2002c)

Teachers' preoccupations often border on social work as they wonder whether their students need shelter, were thrown out by their parents, are hungry, need a shower, or need medical attention. Academics are not a priority for some youth even though they are in school on a given day. Although a class size may be small, teachers have to contend with fifteen or sixteen students who need considerable attention. Smock reports: "It's a charged classroom . . . [and teachers] have to tune into their [students'] needs and know who's suffering from depression, who's having issues with their housing right now, who just lost their parent, who just started having HIV. There are just so many issues. . . . As a teacher it's hard to keep that paramount and focus on teaching when you're dealing with at-risk young people" (Campos 2002c).

Some teachers who have worked at Harvey Milk School were experienced in diversity and multiculturalism and had voiced a desire to work with this population, yet many of them found the work traumatic. They were emotionally unprepared and unable to work with the youth at hand. The teachers and staff now collaborate to find teachers who are able to work with at-risk youth, have the best interest of this population in mind, and are supportive of the youth and the programming. Hiring a teacher who is homophobic or has never worked with an at-risk population, regardless of sexual orientation, would be a disservice to all.

Criticism

The institute and Harvey Milk School receive their share of criticism. Some members of the larger community think that the institute could and should serve all gay, lesbian, bisexual, and transgender youth in the city. (Many other service providers are ambivalent about working with this population and tend to refer GLBT youth rather than work with them directly.) The most prominent criticism is that it is wrong to segregate these youth from society. Rodriguez responds:

> As if they spend all of their waking hours of their lives in the building, in the programs, when in fact most of these children commute long distances on public transportation, are living openly in their community and families, and struggling with these issues outside the agency. I think it's a reflection, a story about the larger community and their lack of understanding, lack of information about the population, about the implicit kinds of issues in sexual orientation and sexual identity. (Campos 2002b)

Community Support

Despite these criticisms, the greater New York City community and the GLBT community remain steadfast in their support of the institute and the school. Much of their support is financial, which generates resources to support the various programs. Some city and state government officials have made it part of their work to promote the institute's mission and talk about the challenges these youth encounter. Many notable citizens have embraced the institute's mission: Hillary Swank,

Madonna, and Rosie O'Donnell are among some of the most well-known supporters. Their prominence can transform public opinion and influence decisionmakers and funders. Kevyn Aucoin, stylist to Hollywood celebrities, contributed a symbolic gift in 2002. As a loyal supporter and honorary Harvey Milk School graduate, he requested that on his passing (May 7, 2002) all contributions offered on his behalf be sent to the Hetrick-Martin Institute. (Sidebar 5.3 is the tribute to Aucoin the institute posted on its website.) In short, the supporters are committed to these youth because they understand that they are the future of the community.

Future

The Hetrick-Martin Institute will continue to collaborate with the New York City Board of Education to expand the school to accommodate about 170 students. The institute does not currently have residential services but nonetheless is searching for a partner to develop a housing project. Its work will then encompass technical assistance, advocacy, education, training, youth leadership development, and collaboration with other youth-serving organizations. The institute has already forged collaborative relationships with the New York State Offices of Children and Family Services, the Child Welfare League of America, the Association of Hispanic Health Care, and a number of other organizations. They provide professional development in areas of sexual orientation, adolescent development, and youth leadership within the context of addressing the needs of gay, lesbian, bisexual, and transgender youth.

Fulfilling a Need

The Hetrick-Martin Institute and Harvey Milk School have grown into a self-sustaining, nonprofit organization providing comprehensive services to thousands of gay, lesbian, bisexual, and transgender youth. Their twenty-year report indicated that the institute serves:

- 7,800 youth members each year from approximately 172 zip codes in the New York City metropolitan area
- 11,000 hot meals each year to hungry youth in Café HMI
- 12,000 homeless youth each year through street outreach in the five boroughs of New York City
- 10,000 youth and adults each year via the institute's training center and technical assistance programs (*The Hetrick-Martin Institute Millennial Report, 20 Years, 20 Stories* 1989)

In one year alone, the institute's peer educators were twice invited to the White House to meet with President Bill Clinton.

They have forged some critical partnerships that have made Harvey Milk School a reality, and now some youth are fortunate to have the opportunity to earn their high school diploma in a safe and supportive atmosphere. They receive significant attention to help them overcome personal obstacles and regain the confidence to enter the world as independent, contributing adults. The greater community remains unaware of these issues and the amount of work that cannot be documented, measured, accounted for, because the demands are ongoing and multifaceted. According to Smock: "Trying to provide comprehensive programming, trying to support young people across a range of challenges, is very, very hard. It's very difficult work. There's a limit to what any single staff person or any group of staff can provide in a given period. Some things are just not in your control. There's just so much to address. And there's so many of them and so few of us" (Campos 2002c).

Despite the seemingly insurmountable deluge of youth, the institute continues to advocate for them and listen to their concerns and interests. Future generations of GLBT youth will benefit from the programs. Rodriguez elaborates:

> They drive everything we do. So everything we have is really fundamentally something they wanted. We started off with a Drop-In Center—they wanted a place to meet and socialize and recreate where it was safe. From there they wanted someone to talk to about their issues and challenges, so there was clinical services and counseling services. After that they wanted support with public assistance and job readiness training, so there was case management. It's just kind of grown and grown and grown. (Campos 2002b)

OASIS AND EAGLES: A SAFE PLACE
FOR YOUTH TO GET AN EDUCATION

The Los Angeles Unified School District has a school program for gay, lesbian, bisexual, and transgender youth similar to Harvey Milk School in that it operates from an alternative high school site. The youth may have similar needs as those attending Harvey Milk School, but the OASIS and EAGLES program serves their needs in unique ways.

Sidebar 5.3 Tribute to Kevyn Aucoin by the Hetrick-Martin Institute

The Hetrick-Martin Institute Remembers Kevyn Aucoin

The Hetrick-Martin Institute is deeply saddened by the death of our dear friend and long-time supporter, Kevyn Aucoin.

In 1999, Kevyn received both an Emery Award, named after cofounder Dr. Emery S. Hetrick, in recognition of his work for HMI, as well as an honorary diploma from the Harvey Milk School.

Kevyn served as a shining example to young people everywhere. He overcame an adolescence in which he was isolated and ostracized for being "different." Through hard work and belief in his abilities, he built an international reputation as the entertainment industry's paramount stylist. He displayed his commitment to the Hetrick-Martin Institute and the Harvey Milk School by speaking and advocating for lesbian and gay youth across the country and around the world.

Bari Mattes, Chairman of the Board of Directors, knew him well. "Kevyn's passion and commitment to HMI was extraordinary. He made the young people feel so special each and every time he visited HMI. His remarks at the 1999 Emery Awards were so powerful—about his responsibility, as a person of note, to be out and proud so that all of America could know a gay person. Kevyn always told the HMI youth how brave he thought they were for being who they are."

She adds, "Kevyn was a remarkable man who is leaving behind a legacy at HMI—his impact upon our young people will live on in perpetuity. I feel privileged to have known him."

The Hetrick-Martin Institute gratefully acknowledges Jeremy Antunes, Kevyn's partner, and the Aucoin family, in allowing Kevyn's legacy to live on through their request that donations in Kevyn's name be made to HMI.

Source: "The Hetrick-Martin Institute Remembers Kevyn Aucoin." 2002. New York: Hetrick-Martin Institute. Available at http://www.hmi.org/news4.htm (cited June 18). Reprinted with permission.

Program's History

In the early 1990s, an AIDS ribbon task force was established with the Los Angeles Unified School District to respond to the high dropout rate among gay and lesbian students in the district. Under the initiative of Jerry Battey, the program's founder and first teacher, district officials opened a classroom in collaboration with Central High School (the district's alternative high school) for gay, lesbian, bisexual, and transgender youth. Battey named the program EAGLES, an acronym for Emphasizing Adolescent Gay Lesbian Education Services, and opened the school in 1992. Classes were first held at the Los Angeles social service agency known as GLASS (Gay Lesbian Adolescent Social Services), but relocated a number of times thereafter.

A second teacher, Sandy Miller, joined the faculty in 1993, and Joe Salvemini started a special education program for these youth in 1994. The three teachers were located at one site, but by July 1996 a fourth teacher joined the faculty, creating a need for additional space. That year the teachers divided themselves into three separate locations and agreed to adopt another program name, Out Adolescent Staying in School—OASIS. The programs or classrooms are located at various sites throughout Los Angeles just as are the other transitional (or alternative) school programs that make up Central High School. There are now four branches or classrooms with one teacher per site: OASIS West Holly-wood, OASIS Crescent Heights, OASIS Long Beach, and OASIS Fellowship. Salvemini, the programs' current director, explains: "Our programs actually work better with one-teacher situations. When we get too many of our students together with the same of type of issues . . . that gets to be too many students and too much drama" (Campos 2002d). Each branch is technically a Central High School classroom operating in donated church space.

Much of what OASIS is today is the result of district support. School officials support a number of initiatives associated with GLBT youth:

- ➡ PROJECT 10 was started in 1984 at Fairfax High School as a support program for youth of this population (see Sidebar 5.4 for details)
- ➡ EAGLES was the second school in the nation designed specifically for this population
- ➡ OASIS and EAGLES sponsored the state's first gay and lesbian prom in 1995
- ➡ The district had a gay and lesbian education commission in the 1990s

The district provides many of the materials and books necessary for the students, but teachers have to find and sustain their own classroom space and fund-raise for excursions, high-end equipment, and so forth.

Conceptual Framework and Program Structure

The school programs exist primarily as a safe haven for youth to finish their high school education. Safety is underscored at OASIS because a lot of the students have not been safe in their neighborhood schools. Most of the students have been out of school for a year or two and want to attend school but are simply afraid to go. This is why the programs are strategically located away from neighborhood high schools. Salvemini explains:

> The main thing is the safety issue. That was what we were created for. One of the things we tell our kids when they come here is that there is to be absolutely no fighting. No threats to kids or saying things like, "I'm going to kick your ass," because many of our kids have lived through things like that and that's why they've come to us. We're not going to have it so that kids are afraid to come to school because of somebody else at the school. If a kid gets into a fight here, nine and a half times out of ten that's the kid's last day of school at OASIS. (Campos 2002d)

The program's mission is centered on providing the students with the skills to return to their neighborhood schools and community, but teachers and staff are aware that many students are too terrified to ever return. To this end, a student might be transitioned into vocational education programs for a half day and attend OASIS for a half day.

OASIS teachers believe that students need to be in neighborhood schools because these are the microcosms of society where youth learn to adapt to real-world situations—all adolescents need to work with one another in tolerating and accepting differences. The teachers unfailingly interrogate school personnel about their referrals to OASIS. When the reply is that the student is being harassed, they ask:

- What are you doing to promote the acceptance of differences in your school?
- What are you doing for the youth who are being harassed?
- What are you doing about the youth who are doing the harassing?

By no means will the gay, lesbian, bisexual, or transgender youth be denied an OASIS program, but quite frequently school personnel are reported to district offices for failing to protect their GLBT students. The district encourages this reporting so that no further safety problems occur in neighborhood schools.

Each OASIS branch averages about fifteen students. In a given year, the programs may have a combined enrollment of seventy students. All the students are bound to the district's curriculum, policies, and procedures, and must pass all coursework and proficiency exams to earn their diploma. Each teacher is responsible for offering and teaching the required coursework and monitoring student progress toward

---

**Sidebar 5.4 PROJECT 10 Brochure Circulated
in the Los Angeles Unified School District**

PROJECT 10 Addressing Lesbian and Gay Issues in Our Schools

PROJECT 10 is a drop-out prevention program that offers emotional support, information and resources to young people who identify themselves as lesbian, gay or bisexual, or who want accurate information about sexual orientation.

PROJECT 10 was started in 1984 at Fairfax High School (Los Angeles Unified School District), by Dr. Virginia Uribe, as a response to suicide, alcohol/substance abuse and risk of AIDS among teenagers in this target group.

We Help Gay and Lesbian Teenagers Cope With:
Low Self-Esteem
Poor Family Communication
Isolation
Verbal and Physical Abuse

We Provide
Understanding
Emotional Workshops
Sensitive School Site Counseling
Accurate Non-Judgmental Information

We Support
Educational Equity
The Right to Safe Schools
Anti-Slur Resolutions
Non-Discrimination Policies for our Lesbian and Gay Children

Source: "PROJECT 10," 2002. Los Angeles: PROJECT 10. Available at http://www.lausd.k12.ca.us/lausd/offices/glec/p10_flyer.html (cited June 25). Reprinted with permission.

---

credit accumulation. One teacher mentioned that the OASIS service delivery model resembles the early twentieth-century one-teacher schoolhouse, which comprised students of varying ages and academic competencies. So that students can earn some of their academic credits, teachers employ the City-as-School program, in which students intern in community-based businesses and agencies. (Sidebar 5.5 is a letter that was sent to the West Hollywood community asking for its participation in the City-as-School program.) Teachers create a portfolio-based assignment that fulfills an academic requirement but is specific to a student's internship. One student, for instance, could intern with a production studio and learn to write effective press releases to satisfy an English requirement. Another student could intern in a bank's bookkeeping department and learn how to manage a small account to satisfy a consumer math credit. City-as-School has been hailed as an enriched curriculum because the opportunities are practical and meaningful for students, and teachers are able to transition their students through their academic course of action.

OASIS students are able to attend more school days than is required by the district. The length of the school day is comparable to that of other high schools, but students go to school for a longer duration. Students may have a week or two off at the end of the school year, but they return to school when other students in the district are off. Ironically, most students appreciate the extended programs. Salvemini adds:

> I tell the kids when they come in for an interview that summer school is a thing of the past. . . . At Christmastime we've been able to choose whether we want two weeks or three weeks off, and the kids have always chosen the two weeks off. And if we could have had no weeks off, they would have chosen no weeks off, because a lot of the response we get from the kids is: "What am I going to do if I'm home? I'd rather come to school." Which is a big difference when you have kids that weren't going to school for a year or more. Now they want to come to school. (Campos 2002d)

OASIS West Hollywood was specifically created for youth who have a special education diagnosis. Unlike Harvey Milk School, OASIS West Hollywood accepts students who have learning disabilities, emotional disturbances, speech/language impairment, and so forth and is able to meet their needs. The program was the brainchild of the special services director, Salvemini, who was a special education teacher working for the district in a psychiatric hospital. He had noticed that as many as 50 percent of the suicidal clients there were also struggling with sexual orientation issues. In many cases, the youth were designated as emotionally disturbed and placed in nonpublic schools. The district was paying up to $25,000 per year for each student to attend those schools. Salvemini realized the potential of creating a special education program modeled after EAGLES and saving the district about $200,000 a year in perpetuity. Shortly thereafter, he was asked to start the special education program.

OASIS West Hollywood only accepts students who have a special education identification and an individualized education plan (IEP—a

Sidebar 5.5 Soliciting Assistance from the West Hollywood Community

Dear West Hollywood Community:

OASIS (Out Adolescent Staying in School) West Hollywood is an LAUSD program of Central High School. We provide a safe haven for students who are between that ages of 14 to 21, and are gay or lesbian. Most of our students are at risk of dropping out of school. Many of our students have been exposed to persistent ridicule, harassment and/or gay bashing while attending more traditional high schools.

OASIS West Hollywood's agreement with LAUSD is to remain a no-cost item to the school district. We, in fact, exist through the generosity of and collaboration with the community (e.g., our classroom space here has been generously donated by the Metropolitan Community Church–Los Angeles and the Bank of America).

OASIS West Hollywood is involved in an exciting new program, City-as-School, whose primary objective is to offer internships in community-based businesses and agencies. These unpaid internships are individually designed by us to meet the student's vocational and academic goals. LAUSD assumes all liability for the intern and provides its own worker's compensation insurance.

You can help our youth. If you would like to mentor one of our youth by providing an internship opportunity, or if you can provide lunch for up to twelve people once every two to four weeks, or if you are able to provide us with any of the items on our wish list below, please call 310-275-0768 (Mon–Fri 9–2 P.M.) or fax us at 310-275-2639. We are supported, in part, by nonprofit 501(c)3 organizations and your gift may be tax deductible.

Sincerely,

Joe E. Salvemini
Special Services Director

Wish List
Fax machine and answering machine
Field trip admission fees
Scanner
Postage stamps and petty cash
Digital camera
Grant Writers
Time at local gym for up to 8 people
Laminating machine & film
Working late model Macintosh or IBM computers
Volunteers to teach sewing, dancing or arts & crafts, personal training, etc.
Incentive rewards (tangibles; coupons or gift certificates for free movies, food, or other items, etc.)

Source: Joe E. Salvemini, 2002, "Letter to West Hollywood Community." Reprinted with permission.

nationally recognized special education plan of action). If a student at OASIS Long Beach has a special education need, for instance, he or she will attend the West Hollywood branch. Transportation is intentionally written into a student's IEP, and most special education students have a district school bus transport them between home and school. Each week a school psychologist works with the West Hollywood students and a psychiatric social worker works with the students at the three other branches. All students have access to a coordinator who case-manages their medical, dental, and vision services.

One striking aspect of the OASIS environment is that the students are taught to reflect on their own reputations. With pride being a common theme in the GLBT community, youth often proclaim their pride in being gay. But at OASIS, youth are taught to be proud of their tangible accomplishments—their grades, their diplomas, their job skills, and so forth—and to feel no shame for their sexual orientation. They are taught the value of self-respect and a reputation and the importance of becoming respectable members of the community. Students are often reminded to behave appropriately in public situations.

Student Body

Students are generally referred to OASIS by counselors, school psychologists, or PROJECT 10 (see Sidebar 5.4) group leaders. In the past, students have made self-referrals, and some heterosexual youth have even referred themselves to benefit from the safe environment and small-group instruction. The district allows for some youth to transfer from surrounding districts, but most youth are directly referred from their neighborhood school. Occasionally, a homeless youth will ask to attend one of the programs. In those situations, the teachers contact the nearest high school and ask that it refer the youth:

> If a kid was homeless here in West Hollywood, they would normally go to Fairfax High School. If that kid came here, I might call up Fairfax in reverse and say, "I've got a kid here that you need to refer over to OASIS." When I first started working here, it seemed like every single week we'd come to school and there would be at least one person waiting for us at the door, saying: "I've heard about the school, and I've been kicked out of my house. I don't know what to do or where to go. I've heard this is a place that I can come to." (Campos 2002d)

Because of prior school experiences, some students are terrified of going to school and distrust school systems and teachers and what they represent. One student was so terrified that on his first day of school at OASIS he would not get off the school bus. Another student was so anxious about his first day that he escaped to the rooftop wanting to jump. These youth have had difficult lives and consequently come to school with low self-esteem. It is up to teachers, counselors, and staff to convince them that they are worthy and should believe in themselves. One student's drug-addicted father was physically abusive and had a criminal record, and his mother's parenting skills were less than adequate, but they believed that their son was bad, evil, and going to hell because he is gay. The youth arrived at OASIS frightened because he believed he was going to hell. It is no wonder that a number of youth have tried to commit suicide before being referred to OASIS. Salvemini discloses:

> Many of our kids have tried to commit suicide. I could point and say "One time, two times, and three times," meaning how many suicide attempts a particular student tried. In the seven years that I have been working in the programs, there have only been two kids that I can recall that have tried to commit suicide [while at OASIS or EAGLES]. They weren't actually serious attempts; they were more of a "please help me" type of attempts. Of course, you didn't want to see either of those happen, but when you consider how many of those kids come in with previous history of suicide attempts, I think we've been pretty successful. (Campos 2002d)

Often families and former schools have treated these youth like throwaways, failing to validate their disparity and dismissing their plight. After considerable attention, support, and counseling, students begin to realize that OASIS and EAGLES personnel do care about their well-being and that their school is a safe environment. Even so, students need constant reassurance. Salvemini explains:

> We're counselor and teacher and everything else for these students, and sometimes we have to refer students to community centers because they've been kicked out of their home and they don't know where to go or what to do. The only people they know who to come to are us. The reality is they know they can talk with us. . . . One of the things that I never realized was how much the kids need us. Even though [the school psychologist] comes in once a week to talk to them, I have to keep pulling the kids in every day and have talks with them. (Campos 2002d)

Transgender youth can pose a challenge because they often have a completely different set of issues from gay, lesbian, and bisexual youth.

A staff member at Harvey Milk School and a teacher at OASIS confirmed that some transgender youth have moved so far from their born gender that they believe their current physical body and their current gender identity are their actual born body and gender. Salvemini says:

> We've had some students come here that vehemently claim that they are in the wrong program. "What the hell am I doing here? I'm a straight girl and I don't need to be in the program for gay and lesbian kids." They felt like they were straight females and in the wrong place even though they were actually boys. (Campos 2002d)

Part of the challenge is that some youth start taking hormones, causing them to have emotional outbursts, and they are somewhat emotionally unbalanced considering that they are adjusting to their new bodies.

Surprisingly, some of the OASIS students have identified themselves as heterosexual. The programs do not discriminate, and the students are not asked if they are gay, lesbian, bisexual, or transgender during their interview. A heterosexual student has never been denied enrollment because of sexual orientation, but teachers must confirm that the youth would be comfortable in the environment: "If they are identifying themselves as straight, then I let them know that most of the students that they will be going to school with are GLBT. I want to know that the incoming student is okay if other people see him with us and assume that he's gay. It can happen. Or I bring up the issue of: 'Well, what would happen if someone here developed a crush on you? How would you handle that? Would you be insulted?'" (Campos 2002d). At any given time in the academic year, about 10 percent of the students identify themselves as heterosexual. Whether the students are or not remains uncertain; however, one year there were three pregnancies among the student body.

Criticism and Challenges

OASIS has its share of criticism, most of which focuses on the idea of segregation. Just like the criticism directed at Harvey Milk School, some community members (gay and heterosexuals alike) believe that the school programs should not segregate gay, lesbian, bisexual, and transgender youth from their neighborhood schools. Salvemini replies:

> My response has always been that our kids were already being segregated in the comprehensive high schools and it was allowed to happen. They were allowed to be picked on, ridiculed, and beaten up. They

dropped out of schools. They slipped through the cracks. People didn't know what happened to them and they just let them go. . . . The reasons we're not located on school campuses is because some of our kids are terrified to go on school campuses because of the baggage they've brought in with them. (Campos 2002d)

Undoubtedly, OASIS teachers want their students in neighborhood schools as long as they are in safe environments and their needs are met. These teachers believe that the Los Angeles Unified School District will be successful when there is no reason to have OASIS: "I don't think we should have programs like this. I think we have to have programs like this. I think it's a shame that we have to have a program like this. I think if kids want to be with other gay, lesbian, bisexual, and transgender youth that there's no reason why they shouldn't be able to meet those needs on a regular school campus without having to worry about their safety" (Campos 2002d).

From time to time, conservative factions surface and accuse the programs of promoting a liberal, homosexual agenda and of spending millions of dollars to operate the programs, neither of which is true. Other factions simply wish the program would go away. Perhaps the most publicity the programs received was when they sponsored the state's first gay and lesbian prom in 1995. It was quite a controversy, with religious congregations picketing and protesting.

At times, OASIS and EAGLES find themselves in challenging situations. Locating adequate space was an initial issue for EAGLES, but each of the OASIS branches now seems secure in its location. Teachers at times find themselves overwhelmed with making sure each student earns the required credits for graduation. Salvemini explains: "I'm required to teach every single subject to every single kid in order to get that high school diploma. And that's a challenge. That's why I like volunteers to come. Let's say someone knows how to sew. I have two sewing machines. Kids would love to learn how to sew. . . . Getting people in here to teach the students how to dance or run a music class or an art class is great for all of us" (Campos 2002d).

Sometimes situations can get difficult when students ask teachers not to tell their parents that the program is for GLBT youth. Teachers cannot lie to parents when students are minor, but they will generically explain that the school is an alternative school for students who have had problems in other schools. When parents ask directly, however, they are told that the school was designed for this specific population.

Future

For the 2002–2003 school year, OASIS will open another branch and possibly open another with a special education emphasis. The name EAGLES has been subsumed by OASIS, and all of the branches are OASIS combined with a moniker identified by the students (such as OASIS San Fernando). Central High School has a history of having its programs become independent schools, which creates the strong impression that OASIS may soon become its own independent school. The greater community has received and supported OASIS since its inception; judging from contributions of classroom space, participation in the City-as-School, and volunteers, the community will continue in this tradition.

Fulfilling a Need

In the early 1990s at the height of AIDS, a progressive task force in Los Angeles determined that some gay, lesbian, bisexual, and transgender youth were in desperate situations and strategized what could be done for them. The idea of a safe and supportive school for these youth came to fruition in 1992. That year, EAGLES became the second school in history to specifically serve this population. EAGLES conjoined with OASIS, and four teachers now teach at four OASIS branches. During this time, teachers have encountered students who were harassed, abused, dismissed, and often forgotten at their neighborhood schools but are still eager to finish school. OASIS and EAGLES have afforded them the opportunity to complete their education. Salvemini stresses: "A lot of our kids have been out of school for a year or two. And then they hear about us, and they want to come back to school. They have the desire to go to school. But they're afraid to go" (Campos 2002d). Teachers continue to teach, structure the academic programs, and do what they can to build student self-esteem and confidence, hoping that these youth become strong enough to return to their neighborhood campus. Until then, teachers are optimistic that a time will come when there will be no need for OASIS. "When we're successful, we're not going to be in operation anymore. . . . As long as we are closing not because of political pressure but because there is no longer the need for us, that's a big success story" (Campos 2000d).

WALT WHITMAN COMMUNITY SCHOOL: A NONTRADITIONAL SCHOOL FOR NONTRADITIONAL STUDENTS

Walt Whitman Community School is different from Harvey Milk School and OASIS in that it is an unaccredited, private, self-sustaining school with a small student body. Walt Whitman gets no financial support from school districts and relies heavily on the generosity of the Dallas community to finance its operations. The youngest and smallest of the three schools, youth from all over the nation can enroll at Walt Whitman to escape whatever unfortunate school or familial circumstances they may have.

School's History

To understand the friendship and professional relationship between the founders of Walt Whitman Community School is to understand the school's history. Becky Thompson and Pamela Stone have known and worked with each other since the late 1980s when Thompson went to work for Stone at an alternative high school as a teacher and then as a counselor. Stone later retired, and Thompson became her successor and hired her as a teacher. The alternative school had an approach that complemented the philosophy shared by the two, in which students' nontraditional behavior was accepted and appreciated. Thompson explains:

> That school was started in the early 1970s for kids who weren't successful in the public schools—they had learning disabilities or difficulties that the public schools were not addressing. The school's philosophy was created around acceptance and tolerance, as well as being one's own person, and named for Walden Pond—from Henry David Thoreau's work. The school became a place for students to seek refuge from the very large classes of some of the North Dallas schools and for students who were being kicked out of those schools for dress code violations, drug problems, and assorted other reasons. Walden's philosophy involves students having natural consequences for their actions and being allowed to make decisions about their course work and their education. Teenagers during the 1970s, 1980s, and 1990s were flourishing at the school, and most who would have dropped out long before were now finishing their education and, in large numbers of cases, going on to college and being more successful. (Campos 2002a)

Then, in 1997, Thompson and Stone became aware of the statistics about gay, lesbian, bisexual, and transgender youth who were being tormented in schools for their sexual orientation, and who often dropped out of school, turned to drugs, and had high rates of suicide because they felt alienated from and rejected by their families and peers. The two colleagues believed that they could offer these students the same type of accepting atmosphere that existed at Walden. First, they visited with Dallas gay and lesbian youth groups and other community members of gay organizations in Dallas to discuss the plausibility of creating such a school. The responses were positive. Thompson recalls that students in those youth groups often asked: "Where were you when we needed you? We're in college now. We dropped out. We got our GEDs. We struggled" (Campos 2002a).

Also, members of the gay and lesbian community suggested that they collaborate with the Cathedral of Hope, a Metropolitan Community Church (MCC) with the largest gay and lesbian congregation in the country. This suggestion led to a meeting with church officials and an agreement to rent space in a nearby shopping center, which the church was converting into a youth center. With the support from the youth and this agreement, Thompson and Stone left their jobs and started Walt Whitman. Although the youth center was later put on hold, the church offered its children's center, and in September 1997 Walt Whitman Community School opened. Its mission remains:

> Because sexual orientation issues in adolescence can adversely affect school success, social acceptance, and the development of positive self-esteem, our mission at the Walt Whitman Community School is to create an atmosphere of tolerance, an acceptance of sexuality confusion, and opportunities for personal growth so that each individual student can become a fully functioning and healthy member of society. (Walt Whitman Community School 2002)

The first year was challenging for Thompson and Stone, who initially believed that Walt Whitman would be a tuition-based school like Walden. They quickly discovered, however, that the students and their parents who needed the school did not have the resources to cover the $7,000 tuition. Despite this awakening, the school enrolled seven students in September and grew to fifteen by the end of the first semester. After that first year, the school moved from the MCC location, in order to be seen as a separate, independent entity form the church, into a small showroom/warehouse building. The school averaged fifteen students until January 2001, when the student body grew to twenty-six. Then it moved into rented space in the White Rock Community Church's classroom area.

The tuition issue was addressed in the summer of 1998, when a financial aid plan was created. Marilyn Alexander was hired as development coordinator, and she helped create a three-part program for tuition. Since the students and their families did not have the means to pay the full tuition, a sliding-scale tuition was created. The parents and students would commit to paying what they could each month, and they would also commit to assisting with fund-raising. The fund-raising portion of the tuition included working with the newly created board of trustees, whose task was to raise funds and establish a permanent financial base for the school. The third part of their tuition was a scholarship that came from the community's financial support of the school. The school's financial base has grown significantly since then, partly because of large corporate donations from the Texas Instruments Foundation and the Freddie Mac Foundation, from grants and individual donors, and from gay and lesbian organizations who have held fund-raisers in honor of the school.

Finances have, however, kept the school from becoming accredited. To become accredited by the Southern Association of Colleges and Schools (SACS), a school must have been in operation for three years and show financial support for three years into the future. On the school's third anniversary, Thompson and Stone applied for accreditation and were denied because the school could not demonstrate that its financial future was secure for three more years. Thompson explains:

> SACS wants us to show where the funding is going to come from three years into the future. We can't even come close to that goal. One of the biggest events that we have is the Dallas/Ft. Worth Black-Tie Dinner, a major fund-raiser for the gay and lesbian community. Last year we received over $35,000 from that event. But the Black Tie Dinner committee's goal and mission is to choose their beneficiaries annually. SACS wants a three-year plan and our events and donors have consistently given us the support we need annually, but not long-term, particularly because the need for accreditation is a difficult message to explain. It is a process that we are getting better at every year. Slowly, more and more donors understand our dilemma and begin to make multiple-year pledges that are helping us move closer to being able to reapply for accreditation.
>
> But for now, we're caught in a Catch 22. There is obviously more funding for accredited schools, but we can't get accredited. A lot of additional corporate funding would also be there if we were accredited. The corporations that are giving us grants now are doing so because we are a nonprofit organization, not because we are a school. (Campos 2002a)

The student body has always consisted of students who came every day and other students whose attendance was rather erratic. The 2001–2002 enrollment was twelve students, although four of them were erratic in their attendance. In February 2002, Thompson, Stone (who sits on the board of directors), and the board met to determine whether the need for the school still existed. They asked themselves:

- ⇢ Are kids still being discriminated against?
- ⇢ What are our goals?
- ⇢ What do we think about our low enrollment?
- ⇢ What about the possibility that we are not needed?
- ⇢ What are our possibilities at this point?

From this meeting, efforts were renewed to get the word out about the school in the form of a newly created marketing plan. More inquiries began coming in during the spring semester of that year, and the board's decision was to continue.

Unlike Harvey Milk and OASIS, Walt Whitman offers students housing. Thompson and the board created the Host Family Program because many of the students were estranged from their families and needed permanent housing. (Sidebar 5.6 explains the host's responsibility.) The program was created in summer 2000, but has not been as promising as expected. Thompson continues to secure hosts for some students but finds the task challenging:

Young people who are out on their own for even a short time have this idea that they are adults. They believe that they already know everything about life. Hosts want to provide a home, but also establish a relationship with these kids and have them follow the rules of the house. The balance is difficult to find.

We had one seventeen-year-old who has had two hosts. He came and took advantage of everything that the hosts had to offer with very little appreciation, with very little giving back. So now, at eighteen, he is on his own, and he's looking back on it and finally getting it. With hosts, he had gone a whole year without paying any rent. The reality is that he has to pay the rent for himself now. It's difficult trying to get the youth to learn that lesson in smaller steps, so they are not out on their own. It is very frustrating. In fact, the board just recently discussed shifting gears to begin looking at the possibilities of having a dorm. The possibility of a dorm is overwhelming to me—the cost of buying a building, the overhead, and a staff for supervising the kids. (Campos 2002a)

Conceptual Framework and School Structure

Stone and Thompson envisioned a school for at-risk, nontraditional students who were unable to succeed in neighborhood schools because of their sexual orientation. The school's tenets are found in Sidebar 5.7 and proclaim that students deserve a safe and secure learning environment where sexual orientation is appreciated and self-concept/esteem is nurtured. One of the most salient aspects of the school's philosophical approach is that students learn to make their own choices about their lives and contend with the direct consequences. Thompson adds:

> We believe that you learn through experiences and that you need to be allowed to make your own decisions in order to learn how to take responsibility. So, if we give young people responsibility, they can learn

---

Sidebar 5.6 Walt Whitman Community School Host Family/Mentor Program

The Walt Whitman Host Family Program will provide a safe, nurturing living environment for Walt Whitman students who need a place to live, so they can complete their educational goals while attending the school. This will be accomplished by placing youths into the homes of volunteer "Host Families." Both volunteers and youths will complete an assessment process that ensures the best possible match between the family and the youth. All host volunteers will be provided adequate training and education on issues related to young people in the program. All participants will be provided ongoing support and will participate in monthly one-on-one evaluations with the Program Coordinator. A "Mentor" component of the program will provide the youth with extended support. Please call for more information.

The Walt Whitman Host Family Program (WWHFP) and Walt Whitman Mentor Program depends on Community volunteers to provide safe, nurturing experiences for the youth in our Community. Therefore, it is important that applicants meet the eligibility requirements listed below to be considered for application into the programs. As always, all applicants who meet the below criteria will be considered for application, regardless of gender, race, ethnic background, socio-economic background, or sexual orientation.

Source: "The Walt Whitman Community School Host Family/Mentor Program." 2002. Dallas: Walt Whitman Community School. Available at http://www. waltwhitmanschool.org/host_families.htm (cited June 6). Reprinted with permission.

---

from success and mistakes. They then know how to take on more re-sponsibility. We allow the youth to make a decision and say "This is your decision; you have to live with the consequences of doing it your way." We allow them to make mistakes—then rethink their decisions and decide again. We let them live their lives. We treat them like adults in incremental steps and assume that they have a better understanding of what's right for their lives. We have had seventy-five to eighty students in the last five years, and a few of them have decided to quit school and have gone into limbo. They've said, "This is the right deci-sion for me." It is difficult to allow them to risk their future on what we think is not the best thing. But you can't really teach them if they are not willing. They know that we're here; they still know that they can come back. But we also have students who come here after they've completed their GEDs to tell us that just having a GED isn't enough. Most of the kids at the school have little parental guidance on this issue. Others have parents who virtually expect them to drop out and get a job. There is always pressure on kids around seventeen to just drop out. (Campos 2002a)

A recent school survey shows how difficult this issue is. Many of the students, when interviewed, wanted the school to have a stricter en-vironment where they would be told what to do and when to do it. The students, however, contradicted this desire when they were asked about the benefits of the school: "We get to make our decisions, and we'll live with those decisions." If they make mistakes, they just have to answer to "Now what are you going to do?" That's a lot like life (Campos 2002a).

Students must earn twenty-four credits to graduate with a high school diploma. The credits encompass traditional academic courses (four credits of English, three credits of math, two credits of science, and so forth), plus credits earned for community service and a class on health issues. Classes are held from Monday through Thursday from 9:00 a.m. until 3:20 p.m. in six periods; Fridays are reserved for commu-nity service projects where students volunteer at other nonprofit organ-izations such as animal shelters, hospitals, food pantries, and churches. Professionals from the community come to the school to speak on top-ics such as career possibilities and HIV/AIDS, smoking, drugs, and alco-hol for the health issues class. To give the students as many educational experiences as possible outside of the classroom, the school takes many field trips to art museums, plays, operas, and so forth. Students also earn one credit of psychology each year by participating in a group ses-sion, discussing physical and mental health issues along with dating and social skills.

Sidebar 5.7 Walt Whitman Community School Philosophy

We believe that all young people, regardless of their sexual orientation, deserve a school situation which guarantees, as much as possible, personal security and physical safety. We believe that adolescence is a time in which people are searching for an identity, including sexual orientation.

We believe that many adolescents, in the process of establishing a genuine sexual orientation, experience extreme intolerance and punishment from most of their peers as well as from the adult society. Approximately one in three teen-age suicides results from the negative attitudes of society toward GLBTQ young people.

We believe that heterosexual adolescents whose parents are GLBT will benefit from a school situation which is free of intolerance and which encourages those young people to gain a realization of sexual orientation issues in order to allow a better understanding of and appreciation for their parents' lifestyles.

We believe that in order for young people to realize a healthy self-concept and esteem, a school situation in which positive reinforcement, access to positive adult role models of various sexual orientations, and an atmosphere of acceptance by their peers is necessary not only for academic success but also for personal growth.

We believe that our society can no longer afford to disenfranchise persons based on sexual orientation, because those individuals are often as not among the most creative, innovative, and intelligent members of the population. These young people may be those individuals who will eventually find the solutions to the problems our world is experiencing.

We believe that a sound education foundation is necessary so that these young people will be able to move successfully into the world of work or pursue further education without the hindrance of poor academic skills.

We believe that because this population of adolescents is at particular risk of contracting HIV/AIDS, a school situation should emphasize realistic and extensive health education.

We believe that GLBTQ young people require a specialized education which will prepare them for membership in a largely heterosexual society. Members of the GLBT community will be able to provide valuable assistance in representing and educating about those unique life issues which these young people will encounter.

We believe that all young people deserve to belong to a community which fosters and reinforces their lifestyles and the development of a sense of self-worth.

We believe that parental involvement in the education process and emotional support of their children is integral to the development of a healthy individual. A school designed to provide services for GLBTQ young people is in a position to provide services to parents as well as to their children. Many parents can benefit from communication-building opportunities and from participating in community activities with other parents struggling with the same issues.

We believe that all young people, including those belonging to minority groups, should receive civics education which emphasizes both community responsibility as well as constitutional rights. Young people who will live in a largely intolerant society will benefit from an educational process which also prepares them to deal with possible conflicts and harassment.

We believe that adolescents should be provided opportunities to donate time and energy to community service activities in order to foster an appreciation of the responsibility that all members of a community owe to the whole.

Source: "Walt Whitman Community School Philosophy." 2002. Dallas: Walt Whitman Community School. Available at http://www.waltwhitmanschool.org/about/philosophy.htm (cited June 6). Reprinted with permission.

The small enrollment allows for individualized attention, and for some students this is a first-time phenomenon. "One of the other skills they get is speaking up in class; some don't have that opportunity in the larger schools. They've hidden in the back of classrooms for years and never answered a question or given an opinion. Well, in our classrooms that's not possible" (Campos 2002a).

Students have a choice of structure in the academic program, as courses can be self-paced, allowing students to progress and earn credits when they have completed the requirements. Some students attend only when they can. Self-pacing allows students who are absent to simply pick up where they left off; no one is scolded, failed, or dismissed for lack of attendance. Other students work in more traditional classroom settings where they are moving along with a class led by the instructor.

In the 2001–2002 school year, all the subject areas were covered by two teachers and Thompson. All three adapted their content for each student; inevitably, they were teaching different skills to the individual students, but the students moved through the different subject areas just as they would in a traditional school. In math classes, for example, a teacher could be teaching beginning algebra, advanced, and geometry to students in the same class. Occasionally seniors who needed a required or elective course that could not be accommodated by their schedule were encouraged to take the courses at community colleges with guidance from the Walt Whitman teachers. Since the school first opened, six students have graduated. One of the graduates has moved on to university; two other graduates are still in community college. Several of the students who did not graduate have taken the GED and are currently enrolled in area community colleges.

Gay and lesbian issues are discussed in the curriculum but not to the extent that is often expected, perhaps because these issues are already a significant part of students' lives. Thompson continues:

> Every year I start psychology class by opening the psychology book and looking at the gay and lesbian section. "What are psychologists saying about gays and lesbians?" The students usually react and say, "That's not the way it is." So we talk about the differences between studies and reality. Of course, gays and lesbians also come up in literature. "Walt Whitman was gay, so what do you see in his poetry about this aspect of his life?" But, we also might ask, "What do you find that gives you an idea of his opinions about the Civil War?" Obviously, we don't teach the students "how to be gay," like many believe, or even offer specific courses on gay studies.
>
> The curriculum of a high school has to be diverse and inclusive, but focused with respect to traditional requirements. We bring in the cultural aspects of what we are studying. A number of people have asked if I would like for them to teach a gay studies or gay history course. I always offer to have them teach it to the Walt Whitman students after school or in evening classes to the community. We have a curriculum that encompasses a general education; colleges and universities offer more specific courses such as women's issues, gay studies, and ethnic and religious group interests. (Campos 2002a)

Additional classes are offered after school, relying heavily on volunteers to teach them; the students have had instruction in music, video production, dance, and so forth. When a student expresses interest in sports or wants to develop a talent, Thompson and her colleagues do what they can to find a teacher or connect the youth with an appropriate organization.

Student Body

Most students learn about the school through Internet searches. One year some students drew attention to the school when they communicated with *XY Magazine* and a story was written; another year informa-tion about the school was continuously displayed locally during the coming-out episode of *Dawson's Creek*. Brochures on Walt Whitman are available for youth groups (see Sidebar 5.8). Students who inquire about the school receive some general information about the program, an admissions application, an application for a host family (if there is a need), and a financial aid application. Students seriously considering the program complete the applications and then come to Walt Whit-man for an interview with the director. Some local students have started school as early as the next day, and out-of-state students have started within a week.

Just like the students at Harvey Milk School and OASIS, Walt Whitman students are considered at risk for emotional problems and cognitive delays; they have unfailingly shown that sexual orientation is one issue among many to be resolved. Some students shared their ordeals:

> "The most difficult part for me is my father. We had never really gotten along, but one time he broke into my email and found out that I was gay, among a couple of other things. If it weren't for my mom's support, I would no longer know or have any communication with my dad."

> "Probably the most difficult part is my family. My mother is awesome about it, but my father's side of the family is not so open-minded. My fa-ther, his new wife, kids, and my grandparents are all Assemblies of God. That whole side of the family, with the exception of a few aunts and cousins, are all saying I'm going to hell."

> "Public school was horrible. No one understood me. My car was van-dalized, and I was constantly harassed. The teachers and principal did-n't do anything."

> "I was chased all the way to my house by a mob of people as things were thrown at me and I was kicked and hit."

Many of the students arrive distrustful, defensive, ready to de-mean and criticize, and in need of social skills remediation. They have survived in environments where adults and peers are enemies, and it is not uncommon for them to be guarded. Thompson explains:

> They come in with that adolescent attitude, and then it will kind of shift to the insult, put-down kind of thing. They come in full of barbs and criticisms for other people. They come in very defensive. The worst thing that we have is the issue of getting along. You have to teach them to get along. If kids who have been rejected by everyone in their lives,

Sidebar 5.8 Brochure on Walt Whitman Community School

Walt Whitman Community School

A private alternative high school specializing in sexual orientation issues of adolescents

DID YOU KNOW…

That Walt Whitman was a homosexual?

That one in three teenage suicides is related to sexual orientation issues?

That all "out" gay and lesbian teenagers experience harassment by peers, teachers, or administrators in schools?

That one of the fastest-growing groups of HIV/AIDS victims is gay and lesbian teenagers?

That sexual orientation honesty can adversely affect school success?

Of course you did. But just knowing the facts doesn't change the circumstances.

High school should be a time when young people can explore, create, and maintain their own integrity in an atmosphere that is safe and nurturing.

The Walt Whitman Community School is among only a very few schools in the country specifically designed to allow homosexual, bisexual, and heterosexual young people to do just that.

Work toward a high school diploma can be organized around a variety of options:

Traditional, small (6–8 student) classes

Self-paced classes

Dual enrollment at community colleges

Credit earned through work programs

Community internships in a variety of career fields

A varied curriculum including all academic areas as well as many fine arts options

For more information, call: (214) 855-1535

Each of us inevitable,
Each of us limitless—each of us with his or
    her right upon the earth,
Each of allow'd the eternal purports of the earth,
Each of us here as divinely as any is here.
                    —Walt Whitman

Source: "Walt Whitman Community School" brochure, 2002. Dallas: Walt Whitman Community School. Reprinted with permission.

sometimes by their own parents, are put into a group, you find that they don't have social skills. So we're trying to teach them to treat other people in a kind way, to simply be nice to someone because they care about them. (Campos 2002a)

Within a month of attending Walt Whitman, the teachers notice, students are less hypercritical of themselves, appear more relaxed at school, and are more introspective about their personal identities. Thompson maintains:

They start searching for who they are and changing a bit. I notice them going through, "Am I this? Am I that? Am I this?" They are trying to figure out what it is to be gay. We have had several gay boys who began wearing makeup once they started attending Walt Whitman. One student told me that last year, when he got to the school in January, he went out and bought makeup and eyeliner. And then there was a point when he said, "That's not me." We allow the students to change into whoever they are becoming, and we try to help all of the students in allowing each other to change from thing to thing, also. (Campos 2002a)

Community Support and Criticism

A number of Dallas community organizations have been very supportive of the school. MCC donated free space, and other religious affiliations (an Episcopalian church, a Jewish temple, and a Catholic organization) publicly endorse the school. Several gay and lesbian nightclubs sponsor fund-raising events, and one gay nightclub adopted the school. Thompson emphasizes that the school would not be in operation had it not been for the generosity of the "drag queens and the leather community." They were among the first wave of donors to financially sustain the school. Some community members were skeptical of the school, but after five years it has proven itself. Thompson explains:

I talked to someone the other day who said: "When we heard you were starting the school, we thought, 'Umm-hmm.' But by the time you stayed open for three years, we were going, 'Okay, this is something to put money into.' So there was a waiting period for a lot of people. Everybody has nifty ideas, but what's really going to float? From the very beginning, we have grown in terms of community support. The entire community supports us. Absolutely, we wouldn't exist without them. (Campos 2002a)

There was some initial backlash from the larger community, including accusations that Thompson and Stone were pedophiles "recruiting" youth into a horrific "lifestyle" and complaints that the youth should not be segregated. But the school keeps a low profile, and consequently the negative attention and ignorant comments have lessened. The larger community often fails to understand that the students are developmentally at risk. Many people are surprised to learn that some students have difficulty reading, often arriving with fourth or fifth-grade reading and math skills. Others question why stricter rules have not been imposed on the students. People often believe that the students should conform to certain standards and have been critical of the youth who are tattooed, pierced, or dressed in drag. Thompson says:

> As much as we are accepted by the community and loved by the community, we are aware of the current attitude about teenagers and adolescents. Our community, as well as the larger community, believes that kids need to be told what to do and controlled a great deal more than follows the philosophy of the school. Also, a lot of adults don't stand back and laugh and say, "Isn't that unusual?" They feel like they have to say "You shouldn't be pierced, you shouldn't be tattooed ... instead, you should be normal." The adult world is about rules, but these kids aren't following the rules. One of the biggest issues with at-risk kids is that they don't like rules. The rules are not working for them.
>
> At Walt Whitman, we choose our battles. Sometimes all we want is for them to learn that they are capable and that they can go out into this world and get what they want by being productive. We don't tell them what to wear or punish them for not looking like everyone else. We are an alternative school, by the way.
>
> One of my favorite sayings to the staff when they become frustrated with students is "If they could do what you want them to do, they'd be back in public school doing that, and we wouldn't be here." We have to keep in mind that somewhere along the line, this population of young people, be it because they are gay, lesbian, bisexual, transgender, or whatever, is not fully capable of functioning in the public schools. That's not working for them. So we have to be creative about how to get through to these young people that an education can change all of that. "Stay in school and finish, and see if it isn't better after you graduate. It isn't going to be any worse than high school." Those are the most difficult years for all adolescents anyway. (Campos 2002a)

The teacher turnover has been high, and many teachers have left over the five years. Thompson explains "Although they may be in the same class, the teachers are dealing with them individually. We're small enough to do that. But we're so small that most of the teachers that we've hired over the last five years have had to have other means of financial support, because most of our positions are part-time. It's a lot for teachers to deal with" (Campos 2002a).

Challenges and Future

Thompson and the board will continue to work toward school accreditation, which means that substantial funding will have to be raised to demonstrate that the school is financially stable. They will have to find a solution to the ongoing housing issue. Housing is a central issue because willing host families are difficult to find and the alternative of financing a dorm is also daunting. In terms of Walt Whitman's future, the board will be reconstructed so the members represent the demographic make-up of the student body. In addition, public relations, marketing, and business professionals will be asked to join the board and contribute their expertise. The board is expected to become more stable, constructive, and powerful enough to advise the next executive director (Thompson's successor) and approve all courses of action. The student body has yet to reach thirty students, so the board will also work toward increasing enrollment.

Fulfilling a Need

In the five years of its existence, Walt Whitman has come a long way. What started as an idea between two friends is now a private, community-supported school for gay, lesbian, bisexual, and transgender youth. Unlike Harvey Milk School and OASIS, youth from all over the nation can enroll at Walt Whitman. Despite some inherent challenges—getting accredited, becoming financially stable, finding host families for students, having a low enrollment—the school remains a small, safe haven for some youth and this is reassuring even to those who will never attend the school:

> Someone called me a couple of weeks ago from Canada: "Can I come to that school?" "Sure, sure, sure, I'll send you this and I'll send you that." It's not that they're really going to come, it's just knowing that we're here. They don't have to pick up from Canada and move everything down to Dallas. The idea of it is that "Yes, you are invited to come," and

that takes the pressure off. When we have eight kids, we have to remind ourselves, especially the teachers, that we're not just here for these kids; we're here with the idea of the school for kids from other places. (Campos 2002a)

For now, Thompson and her colleagues will continue to be consistent, stable forces in the students' lives ready to listen, give advice, and show they care. Thompson concludes:

We now have research that shows that we're not just attempting to educate; we're saving lives. That needs to be our message—that we're saving these kids from falling through the cracks or getting addicted to substances, or committing suicide. What I think I'm doing here is a high school, but what keeps coming back to me is that we're doing so much more than that—more like a social service. I'm starting to let go of my own need for them to get a diploma, and I'm starting to focus on the other things we're doing. Although that diploma will always be my goal for them, I'm allowing them to make their own choices. (Campos 2002a)

REFERENCES

Campos, David. 2002a. Personal interview with Becky Thompson, director, Walt Whitman Community School, Dallas, TX, 9–10 May.

———. 2002b. Personal interview with Christopher R. Rodriguez, assistant executive director, the Hetrick-Martin Institute, New York, NY, 23 May.

———. 2002c. Personal interview with Debra Smock, director of educational and recreational services, the Hetrick-Martin Institute, New York, NY, 24 May.

———. 2002d. Personal interview with Joe E. Salvemini, special service director, OASIS West Hollywood, a branch of Central High School, West Hollywood, CA, 6 June.

Hetrick-Martin Institute. 1987. *Tales of the Closet: Graphic Book Two, Falldown.* 1987. New York: Hetrick-Martin Institute.

———. *The Hetrick-Martin Institute Millennial Report: 20 Years, 20 Stories.* 1989. New York: Hetrick-Martin Institute.

Hogan, Steven, and Lee Hudson. 1998. *Completely Queer: The Gay and Lesbian Encyclopedia.* New York: Henry Holt.

Walt Whitman Community School. 2002. "About Walt Whitman Community School," http://www.waltwhitmanschool.org/about.htm (cited May 6, 2002).

Woog, Dan. 1995. *School's Out: The Impact of Gay and Lesbian Issues on America's Schools.* Los Angeles: Alyson Books.

Chapter Six

•❖ Advocacy Organizations, Associations, and Government Agencies

My biggest issue was knowing I was different. I really wanted to be like everyone else. I eventually got really depressed and had two suicide attempts, and I am now struggling with self-mutilation, all of which I associate with being gay and living in a society that does not openly accept GLBT youth. We are really not accepted by our straight peers.
—Christian, Eighteen, Dallas, Texas

Christian is one of thousands of gay, lesbian, bisexual, and transgender youth who are isolated and ostracized by their families and school communities. Even as some of these youth struggle to survive each day in unsafe, unsupported, and uncaring environments, there are organizations working to transform social attitudes and behaviors toward these youth and lobby for safe, violence-free schools. Because of these endeavors, more and more youth are now able to access support services and establish cyberspace social networks. The organizations discussed here are presented in this order: advocacy organizations and resources.

ADVOCACY ORGANIZATIONS

Advocates for Youth
1025 Vermont, NW, Suite 200
Washington, DC 20005
Telephone: (202) 347-5700
http://www.advocatesforyouth.org

The organization develops programs and policies for youth so that they are better informed about sex and their sexual health. A comprehensive website allows users to access a variety of information about sexuality, including information for youth with diverse sexualities. Advocates want youth to make responsible decisions in their sex lives, and to accomplish this, members support a sex education that respects diversity.

AIDS Alliance for Children, Youth, and Families
1600 K Street, NW, Suite 300
Washington, DC 20006
Telephone: (888) 917-AIDS
http://www.aids-alliance.org

Much of the alliance's mission is to advocate for children, youth, and families infected, affected, or at risk of acquiring HIV/AIDS. The alliance conducts policy analysis, education, and training, and disseminates information through its clearinghouse database, publications, and yearly conferences. Members of the alliance provide current HIV/AIDS information to policymakers, Congress, and congressional committees. A website button allows users to access current topics associated with HIV/AIDS (sex education, sexually transmitted diseases, and so forth).

American Civil Liberties Union (ACLU)
Lesbian and Gay Rights Project
American Civil Liberties Union
125 Broad Street, 18th Floor
New York, NY 10004-2400
Telephone: (212) 549-2627
http://www.aclu.org/issues/gay/hmgl.html

This ACLU division advocates for the equal treatment and dignity of gay, lesbian, bisexual, and transgender people. It helps ensure that government and public and private enterprises treat the community rightfully in employment, service, and accommodations. The division has helped enact many laws and policies promoting the protection of and access to the larger community. The website comprises a variety of links to news associated with GLBT people, antigay initiatives and violence, civil rights and criminal law, domestic partnership, job discrimination, and so forth.

American Counseling Association (ACA)
Association for Gay, Lesbian, and Bisexual Issues in Counseling
5999 Stevenson Avenue
Alexandria, VA 22304
Telephone: (800) 347-6657
http://www.aglbic.org

This ACA division educates mental health counselors about gay, lesbian, bisexual, and transgender issues. It publicly acknowledges that these people experience inequalities and injustices in their lives and therefore have unique needs. The association informs and consults with teachers and school counselors, helping them better understand sexual diversity and identity. A website button accesses the ACA's premier online journal, which contains articles on counseling youth with diverse sexualities.

American Psychological Association (APA)

Lesbian, Gay, and Bisexual Concerns Office
750 First Street, NE
Washington, DC 20002-4242
Telephone: (800) 374-2721
http://www.apa.org/pi/lgbc

This two-decade-old committee seeks to ensure that effective psychological services are available to gay, lesbian, bisexual, and transgender people. The office is involved in a variety of advocacy efforts, including policy analysis and development, psychological knowledge development and dissemination, technical assistance, and information and referral. The office also has the Healthy Lesbian, Gay, and Bisexual Students Project, which trains school counselors, nurses, psychologists, and social workers to help them meet the needs of these youth. The website has a button to access a database of articles, books, and reports on gay, lesbian, bisexual, and transgender youth.

Anti-Defamation League (ADL)

Department DJ
823 United Nations Plaza
New York, NY 10017
Telephone: (212) 885-7700
http://www.adl.org

For more than eighty-eight years, the ADL has combatted hate propaganda aimed at Jews and other minority groups, which most recently has included gay men and lesbians. It protests against any faction that denounces or causes emotional or physical injury, property destruction, and death to any group of Americans. In short, its mission is to "stand up for the core values of America against those who seek to undermine them through word or deed." The website comprises a variety of buttons addressing topics including terrorism, extremism, civil rights, the Holocaust, and religious freedom. An education button allows users to download material for teaching antihate and antiviolence behavior to children.

Gay, Lesbian, and Straight Education Network (GLSEN)

121 West 27th Street, Suite 804
New York, NY 10001

Telephone: (212) 727-0135

http://www.glsen.org

GLSEN is the leading organization fighting to eradicate discrimination against students with diverse sexualities. Part of the network's mission reads: "to assure that each member of every school community is valued and respected regardless of sexual orientation or gender identity/expression. We believe that such an atmosphere engenders a positive sense of self, which is the basis of educational achievement and personal growth." GLSEN educates school personnel and youth about antigay bias and provides technical assistance to help schools establish healthier environments. The website is resourceful, with buttons that locate news about GLBT youth and teachers, teaching materials, the organization's research, and information for and about gay-straight alliances.

Gay-Straight Alliance Network

160 14th Street

San Francisco, CA 94103

Telephone: (415) 552-4229

http://www.gsanetwork.org

The network is a California-based organization helping youth start, maintain, and strengthen gay-straight alliances (GSAs) in their schools. The website has buttons that allow users to learn how to start, register, and locate resources for a GSA.

Gender Education and Advocacy

http://www.gender.org/index.html

This organization is focused on the needs and issues of transgender persons. It asserts, "We seek to educate and advocate, not only for ourselves and others like us, but for all human beings who suffer from gender-based oppression in all of its many forms." The website provides users with access to current news about the population, descriptions of projects in the works, and resources on such issues as child custody, surgeons, and employment. Users can also search the website clearinghouse for transgender-specific information.

Gender Public Advocacy Coalition (GenderPAC)

1743 Connecticut Avenue, NW, 4th Floor

Washington, DC 20009

Telephone: (202) 462-6610

http://www.gpac.org/index.html

GenderPAC educates the public about gender stereotypes and the impact these have on discrimination and violence, and advocates for the gender rights of all people (including transgender people). In addition to containing the latest news, the website enables users to access information on job discrimination, hate crimes, youth outreach, congressional advocacy, and gender law.

Human Rights Campaign (HRC)

919 18th Street, NW, Suite 800
Washington DC 20006
Telephone: (202) 628-4160
http://www.hrc.org

The HRC is most widely identified by the yellow equal sign (in a blue box) that symbolizes equal rights for GLBT people. The HRC lobbies state and federal officials to pass legislation on issues such as domestic partner benefits, adoption by gay and lesbian couples, and hate crime laws. The website posts daily news that affects this community and the search engine can be used to retrieve articles from an extensive database.

Human Rights Watch (HRW)

350 Fifth Avenue, 34th Floor
New York, NY 10118-3299
Telephone: (212) 290-4700
http://www.hrw.org

The HRW is an international organization committed to "defending human rights worldwide." It defends victims who have been discriminated against and had their human rights violated, and it challenges political entities that continue to deny people their freedom. The website contains various buttons linking to stories on human rights violations throughout the world. The HRW published *Hatred in the Hallways* in 2001, which found that GLBT youth suffer from continual harassment. The publications button accesses *Hatred in the Hallways* and an assortment of youth testimonies.

Lambda Legal Defense and Education Fund

120 Wall Street, Suite 1500
New York, NY 10005-3904
Telephone: (212) 809-8585
http://www.lambdalegal.org

Lambda LDEF is a national organization that upholds and protects the civil rights of GLBT people as well as people living with HIV or AIDS. It investigates and exposes violators of civil rights and brings them to justice through litigation. It has been actively defending same-sex marriages, domestic partnerships, and protection of youth in schools. The youth and schools button on the website retrieves memos, litigation decisions and briefs, resources, and publications regarding the organization's work with youth with diverse sexualities.

National Center for Lesbian Rights (NCLR)
Youth Project
870 Market Street, Suite 570
San Francisco, CA 94102
Telephone: (800) 528-6257
http://www.nclrights.org

NCLR is a legal resource center committed to eliminating prejudice, violence, and injustices against lesbians and their families. Legal representation, policy advocacy, legal advice, and public education are some of the services available through the center. The center also provides services and resources to GLBT people when their issues affect or advance lesbian rights. The Youth Project provides youth free and confidential legal counsel related to safety in schools, psychiatric abuse, homelessness, discrimination, and so forth. The project's button on the website directs users to an assortment of publications and cases regarding GLBT youth.

National Education Association (NEA)
Gay and Lesbian Caucus
1201 16th Street, NW
Washington, DC 20036-3290
Telephone: (202) 833-4000
http://www.nea-glc.org

The caucus collaborates with the NEA to ensure that national educational and political policies and activities are developed with GLBT people in mind. It attempts to eliminate homophobia and discrimination in schools by educating state education agencies on sexual orientation issues.

National Gay and Lesbian Task Force (NGLTF)
1700 Kalorama Road, NW
Washington, DC 20009-2624
Telephone: (202) 332-6483
http://www.ngltf.org

This thirty-year-old organization is committed to eliminating "prejudice, violence and injustice against gay, lesbian, bisexual and transgender people at the local, state and national level." The task force envisions a society where people have complete justice and freedom to express and celebrate their sexual differences. The website has links to current news and issues related to the community, and the school and youth button retrieves respective information.

National Youth Advocacy Coalition (NYAC)
1638 R Street, NW, Suite 300
Washington, DC 20009
Telephone: (202) 319-7596
http://www.nyacyouth.org

NYAC is a social justice organization that focuses on improving the lives of youth with diverse sexualities. It works to end discrimination toward these youth and promote a movement to meet their emotional and physical needs. The coalition operates a five-region infrastructure comprising local, grassroots organizations seeking to transform state and national policy. The website allows users to learn about critical issues impacting the community, write to elected officials, and search the site.

Parents, Friends, and Families of Lesbians and Gays (PFLAG)
1726 M Street, NW, Suite 400
Washington, DC 20036
Telephone: (202) 461-8180
http://www.pflag.org

PFLAG has more than 80,000 members who "celebrate diversity and envision a society that embraces everyone, including those of diverse sexual orientations and gender identities." To this end, it professes: "Only with respect, dignity and equality for all will we reach our full potential as human beings, individually and collectively." Members help their friends and/or family members achieve emotional and physical well-being by supporting them, educating the public about them, and advocating for their civil rights and equal treatment. Users can access information about youth and schools via the education button. "From Our House to the School House: Safe School News from across the Country," "A Brochure for Educators," "2001 Safe Schools Campaign," "Safe Schools Resources," "Tips for Working with GLBT Youth," and so forth are available through the issues button.

Safe Schools Coalition
814 NE 40th Street
Seattle, WA 98105
Telephone: (888) 307-9275 (crises)
(206) 632-0662 ext. 49 (messages)
http://www.safeschoolscoalition.org/index.html

This coalition of seventy-plus organizations strives to make schools safe places "where every family can belong, where every educator can teach, and where every child can learn, regardless of gender identity or sexual orientation." The coalition provides resources to schools and the public, increases the community's awareness about sexual diversity, provides professional development to schools, and conducts and disseminates research. Buttons allow users to access legislation, resources, position statements, handouts, and so forth. A button is designated for youth and directs them to various adolescent-based issues.

Sexuality Information and Education Council of the United States (SIECUS)
130 West 42nd Street, Suite 350
New York, NY 10036-7802
Telephone: (212) 819-9770
http://www.siecus.org

SIECUS promotes and affirms that sexuality is a natural and healthy part of human life. The organization has extensive resources providing information and support to schools and the general public. It actively engages in public policy work advocating for comprehensive sex education that affirms that sexual diversity is common in society and should be respected. *Guidelines for Comprehensive Sexuality Education: K–12th Grade,* developed in 1991 and updated in 1996, encompasses elements related specifically to sexual orientation. See Chapter 7 for more information. A search of the SIECUS clearinghouse yields an annotated bibliography of GLBT resources.

Society for Adolescent Medicine
Gay and Lesbian Special Interest Group
1916 NW Copper Oaks Circle
Blue Springs, MO 64015
Telephone: (816) 224-8010
http://www.adolescenthealth.org

The society engages in scholarly discourse about the medical well-being of adolescents. In addition to publishing the *Journal of Adolescent*

Health, the society seeks to increase public awareness about adolescents' health needs and improve the provision of their health care. The SIG button presents a list of medical experts in the field of GLBT youth health.

RESOURCES

Adolescent AIDS Program (AAP)
Children's Hospital at Montefiore Medical Center
111 East 210th Street
Bronx, NY 10467
Telephone: (718) 882-0232
http://www.hivgettested.com

The AAP is considered a leader in the field of HIV/AIDS among adolescents and serves as a national resource center for the populations of youth (and their families) who are living with AIDS, at risk for acquiring the disease, and/or are GLBT. Website buttons are designed for youth and service providers, and the resource center button accesses a collection of material on youth and HIV, gay and lesbian youth, and professional education. The AAP library button allows users to download an annotated bibliography of articles on youth and HIV and gay and lesbian youth.

American Education Gender Information Service (AEGIS)
P.O. Box 33724
Decatur, GA 30033
Telephone: (404) 939-2122
http://gender.org/aegis

AEGIS is committed to serving transgendered and transsexual persons and their service providers. "We promote nonjudgemental treatment and depathologicalization of persons with transgender and transsexual issues. We seek to do so in an atmosphere of respect and toleration." AEGIS provides a clearinghouse of information about transgender and transsexual issues. It publishes *Chrysalis: The Journal of Transgressive Gender Identities, AEGIS News,* the *Transgender Treatment Bulletin,* and other resources.

American Friends Service Committee (AFSC)
1501 Cherry Street
Philadelphia, PA 19102
Telephone: (215) 241-7000
http://www.afsc.org

This is a Quaker organization comprising members of various faiths who dedicate themselves to social justice, peace, and humanitarian services. Members believe that every human is worthy and that love can overcome violence or injustices. Current issues about international violence are found on the website, and a search engine retrieves articles about GLBT youth.

American Library Association (ALA)
GLBT Round Table
50 East Huron
Chicago, IL 60611
Telephone: (800) 545-2433
http://www-lib.usc.edu/~trimmer/ala_hp.html

The Round Table is one of the first gay, lesbian, bisexual, and transgender professional organizations in the nation. It seeks to ensure that people of diverse sexualities are represented accurately and positively in books in (public and school) libraries; patrons have easy access to these materials, and librarians can guide readers to the appropriate resources with respect and confidentiality. The Round Table presents two (fiction and nonfiction) awards each year for the best GLBT-themed books. A website button retrieves previous award winners, locates bibliographies appropriate for youth, and directs users to the children's literature evaluation guidelines.

Children of Lesbians and Gays Everywhere (COLAGE)
3543 18th Street, Suite 17
San Francisco, CA 94110
Telephone: (415) 861-5437
http://www.colage.org

COLAGE supports youth whose parents are gay, lesbian, bisexual, or transgender. It sponsors a pen pal service and several events each year to bring these youth and their families together. The organization's publications (*Books for Parents, Books for Children and Young Adults, Tips for Making Classrooms Safer,* and so forth) can be downloaded via the website's resources button.

Gay and Lesbian Alliance Against Defamation (GLAAD)
5455 Wilshire Blvd., Suite 1500
Los Angeles, CA 90036
Telephone: (323) 933-2240
http://www.glaad.org

GLAAD works to protect the way GLBT people are portrayed in the entertainment industry and the news media. It educates decisionmaking officials associated with newspapers, magazines, motion pictures, television, and political campaigns about the community and exposes and challenges those who blatantly portray such people in an offensive manner. GLAAD offers several publications about the dynamics of sexual orientation, gender identity, and media representations. A search button on the website retrieves information on gay and lesbian youth.

Gay Men's Health Crisis (GMHC)
119 West 24th Street
New York, NY 10011
Telephone: (800) 243-7692
http://www.gmhc.org

GMHC was established in 1981 to care for New York City gay men who had acquired AIDS and needed care. The organization continues to provide care but also advocates for effective public policy and educates New York residents about maintaining healthy lives. The website contains current news regarding HIV/AIDS, and buttons retrieve information about drugs, sex and HIV, and living with HIV.

Health Initiatives for Youth (HIFY)
235 Montgomery Street, Suite 430
San Francisco, CA 94104
Telephone: (415) 274-1970
http://www.hify.org

HIFY works to improve the health and well-being of youth, fight against the spread of HIV among adolescents, and create a support network for those youth at risk of or living with HIV. Website buttons allow users to access HIFY publications, retrieve health information, and learn how to become actively involved in health fairs and youth events.

Hetrick-Martin Institute
2 Astor Place
New York, NY 10003
Telephone: (212) 674-2400
http://www.hmi.org/main.html

The Hetrick-Martin Institute (described in Chapter 5) is a social service agency for gay, lesbian, bisexual, and transgender youth of New York City. The institute provides various services for these youth including the Harvey Milk School, a GED program, the After-School Drop-In Center, street outreach, and counseling. The website has buttons that locate information about the institute's work, and the resources button links to youth-serving organizations.

International Foundation for Gender Education (IFGE)
P.O. Box 540229
Waltham, MA 02454
Telephone: (781) 899-2212
http://www.ifge.org

The foundation is considered "a leading advocate and educational organization for promoting the self-definition and free expression of individual gender identity." IFGE has a clearinghouse of information on gender expression and identity, cross-dressing, transsexualism, intersexuality, drag kings and queens, and so forth. The foundation also publishes *Transgender Tapestry,* and website buttons retrieve a bibliography of books and movies with transgender themes.

LAMBDA GLBT Community Services
P.O. Box 31321
El Paso, TX 79931
Telephone: (915) 329-GAYS
http://www.lambda.org

LAMBDA advocates for "reducing homophobia, inequality, hate crimes, and discrimination by encouraging self-acceptance, cooperation, and nonviolence." It operates a hate crime network (resources for victims of hate crimes) and offers an assortment of online resources, including coming-out support. A section of the website is devoted to queer and questioning youth, and various publications can be downloaded from this link. Victims of hate crimes can call the GLBT Hate Crimes Hotline at (800) 686-HATE for emotional support and guidance.

Massachusetts Governor's Commission on Gay and Lesbian Youth
State House, Room 111
Boston, MA 02133
Telephone: (617) 727-3600 ext. 312
http://www.state.ma.us/gcgly

Governor Weld established the commission in 1992 to help reduce the incidence of suicide among and violence toward gay and lesbian youth. Since its inception, the commission has been instrumental in creating safe schools for gay, lesbian, bisexual, and transgender youth. In fact, Massachusetts is considered the leader among the states for its support of these youth. The commission's reports, newsletters, and official proclamation can be downloaded via buttons found on the website's homepage.

**National Coalition for Gay, Lesbian, Bisexual,
and Transgender Youth**
OutProud
369 Third Street, Suite B-362
San Rafael, CA 94901
http://www.outproud.org

The coalition/OutProud provides outreach information, resources, and support to adolescents who are out, coming out, or considering coming out. A score of resources are available on the website, including coming-out stories, archives of role models, a library, online brochures, survey results, agencies for support, and an online magazine.

**National Institute for Gay, Lesbian, Bisexual,
and Transgender Education**
3932 Broadway
P.O. Box 45600
Kansas City, MO 64171
Telephone: (816) 960-7200
http://www.thenationalinstitute.org/index1.html

The institute provides educational programs to help any individual or organization contend with gay, lesbian, bisexual, or transgender issues. "The intent of the National Institute is to reduce individual and family distress and diminish the current systems of oppression, discrimination and homophobia in mainstream America." The website has buttons that allow users to access a resource center, a list of speakers and trainers, a bookstore, a calendar of national events, the Endangered Youth Campaign (a national program to keep youth alive), and the Youth Recognition Project. The organization's online magazine, *Authenticity,* is also available to users.

**PERSON (Public Education Regarding Sexual
Orientation Nationally) Project**
586 62nd Street
Oakland, CA 94609
http://www.youth.org/loco/PERSONProject

The project educates the public about GLBT people by providing fair, accurate, and unbiased information about this population on a website. Members meet with political and school policymakers to advocate "for an end to the censorship of information about our communities in text-books, course content, resource materials, and library offerings associated with public education." The project's brochure and organizing handbook, a score of news and action alerts, and resources can be accessed via the buttons found on its homepage.

Planned Parenthood Federation of America (PPFA)
810 Seventh Avenue
New York, NY 10019
Telephone: (212) 541-7800
http://www.plannedparenthood.org

Planned Parenthood offers an array of services to the public inclusive of comprehensive reproductive and complementary health care. The website is complete with current news on this topic, and buttons retrieve information on contraceptives, family planning, and sex education. The Young People Speak Out button links users to teenwire.com—an informational website for youth. The search button on teenwire.com directs users to resources including Helping Your Buddy Out, How To Be an Ally, Coming Out—Keeping It Real, What Does It Mean to be Gay? and Safer Sex for Lesbians.

PROJECT 10
Los Angeles Unified School District
Health Education Programs
1320 West 3rd Street, Room 34
Los Angeles, CA 90017
Telephone: (213) 625-6411
http://www.lausd.k12.ca.us/lausd/offices/hep/index2.html
http://www.project10.org

PROJECT 10 (described in Chapter 5) is an educational and support program for gay, lesbian, bisexual, and transgender youth. The project assists schools in helping youth come to terms with their sexual orientation, and teaches them about HIV/AIDS, sexually transmitted diseases, substance abuse, and so forth. Friends of PROJECT 10 works with PROJECT 10 to sponsor a gay and lesbian prom, a yearly conference, a scholarship program, and other significant projects. The first website address directs users to a compilation of resources, and the second website contains buttons to access the project's accomplishments, tips to facilitate healthy and safe school environments, and the founder's advice column.

PROJECT 10 East
P.O. Box 382401
Cambridge, MA 02238
Telephone: (617) 864-GLBT
http://www.project10east.org

PROJECT 10 East seeks to "create safe and affirming space for gay, lesbian, bisexual and transgender (GLBT) youth and their allies." To accomplish this mission, the project provides accurate information about GLBT issues, works with teachers, schools, and educational organizations to ensure that the rights of these youth are upheld, trains and consults with education officials, and develops materials for and about these youth. The website buttons retrieve information about technical support services, upcoming events, and other resourceful organizations.

Southern Poverty Law Center
Tolerance Website
400 Washington Avenue
Montgomery, AL 36104
Telephone: (334) 956-8200
http://www.tolerance.org

The center operates a website to inform the general public about hate in society and ways that tolerance is promoted and implemented. The site comprises buttons that allow users to watch out for and learn how to eradicate hate and learn about hidden biases in society. A search engine locates gay and lesbian information.

U.S. Department of Education
Office of Civil Rights
400 Maryland Avenue, SW
Washington, DC 20202
Telephone: (800) US-LEARN
http://www.ed.gov/offices/OCR

The office protects the civil rights of all youth regardless of their gender, ethnicity, ability, sexual orientation, and so forth by "ensuring equal access to education and promoting educational excellence throughout the nation through vigorous enforcement of civil rights." The website search engine allows users to access information about gay and lesbian youth including *Sexual Harassment: It's Not Academic* and *Protecting Students from Harassment and Hate Crimes.*

Youth and AIDS Project (YAP)
University of Minnesota
Adolescent Health Project
428 Oak Grove Street
Minneapolis, MN 55403
Telephone: (612) 627-6820
http://www.yapmn.com/index.cfm

YAP informs youth about HIV/AIDS, teaches them to make responsible decisions in their lives, cares for youth (and their families) suffering from the disease, and attends to their health care needs. The website allows users to ask confidential questions, learn current information about HIV/AIDS, and read online publications about diverse sexuality.

Chapter Seven

⚫ Print and Nonprint Resources

My gay friends know that I'm bisexual. Everyone thinks that I'm gay because of the way I act, but I know that I want to be with a girl one day. My dream would be to have a girlfriend for the fun of it and like a really cool guy for other times—you know, like if I wanted him to hold me or for times like that. I could see that happening. I get turned on by guys; I love them, but with girls it's different. You know, I want the romantic kinds of things with them. I like to hold hands with them. Brush their hair. Hold them. You know, things like that. . . . And I *can* have sex with them. . . . It would be nice [to have that relationship] because when I would feel like being a femme for a day, I could wear her clothes, and when I feel like being all macho, I could wear his. Just kidding. Like Britney Spears could be my girlfriend and Tobey Maguire could be my boyfriend. Never mind. I would want to be with Tobey Maguire all the time. . . . Okay, I guess I could be gay. But the thing is, even though I can't stand kids, I know that I want some, and my girlfriend will be able to give that to me. Tobey can't. . . . People just don't understand. Not even my friends. Why can't they just say, "Okay, he's bi." Why do they have to say: "No, you're not. You're gay. Just accept that you're gay." I'm like: "Come on, people. You're supposed to be my friends. Hello! Friends support each other like they do on that show." And then they go off on me when I put on makeup. Aye yayaye. Then it's, "Make up your mind."

—Michael, Fifteen, St. Louis, Missouri

Michael is an interesting youth. Despite many challenges in his life, his family (mother and a younger sister) has remained very supportive of him. His mother drove him considerable distances just to meet with a group of other gay, lesbian, and bisexual youth. For nearly two years he developed ongoing relationships with these youth, and he attributed his humor, happiness, and positive outlook on life to having this circle of friends. Michael's brief testimony is insightful because it underscores that even the closest of his friends failed to understand how he regarded his own sexuality. This raises the question, If the closest of his friends cannot understand him, how can we expect teachers, principals, school officials, and other youth to understand him?

Youth with diverse sexualities have heterogeneous needs, and school personnel should do what they can to better understand and learn how to meet these needs. Valuable print and nonprint material are available to help accomplish this task. Some of these publications are presented in this chapter under the rubrics: books, journals, popular magazines, reports and studies available online, and websites for youth.

BOOKS

Two national publishers develop, promote, and disseminate scholarly and literary books specific to GLBT issues: Alyson Publications and Harrington Park Press. Their websites allow users to peruse and purchase items directly from their online catalogs.

Alyson Books
Alyson Wonderland
Alyson Publications
6922 Hollywood Blvd., Suite 1000
Los Angeles, CA 90028
Telephone: (800) 525-9766
http://www.alyson.com

Alyson serves the literary needs of GLBT and questioning people. Its publications include literary and erotic fiction, and nonfiction about politics, medicine and health, law, meditation and spirituality, sexuality, finances, and so forth.

Harrington Park Press
The Haworth Press
10 Alice Street
Binghamton, NY 13904
Telephone: (800) 429-6784
http://www.haworthpressinc.com

Harrington Park Press is an imprint of The Haworth Press. Its publications are grounded in issues largely associated with GLBT and questioning people. The press also publishes fiction.

The following books encompass an array of topics concerning GLBT youth, the challenges presented in their lives, how they have overcome these, and how youth workers can empower them to surmount the obstacles they have in their families, schools, and society.

Baker, Jean M. 2002. *How Homophobia Hurts Children: Nurturing Diversity at Home, at School, and in the Community.* Binghamton, NY: Harrington Park Press.

Baker, a clinical psychologist, became active in the GLBT community soon after her sons disclosed they were gay. She has written *Family Secrets: Gay Sons—A Mother's Story,* and has received accolades for her advocacy efforts. This eighteen-chapter book discusses the detrimental affect homophobia has on children. Baker begins by addressing what it is like to grow up gay in a homophobic society and proceeds to dispel the myths associated with diverse sexualities. She also writes about the coming-out process, what this population of youth experiences at school, and how school officials can help, and she concludes with the experiences of transgender persons.

Bass, Ellen, and Kate Kaufman. 1996. *Free Your Mind: The Book for Gay, Lesbian, and Bisexual Youth—and Their Allies.* New York: Harper-Perennial.

Bass, author of several books on sexual abuse, teamed up with Kaufman to write this guide for youth, but the book is a resource for any person who works with or wants to better understand this population. Bass and Kaufman, both lesbian mothers, have divided their text into six parts: self-discovery, friends and lovers, family, school, spirituality, and community. In short, youth learn what their sexual orientation means in society and how to reach out to others for support, and adults learn how to affirm youth with diverse sexualities.

Bernstein, Robert A. 1999. *Straight Parents, Gay Children: Inspiring Families to Live Honestly and with Greater Understanding.* New York: Thunder's Mouth Press.

A former national vice president of PFLAG, Bernstein has written this text from the viewpoint of a father with a gay son. The book is an education for any adult coming to terms with a family member's sexual orientation. Chapters discuss what it is like to grow up gay, coping with the member's sexual orientation, the gay rights movement, myths, and so forth. Other parents of children with diverse sexualities share their stories, and one chapter discusses public figures and their gay relatives.

Bohan, Janis S. 1996. *Psychology and Sexual Orientation: Coming to Terms.* New York: Routledge.

This text is appropriate for higher education classrooms and any reader interested in learning about the psychology of sexual orientation. The eight-chapter book is divided into three parts: Conceptual Framework comprises the meaning of sexual orientation and homophobia; Lesbian/Gay/Bisexual Identity describes such matters as origins of sexual orientation, stigma management, identity formation, coming out, and lifespan development; and Lesbian/Gay/Bisexual Relationships discusses social dynamics. The text is well referenced as it explores the categories and experiences often assigned to sexual orientation.

Chandler, Kurt. 1995. *Passages of Pride: Lesbian and Gay Youth Come of Age.* New York: Time Books.

This is a collection of stories about the true lives of gay and lesbian youth. The book includes thirty-two essays about youth who discuss everything from what it was like living in the closet to a son's liberation. The stories are essential for anyone interested in reading the life histories of some youth.

Clendinen, Dudley, and Adam Nagourney. 2001. *Out for Good: The Struggle to Build a Gay Rights Movement in America.* New York: Simon and Schuster.

This thirty-seven-chapter text provides a thorough presentation of the gay rights movement from the Stonewall Riots of 1969 to the peak of AIDS activism in 1988 (although the book does not specifically address adolescents). Each chapter discusses an event from the gay activists' viewpoint, exploring their opponents' beliefs and actions and the impact the event had on the movement.

D'Augelli, Anthony R., and Charlotte J. Patterson. 2001. *Lesbian, Gay, and Bisexual Identities and Youth: Psychological Perspectives.* New York: Oxford University Press.

D'Augelli and Patterson have gathered leaders in GLBT youth research to discuss the progress in their respective fields. The twelve chapters are divided into three sections: Conceptual Frameworks, Psychological Challenges, and Issues for Intervention and Social Change. The chapters explore lesbian, gay, and bisexual identities in youth through early adulthood, addressing biological, social, psychological, and cultural factors.

DeCrescenzo, Teresa. 1994. *Helping Gay and Lesbian Youth: New Policies, New Programs, New Practice.* Binghamton, NY: Harrington Park Press.

This book is a compilation of articles on serving gay and lesbian youth that appeared in the *Journal of Gay and Lesbian Social Services.* The articles discuss counseling strategies, legal challenges, HIV risks, service organizations, and so forth, with implications for policy and program development.

Fone, Byrne. 2000. *Homophobia: A History.* New York: Metropolitan Books.

Fone traces the history of homophobia in societies ranging from the ancient Greeks to the Victorian Age to the modern day. The twenty-one chapters are divided into eight eras, and even though youth are not addressed specifically in the text, readers learn that homophobia has been and remains an aspect of society evident in today's law, science, religion, and literature.

Harbeck, Karen M., ed. 1992. *Coming Out of the Classroom Closet: Gay and Lesbian Students, Teachers, and Curricula.* Binghamton, NY: Harrington Park Press.

This text is an anthology of essays and studies that appeared in a *Journal of Homosexuality* issue. Ten articles discuss the school community and its gay, lesbian, and bisexual constituents, including the origins of PROJECT 10, empowerment of gay and lesbian educators, gay and lesbian images in sexuality and health books, and HIV education.

Harris, Mary B., ed. 1997. *School Experiences of Gay and Lesbian Youth: The Invisible Minority.* Binghamton, NY: Harrington Park Press.

This text is a compilation of articles that appeared in the *Journal of Gay and Lesbian Social Services.* Seven essays address an aspect of the dynamics between school and gay and lesbian youth (career development, survival in high school, lesbians in high schools, coming-out experiences, and so forth). Four of the articles present the findings of studies, and three reflect on the population, with recommendations for school personnel.

Herdt, Gilbert, ed. 1989. *Gay and Lesbian Youth.* Binghamton, NY: Harrington Park Press.

The book comprises articles from a *Journal of Homosexuality* two-part issue. The articles cover a range of topics (see Sidebar 3.5).

Herdt, Gilbert, and Andrew Boxer. 1996. *Children of Horizons: How Gay and Lesbian Teens are Leading a New Way Out of the Closet.* Boston: Beacon Press.

In *Children of Horizons,* Herdt and Boxer discuss their work with a social service agency in Chicago serving gay, lesbian, bisexual, and transgender youth. The authors interviewed 202 gay and lesbian youth and analyzed their coming-out experiences, the milestones in their development, what it meant to be out in the community, the dynamics of youth and gay cultures, and what it was like growing up in the era of AIDS. Their voices and suggestions for youth workers are presented in this seven-chapter text.

Heron, Ann, ed. 1994. *Two Teenagers in 20: Writings by Gay and Lesbian Youth.* Los Angeles: Alyson Publications.

Heron presents an anthology of essays by youth in this text. Forty-three youth from across the country write about their experiences with school and what it is like for them to be gay or lesbian in contemporary society. This book is an updated version of the original publication *One Teenager in Ten.* The stories are realistic and appropriate for adolescents.

Hogan, Steven, and Lee Hudson. 1999. *Completely Queer: The Gay and Lesbian Encyclopedia.* New York: Henry Holt.

Completely Queer is a thorough, up-to-date reference manual with entries ranging from notable/public persons in history and today to plays, magazines, books, organizations, countries, plays, words, and symbols, and why they are associated with the community. The entries appear in a dictionary fashion (with considerable detail), and a chronology concludes the more than 700-page text.

Hunter, Ski, Coleen Shannon, Jo Knox, and James I. Martin. 1998. *Lesbian, Gay, and Bisexual Youths and Adults: Knowledge for Human Services Practice.* Thousand Oaks, CA: Sage.

Much of the content in this text is presented from the viewpoint of the human service clinician. The text is far more appropriate for the higher education classroom; however, a chapter complete with statistical references is provided on adolescence.

Isay, Richard A. 1997. *Becoming Gay: The Journey to Self-Acceptance.* New York: Henry Holt.

This seven-chapter book explores the gay man's odyssey, dilemmas, and lifespan development. Isay, a practicing psychiatrist, presents his content in a clear, easy-to-understand fashion, often drawing on his patients' cases to emphasize a point. He believes that gay males should accept their homosexuality and develop a positive identity. One chapter is devoted to gay adolescence.

Jennings, Kevin, ed. 1994. *Becoming Visible: A Reader in Gay and Lesbian History for High School and College Students.* Los Angeles: Alyson Publications.

Jennings, founder of the Gay, Lesbian, and Straight Education Network and former high school history teacher, served as the editor for this book because he wanted readers to learn more about gay history and he wanted teachers to have the resources to teach about it. Seventeen chapters present how gay, lesbian, bisexual, and transgender persons have been treated by past and contemporary cultures. Each chapter consists of a published essay (a historical reference on homosexuality) with questions and activities for follow-up. The chapters are divided into three parts: (1) Homosexuals before "Homosexuality": Looking at "Gay" People in Pre-Modern Societies; (2) The Emergence of the Modern Gay Movement; and (3) The Ongoing Struggle: Gays and Lesbians in the Eighties and Nineties.

Lipkin, Arthur. 1999. *Understanding Homosexuality: Changing Schools.* Boulder, CO: Westview Press.

Lipkin, a former high school teacher for twenty years, gives readers insight into GLBT people through his discussions regarding attitudes toward homosexuality, theories about homosexuality, homophobia, homosexuality in U.S. history, counseling issues, gay and lesbian families and teachers, school curricula, and transforming schools. His fourteen-chapter text is comprehensive and critical for those who want to better understand the population and work toward a more inclusive school environment.

Mallon, Gerald P., ed. 1999. *Social Services with Transgendered Youth.* Binghamton, NY: Harrington Park Press.

This text is a compilation of articles that appeared in a *Journal of Gay and Lesbian Social Services* issue. Very few texts are available on transgender youth, making articles such as "Knowledge for Practice with Transgendered Persons" and "Ethical Issues in the Mental Health Treatment of Gender Dysphoric Adolescents" insightful and appropriate for human services professionals.

———. 2001. *Lesbian and Gay Youth Issues: A Practical Guide for Youth Workers.* Washington, DC: Child Welfare League of America.

Mallon begins this guide with answers to basic questions about GLBT issues. He describes the coming-out process and family, school, and mental health issues, with recommendations for teachers, schools, and other youth-serving professionals. A glossary of terms and resources conclude the ten-chapter text.

Marcus, Eric. 1999. *Is It a Choice? Answers to 300 of the Most Frequently Asked Questions about Gay and Lesbian People.* San Francisco: HarperSanFrancisco.

The book is a collection of questions and answers found grouped in twenty areas (coming out, work, sports, AIDS, aging, and so forth). This is an ideal text for any person who does not know about gay and lesbian people and wants to better understand them. The answers are easy to read, insightful, frank, and sincere.

———. 2000. *What if Someone I Know Is Gay? Answers to Questions about Gay and Lesbian People.* New York: Price Stern Sloan.

Marcus presents a score of questions about gay and lesbian people that could be asked by adolescent readers (What does "gay" mean? Do you have to have sex to know if you're gay or not? Can gay people have children?). The questions and answers are grouped into seven categories: the basic stuff; friends and family; dating, getting married, having kids; sex; God and religion; school; activism and discrimination. A list of resources concludes the text.

Nycum, Benjie. 2000. *The XY Survival Guide: Everything You Need to Know About Being Young and Gay.* San Francisco: XY Publishing.

The content of Nycum's text is intended for gay male youth who want answers to questions ranging from safe sex to how to start a gay-straight alliance. The writing is frank, amusing, lighthearted, and clearly focused on solutions for adolescents and young adults. Some of the content may be offensive to some readers.

Owens, Robert E. 1998: *Queer Kids: The Challenges and Promise for Lesbian, Gay, and Bisexual Youth.* Binghamton, NY: Harrington Park Press.

Queer Kids is a twelve-chapter text that describes what home, school, and community life is like for some gay, lesbian, and bisexual youth. This book is ideal for teachers, counselors, and parents who desire to accept, help, or counsel this population. A list of resources concludes the text.

Perrotti, Jeff, and Kim Westheimer. 2001. *When the Drama Club Is Not Enough: Lessons from the Safe Schools Programs for Gay and Lesbian Students.* Boston: Beacon Press.

This book shares what Perrotti and Westheimer learned from the Massachusetts Safe Schools Program for Gay and Lesbian Students. The authors reflect on what worked well in the schools and why, providing student testimonies and sound advice throughout the eight chapters. This book is for the reader who wants to learn how to change a school culture and climate so that all youth are valued and respected.

Ryan, Caitlin, and Donna Futterman. 1998. *Lesbian and Gay Youth: Care and Counseling.* New York: Columbia University Press.

The text is a valuable resource for mental health professionals who provide prevention and intervention services for this population of youth. In fourteen chapters the authors discuss this population's experiences, vulnerabilities, health challenges, and risks and instruct service providers on how to administer effective mental health and medical treatment. The chapters are divided into three parts: Overview: Lesbian and Gay Adolescents—Experiences and Needs; Primary Care and Prevention; and HIV/AIDS.

Savin-Williams, Ritch C., and Kenneth M. Cohen. 1996. *The Lives of Lesbians, Gays, and Bisexuals: Children to Adults.* New York: Harcourt Brace.

This book was designed as a college textbook but nonetheless is for any concerned parent, clinician, or researcher who wants to know more about GLBT people. The twenty chapters cover various aspects of diverse sexuality within the lifespan (from perinatal factors to adolescence to adulthood and aging) and conclude with discussion of cultural and mental health issues. The book deals with a score of topics, such as identity development, relationships, gay and lesbian parents, myths, and gay and lesbian teachers and lawyers.

Sonnie, Amy, ed. 2000. *Revolutionary Voices: A Multicultural Queer Youth Anthology.* Los Angeles: Alyson Publications.

As the title indicates, this is a collection of essays, poems, and letters by youth for other youth. More than fifty youth express themselves through inquiry about their identities, cultural standards, gender inequity, religion, social class, ability, and so forth.

Unks, Gerald, ed. 1995. *The Gay Teen: Educational Practice and Theory for Lesbian, Gay, and Bisexual Adolescents.* New York: Routledge.

This is a collection of articles that appeared in an issue of the *High School Journal* devoted to GLBT youth (see Sidebar 3.8). The seventeen chapters are divided into four parts: The Gay Teenager; Educational Practice and Lesbian, Gay, and Bisexual Teenagers; Educational Theory and Lesbian, Gay, and Bisexual Teenagers; and The Development of Safe Space for Lesbian, Gay, and Bisexual Teenagers.

Walling, Donovan R, ed. 1996. *Open Lives: Safe Schools: Addressing Gay and Lesbian Issues in Education.* Bloomington, IN: Phi Delta Kappa Educational Foundation.

Walling is the editor of these essays on schools and gay and lesbian students, teachers, curricula, and resources. Some of the topics include coaching and homosexuality, bringing gay and lesbian literature out of the closet, whether people are born with the lifestyle or choose it, and preventing gay teen suicide.

Woog, Dan. 1995. *School's Out: The Impact of Gay and Lesbian Issues on America's Schools.* Los Angeles: Alyson Publications.

Woog compiled interviews and discussions with nearly 300 people into an anthology of essays about people, places, and programs associated with gay, lesbian, bisexual, and transgender youth. Readers can learn about the experiences of an openly gay coach, a gay youth who ended up in a hospital, a teacher and principal gay couple, an openly gay guidance counselor, and so forth. This text is ideal for readers who want to learn more about gay and lesbian youth or school personnel who have made significant strides in their school community.

JOURNALS

Much of the content in this text was gathered from professional journals devoted to GLBT issues. The articles in these journals are largely research based, theory oriented, and conceptual in nature, often having implications for school personnel and field practitioners. For the most part, the title of the journal suggests the content of its articles. Harrington Park Press publishes these journals, and university-affiliated professionals serve as the editors.

Journal of Bisexuality
Editor: Fritz Klein, M.D., San Diego, CA

Journal of Gay and Lesbian Politics
Editor: Steven H. Haeberle, Ph.D., University of Alabama, Birmingham

Journal of Gay and Lesbian Social Services
Editor: James J. Kelly, Ph.D., California State University, Hayward

Journal of Homosexuality
Editor: John P. De Cecco, Ph.D., San Francisco State University

Journal of Lesbian Studies
Editor: Esther D. Rothblum, Ph.D., University of Vermont, Burlington

A momentum now exists in the body of literature regarding gay, lesbian, bisexual, and transgender youth. More articles are now available in professional journals than ever before. In addition to the articles cited at the end of the chapters in this text, the following groups of articles are critical for any youth-serving professional who wants to become an ally to the community.

Family Issues

These articles discuss the dynamics of GLBT youth and their families and strategies for working effectively with them. Readers can learn how to connect with or support students or those whose parents or family members are gay, lesbian, or bisexual.

Bontempo, Daniel E., and Anthony R. D'Augelli. 2002. **"Effects of At-School Victimization and Sexual Orientation on Lesbian, Gay, or Bisexual Youths' Health Risk Behavior."** *Journal of Adolescent Health* 30(5): 364–374.

Coenen, Matthew E. 1998. **"Helping Families with Homosexual Children: A Model for Counseling."** *Journal of Homosexuality* 36(2): 73–85.

D'Augelli, Anthony R., Scott L. Hershberger, and Neil W. Pilkington. 1998. **"Lesbian, Gay, and Bisexual Youth and Their Families: Disclosure** of Sexual Orientation and Its Consequences." *American Journal of Orthopsychiatry* 68(3): 361–371.

Mallon, Gerald P. 1999. **"Gay and Lesbian Adolescents and Their Families."** *Journal of Gay and Lesbian Social Services* 10(2): 69–88.

Sanders, Gary L., and Ian T. Kroll. 2000. **"Generating Stories of Resilience: Helping Gay and Lesbian Youth and Their Families."** *Journal of Marital and Family Therapy* 26(4): 433–442.

Sears, James T. 1994. **"Challenges for Educators: Lesbian, Gay, and Bisexual Families."** *High School Journal* 77 (1/2): 138–156.

General Information

These articles offer general information about the population, from descriptions of developmental needs and experiences to recommendations for professionals. These are ideal for readers new to the body of literature who want general knowledge about the population. The articles lend themselves well to circulation in professional development/training seminars.

Harbeck, Karen M. 1994. **"Invisible No More: Addressing the Needs of Gay, Lesbian, and Bisexual Youth and Their Advocates."** *High School Journal* 77 (1/2): 169–176.

Sanelli, Maria, and George Perreault. 2001. **"'I Could Be Anybody': Gay, Lesbian, and Bisexual Students in U.S. Schools."** *NASSP Bulletin* 85(622): 69–78.

Sanford, Gary. 1999. **"Breaking the Silence: Supporting Gay, Lesbian, Bisexual, Transgender, and Questioning Youth."** *New Designs for Youth Development* 15(2): 19–24.

Stevens, Patricia E., and Sarah Morgan. 1999. **"Health of Lesbian, Gay, Bisexual, and Transgender Youth."** *Journal of Child and Family Nursing* 2(4): 237–249.

Homophobia and Associated Challenges

This group of articles contends specifically with hatred, discrimination, prejudice, harassment, and violence toward GLBT youth and the impact these have had on their lives. Readers learn how and why homophobia develops in society (and schools) and understand the importance of teaching about acceptance and tolerance of diversity. The articles also strategize about how to reduce homophobia in classrooms.

Baker, Janet G., and Harold D. Fishbein. 1998. **"The Development of Prejudice towards Gays and Lesbians by Adolescents."** *Journal of Homosexuality* 36(1): 89–100.

De Rosa, Christine Johnson, Susanne B. Montgomery, Justeen Hyde, Ellen Iverson, and Michele D. Kipke. 2001. **"HIV Risk Behavior and HIV Testing: A Comparison of Rates and Associated Factors among Homeless and Runaway Adolescents in Two Cities."** *AIDS Education and Prevention* 13(2): 131–148.

Farrow, James A., Robert W. Deisher, Richard Brown, John W. Klug, and Michele D. Kipke. 1992. **"Health and Health Needs of Homeless and Runaway Youth."** *Journal of Adolescent Health* 13(8): 717–726.

Griffin, Pat. 1994. **"Homophobia in Sports: Addressing the Needs of Lesbian and Gay High School Athletes."** *High School Journal* 77 (1/2): 80–87.

Grossman, Arnold H. 1997. **"Growing Up with a 'Spoiled Identity': Lesbian, Gay, and Bisexual Youth at Risk."** *Journal of Gay and Lesbian Social Services* 6(3): 45–56.

Grossman, Arnold H., and Matthew S. Kerner. 1998. **"Self-Esteem and Supportiveness as Predictors of Emotional Distress in Gay Male and Lesbian Youth."** *Journal of Homosexuality* 35(2): 25–39.

Gustavsson, Nora S., and Ann E. MacEachron. 1998. **"Violence and Lesbian and Gay Youth."** *Journal of Gay and Lesbian Social Services* 8(3): 41–50.

Kruks, Gabe. 1991. **"Gay and Lesbian Homeless/Street Youth: Special Issues and Concerns."** *Journal of Adolescent Health* 12(7): 515–518.

Lock, James, and Hans Steiner. 1999. **"Gay, Lesbian, and Bisexual Youth Risks for Emotional, Physical, and Social Problems: Results from Community-Based Survey."** *Journal of the American Academy of Child and Adolescent Psychiatry* 38(3): 297–304.

Marsiglio, William. 1993. **"Attitudes toward Homosexual Activity and**

Gays as Friends: A National Survey of Heterosexual 15- to 19-Year-Old Males." *Journal of Sex Research* 30(1): 12–17.

Walters, Andrew S., and David M. Hayes. 1998. **"Homophobia within Schools: Challenging the Culturally Sanctioned Dismissal of Gay Students and Colleagues."** *Journal of Homosexuality* 35(2): 1–23.

Identity Development, Coming Out

The following articles are well suited for readers interested specifically in the patterns found in sexual identity development. These articles provide a glimpse of what youth may experience when they come out to friends, family, or teachers. The content, directly or indirectly, suggests how readers can accept, comfort, affirm, or support these youth during this challenging process.

Anderson, Dennis A. 1994. **"Lesbian and Gay Adolescents: Social and Developmental Considerations."** *High School Journal* 77 (1/2): 13–19.

Armesto, Jorge C., and Amy G. Weisman. 2001. **"Attributions and Emotional Reactions to the Identity Disclosure ('Coming Out') of a Homosexual Child."** *Family Process* 40(2): 145–161.

Harris, Mary B., and Gail K. Bliss. 1997. **"Coming Out in a School Setting: Former Students' Experiences and Opinions about Disclosure."** *Journal of Gay and Lesbian Social Services* 7(4): 85–100.

Johnson, Don. 1996. **"The Developmental Experience of Gay/Lesbian Youth."** *Journal of College Admission* 152–153: 38–41.

McFarland, William P. 1993. **"A Developmental Approach to Gay and Lesbian Youth."** *Journal of Humanistic Education and Development* 32: 17–29.

Waldner, Lisa K., and Brian Magruder. 1999. **"Coming Out to Parents: Perceptions of Family Relations, Perceived Resources, and Identity Expression as Predictors of Identity Disclosure for Gay and Lesbian Adolescents."** *Journal of Homosexuality* 37(2): 83–100.

School Issues

These school-based articles have implications for curricula, teachers, counselors, and other school officials and personnel. Studies and discussions are presented with the goal of helping readers understand the importance of having supportive, safe school communities for youth with diverse sexualities. Readers can learn how to mentor, counsel, or protect youth; include gay and lesbian topics in classes; create support networks for GLBT youth; meet the needs of gifted youth; and so forth. The articles can be circulated to specific groups of teachers or counselors trying to understand how to create more inclusive classrooms.

Alexander, Christopher J. 1999. **"Mentoring for Gay and Lesbian Youth."** *Gay and Lesbian Social Services* 10(2): 89–92.

Allan, Christina. 1999. **"Poets of Comrades: Addressing Sexual Orientation in the English Classroom."** *National Council of Teachers of English* 88(6): 97–101.

Anderson, John D. 1997. **"Supporting the Invisible Minority."** *Educational Leadership* 54(7): 65–68.

Brogan, Jim. 1994. **"Gay Teens in Literature."** *High School Journal* 77 (1/2): 50–57.

Buckel, David S. 2000. **"Legal Perspective on Ensuring a Safe and Nondiscriminatory School Environment for Lesbian, Gay, Bisexual, and Transgendered Students."** *Education and Urban Society* 32(3): 390–398.

Callahan, Connie J. 2001. **"Protecting and Counseling Gay and Lesbian Students."** *Journal of Humanistic Counseling, Education, and Development* 40(1): 5–10.

DuBeau, Tania. 1998. **"Making a Difference in the Lives of Gay and Lesbian Students."** *Reclaiming Children and Youth: Journal of Emotional and Behavioral Problems* 7(3): 164–168.

Edwards, Ann T. 1997. **"Let's Stop Ignoring Our Gay and Lesbian Youth."** *Educational Leadership* 54(7): 68–70.

Fontaine, Janet H. 1998. **"Evidencing a Need: School Counselors' Experiences with Gay and Lesbian Students."** *Professional School Counseling* 1(3): 8–14.

Fontaine, Janet H., and Nancy L. Hammond. 1996. **"Counseling Issues with Gay and Lesbian Adolescents."** *Adolescence* 31(124): 817–830.

Gill, Kathy J. 1998. **"Maintaining the Dignity and Rights of Gay and Lesbian Students."** *Reclaiming Children and Youth: Journal of Emotional and Behavioral Problems* 7(1): 25–27.

Herr, Kathryn. 1997. **"Learning Lessons from School: Homophobia, Heterosexism, and the Construction of Failure."** *Journal of Gay and Lesbian Social Services* 7(4): 51–64.

Jones, Rebecca. 1999. **"'I Don't Feel Safe Here Anymore': Your Legal Duty to Protect Gay Kids from Harassment."** *American School Board Journal* 186(11): 27–31.

Kozik-Rosabal, Genet. 2000. **"'Well, We Haven't Noticed Anything Bad Going On,' Said the Principal: Parents Speak about Their Gay Families and Schools."** *Education and Urban Society* 32(3): 368–389.

LeCompte, Margaret D. 2000. **"Standing for Just and Right Decisions: The Long, Slow Path to School Safety."** *Education and Urban Society* 32(3): 413–429.

Macgillivray, Ian K. 2000. **"Educational Equity for Gay, Lesbian, Bisexual, Transgendered, and Queer/Questioning Students: The Demands of Democracy and Social Justice for America's Schools."** *Education and Urban Society* 32(3): 303–323.

Mallon, Gerald P. 1997. **"When Schools Are Not Safe Places: Reconnecting Gay and Lesbian Young People to Schools."** *Reaching Today's Youth: The Community Circle of Caring Journal* 2(1): 41–45.

Marinoble, Rita M. 1998. **"Homosexuality: A Blind Spot in the School Mirror."** *Professional School Counseling* 1(3): 4–7.

Mathison, Carla. 1998. **"The Invisible Minority: Preparing Teachers to Meet the Needs of Gay and Lesbian Youth."** *Journal of Teacher Education* 49(2): 151–155.

McFarland, William P., and Martin Dupius. 2001. **"The Legal Duty to Protect Gay and Lesbian Students from Violence in Schools."** *Professional School Counseling* 4(3): 171–179.

Nesmith, Andrea A., David L. Burton, and T. J. Cosgrove. 1999. **"Gay, Lesbian, and Bisexual Youth and Young Adults: Social Support in Their Own Words."** *Journal of Homosexuality* 37(1): 95–108.

Nichols, Sharon L. 1999. **"Gay, Lesbian, and Bisexual Youth: Understanding Diversity and Promoting Tolerance in Schools."** *Elementary School Journal* 99(5): 505–519.

Peterson, Jean Sunde, and Heather Rischar. 2000. **"Gifted and Gay: A Study of the Adolescent Experience."** *Gifted Child Quarterly* 44(4): 231–246.

Reynolds, Amy L. 1994. **"Lesbian, Gay, and Bisexual Teens and the School Counselor: Building Alliances."** *High School Journal* 77 (1/2): 88–93.

Riddle, Bob. 1996. **"Breaking the Silence: Addressing Gay and Lesbian Issues in Independent Schools."** *Independent School* 55(2): 38–41.

Rienzo, Barbara A., James W. Button, and Kenneth D. Wald. 1997. **"School-Based Programs Addressing Gay/Lesbian/Bisexual Youth Issues."** *Journal of the International Council for Health, Physical Education, Recreation, Sport, and Dance* 33(2): 20–25.

Schneider, Monica E., and Robert E. Owens. 2000. **"Concern for Lesbian, Gay, and Bisexual Kids: The Benefits for All Children."** *Education and Urban Society* 32(3): 349–367.

Telljohann, Susan K., James H. Price, Mohammed Poureslami, and Alyssa Easton. 1995. **"Teaching about Sexual Orientation by Secondary Health Teachers."** *Journal of School Health* 65(1): 18–22.

Underwood, Jackie, and Janet Black. 1998. **"Young, Female, and Gay: Lesbian Students and the School Environment."** *Professional School Counseling* 1(3): 15–20.

Suicide

The articles in this group are specific to suicide, suicide attempts, and suicide prevention. Discussions ensue on suicide statistics for GLBT youth, explanations for why they commit or attempt suicide, and ways youth-serving professionals and parents can help them find alternatives to this devastating, unnecessary option.

Hershberger, Scott L., and Anthony R. D'Augelli. 1995. **"The Impact of Victimization on the Mental Health and Suicidality of Lesbian, Gay, and Bisexual Youth."** *Developmental Psychology* 31(1): 65–74.

Kulkin, Heidi S., Elizabeth A. Chauvin, and Gretchen A. Percle. 2000. **"Suicide among Gay and Lesbian Adolescents and Youth Adults: A Review of the Literature."** *Journal of Homosexuality* 40(1): 1–29.

McFarland, William P. 1998. **"Gay, Lesbian, Bisexual Student Suicide."** *Professional School Counseling* 1(3): 26–29.

Proctor, Curtis D., and Victor K. Groze. 1994. **"Risk Factors for Suicide among Gay, Lesbian, and Bisexual Youths."** *Social Work* 39(5): 504–513.

Remafedi, Gary, James A. Farrow, and Robert W. Deisher. 1991. **"Risk Factors for Attempted Suicide in Gay and Bisexual Youth."** *Pediatrics* 87(6): 869–875.

Sandoval, Jonathan, and Stephen E. Brock. 1996. **"The School Psychologist's Role in Suicide Prevention."** *School Psychology Quarterly* 11(2): 169–185.

POPULAR MAGAZINES

The following magazines can be found in libraries, on newsstands, and in bookstores. Like all lifestyles magazines, the content of these is made up of celebrity interviews, political discourse, arts and entertainment reviews, fashion pieces, and so forth, but is completely geared to the GLBT community.

The Advocate
6922 Hollywood Blvd., Suite 1000
Los Angeles, CA 90028
Telephone: (323) 871-1225
http://www.advocate.com

The Advocate is a national magazine for and about the gay and lesbian community. The magazine contains the latest news and entertainment, featuring groundbreaking stories and interviews with prominent celebrities, politicians, and notable community members. The magazine is published biweekly (except for monthly in January and August) and has historically addressed gay, lesbian, bisexual, and transgender youth and schools.

Curve Magazine
1 Haight Street, Suite B

San Francisco, CA 94102
Telephone: (800) 998-5565
http://www.curvemag.com

Curve is written for lesbian women and youth throughout the nation. Every issue presents an in-depth interview with women eager to challenge the social norm. Issues feature an advice column, Hollywood gossip, and arts and entertainment reviews. *Curve* is considered the best-selling lesbian magazine.

Genre Magazine

7080 Hollywood Blvd., Suite 818
Hollywood, CA 90028
Telephone: (323) 467-8300
http://www.genremagazine.com

Genre is considered the affluent gay man's magazine and features items related to fashion, travel, advice, entertainment, news, and health and fitness. The magazine "reflects the growing diversity and interests of the gay community, and hopes to become the ultimate lifestyle resource for gay men." *Genre* has been promoted as America's favorite gay men's magazine.

Girlfriends Magazine

3415 Cesar Chavez, Suite 101
San Francisco, CA 94110
Telephone: (415) 648-9464
http://www.gfriends.com

Girlfriends is designed for lesbian women and youth interested in lesbian perspectives on politics, culture, and entertainment. Each issue features "herSTORIES"—interviews with prominent women in various fields, advice on health and relations, and arts and entertainment reviews.

Instinct Magazine

15335 Morrison Street, Suite 325
Sherman Oaks, CA 91403
Telephone: (818) 205-9033
http://www.instinctmag.com

Instinct is a gay men's magazine that presents its content in a light (at times brash) fashion. Entertainment, fitness, travel, and fashion are discussed from a humorous perspective. The editors write, "While we will always include something of the inspiring, heart-felt, 'this is touching, isn't it?' moment of seriousness in each issue, the rest is a much-needed vacation from the overkill of a politically correct world." Some partially nude men appear throughout the issues.

Metrosource
180 Varick Street, 5th Floor
New York, NY 10014
Telephone: (212) 691-5127
http://www.metrosource.com

Metrosource is published for the gay community five times each year and features articles on intriguing people and the latest fashion, as well as critical reviews of films, television, music, and books. Readers will find departments devoted to health, fitness, travel, interior design elements, and so forth.

Out
6922 Hollywood Blvd., Suite 1000
Los Angeles, CA 90028
Telephone: (323) 871-1225
http://www.out.com/home.asp

In 2002 *Out* celebrated ten years of providing the gay and lesbian community articles on current affairs and pop culture and celebrities, and featuring advice on fitness and health, relationships, and finances. *Out* is published each month and is composed of Outfront (reviews of television, film, books, arts, and music), Voices (analysis of gay culture, politics, interviews with community members, and so forth), Features (celebrity interviews, fashion spreads, critical issues of concern), and Essentials (calendars, style, advice, horoscopes) departments.

POZ
1 Little West 12th Street, 6th Floor
New York, NY 10014
Telephone: (800) 973-2376
http://www.poz.com

POZ is for those living with HIV/AIDS. Each issue seeks to inform readers about advances in medicine, offer health and lifestyle support, share the encouraging stories of others, and investigate newsworthy developments. More importantly, *POZ* challenges persons living with a life-threatening illness to view themselves in a hopeful perspective. "If we believe ourselves to be 'terminally ill,' then we void everything else about our lives. Our love, passion, vision, and vitality. Our hopes and dreams. We might as well just plan the funeral and wait to die. *POZ* delivers the possibility of survival in an inspiring, hopeful manner."

REPORTS AND STUDIES AVAILABLE ONLINE

In a concerted effort to educate policymakers, school personnel, parents, youth service providers, and communities, some organizations will conduct, publish, and disseminate studies and reports to the general public. Some of the documents listed below contend directly with the population, others suggest how adults and youth can transform their school community to become supportive of all youth, and the remaining are general sources of information to be used for curricula and program development. These documents can be downloaded directly from their respective websites.

101 Ways to Combat Prejudice
Barnes and Noble and the Anti-Defamation League
http://a1055.g.akamai.net/f/1055/979/5h/www.barnesandnoble.com/
boutiques/children/adl/resources/closethebook.pdf

101 Ways is a joint-effort campaign to reduce hatred, violence, prejudice, discrimination, and harassment in various environments. The strategies begin in the home and branch toward ideas for the communities. Some terms and definitions, a reading list (for juveniles and adults), and a resource and ally list are included in the document.

The 2001 National School Climate Survey: The School Related Experiences of Our Nation's Lesbian, Gay, Bisexual, and Transgender Youth
Gay, Lesbian, and Straight Education Network (GLSEN)
http://www.glsen.org/binary-
data/GLSEN_ARTICLES/pdf_file/1307.pdf

This study surveyed 1,000 gay, lesbian, bisexual, and transgender students from forty-eight states to determine the climates in schools across the country. The results were startling with one finding that 84 percent had said they heard words such as faggot and dyke routinely, and another finding that nearly 25 percent had heard a faculty or staff member make a homophobic remark at least some of the time. This document presents the results on such factors as biased language, experiences with harassment and assaults, feeling safe at school, and so forth.

Creating Safe Schools for Lesbian and Gay Students:
A Resource Guide for School Staff
Youth Pride
http://members.tripod.com/twood/guide.html

This report was written so that teachers and school personnel would better understand GLBT youth and learn some teaching strategies to implement in classrooms. Statistics on the population, suggestions for reducing homophobia, some information about sexual orientation, lesson ideas, and recommendations for a nondiscrimination policy are some of the elements of the report.

Defending Gay/Straight Alliances and Other Gay-Related
Groups in Public Schools Under the Equal Access Act
Lambda Legal Defense and Education Fund
http://www.lambdalegal.org

Lambda LDEF has valuable online resources that teachers and youth can use to establish effective gay-straight alliances. This question-and-answer document discusses the Equal Access Act, what to do if school officials do not allow youth to form a club, and what to do if others are complaining about the club's formation and meetings. *Defending* is easy to follow and critical for educating those who oppose such school clubs.

Each Child That Dies: Gays and Lesbians in Your Schools
OutProud, reprinted from *Multicultures, Unity through Diversity—A Monograph of Diversity in the Field of Education,* edited by Jean M. Novak and Louis G. Denti, Volume 1, 1995.
http://www.outproud.org/article_each_child.html

This monograph discusses why teachers should be more accepting and supportive of gay and lesbian youth. The authors elaborate on five suggestions for schools and explain that teaching about homosexuality is worthwhile and beneficial for all students.

Eighty-Three Thousand Youth: Selected Findings of Eight
Population-Based Studies as They Pertain to Anti-gay Harassment
and the Safety and Well-Being of Sexual Minority Students
Safe Schools Coalition
http://www.safeschoolscoalition.org/83000youth.pdf

The Safe Schools Coalition brought together studies of middle and high school students to determine the degree of antigay sentiment in schools.

The studies investigated many aspects of harassment and violence toward gay, lesbian, bisexual, and transgender youth, including whether respondents had been bullied because others thought they might be gay or lesbian, had been threatened and assaulted at school, were fearful at school, or engaged in self-endangering behaviors. Most of the studies used the Youth Risk Behavior Survey and sampled youth from Connecticut, Minnesota, Native American tribes, Vermont, Wisconsin, Seattle, San Francisco, Massachusetts, and Wisconsin.

Focus on Gays, Lesbians, and Bisexuals
National Education Association (NEA)
http://www.nea.org/bt/1-students/gays.pdf

The NEA has produced this document to inform schools that they are legally obligated to protect GLBT youth from antigay harassment and assaults. The document provides answers to questions conceived by people unfamiliar with gay, lesbian, or bisexual people.

A Guide to Effective Statewide Laws/Policies: Preventing Discrimination against LGBT Students in K–12 Schools
Lambda Legal Defense and Education Fund and Gay, Lesbian, and Straight Education Network
http://www.lambdalegal.org/binary-data/LAMBDA_PDF/pdf/61.pdf

This document provides direction to concerned citizens eager to create and change state laws and policies in order to positively transform schools. "This document is a part of our ongoing educational outreach to the youth and their advocates who struggle everyday in schools to get a safe and sound education. . . . Lambda presents the key legal considerations that should inform advocates' decisions about what actions to take at the state level. Then GLSEN fills in the legal framework with the important political considerations for advocates."

Guidelines for Comprehensive Sexuality Education, 2d **Edition**
Sex Information and Education Council of the United States
http://www.siecus.org/pubs/guidelines/guidelines.pdf

A national task force created the *Guidelines* to serve as a model for the development of health and sexuality education curricula. Teachers and curricula administrators are to use the guidelines to develop lessons most appropriate for their school community. This framework of concepts has four goals for sexuality education: information; attitudes, values, and insights; relationships and interpersonal skills; and responsibility. Diverse sexualities are addressed throughout the developmental messages.

Hate-Motivated Behavior in Schools: Response Strategies for School Boards, Administrators, Law Enforcement, and Communities
Alameda County Offices of Education
http://www.acoe.k12.ca.us/acoe/HATECRIMES/manual.htm

Although this is a local publication, the information can be used by school districts across the country. The document defines hate-motivated behavior; discusses ideas for dealing with, preventing, and responding to the behavior; and follows with strategies for working with victims and perpetrators. The website homepage allows users to download an accompanying document, *Tool Kit,* which is a compilation of classroom activities and resources.

Homosexuality and Adolescence
American Academy of Pediatrics
http://www.medem.com/search/article_display.cfm?path=n:&mstr=/Z ZZUHJP3KAC.html&soc=AAP&srch_typ=NAV_SERCH

This publication is the academy's official position on homosexuality and adolescence. Included are discussions on etiology and prevalence, special concerns, special aspects of care, and psychosocial issues. One table presents definitions and terms, and another underscores the stages of identity development.

How to Start a Gay-Straight Alliance
Gay, Lesbian, and Straight Education Network (GLSEN)
http://www.glsen.org/binary-data/GLSEN_ARTICLES/pdf_file/258.pdf

GLSEN has produced this publication offering advice to students and teachers who want to start and maintain a gay-straight alliance in their school. The publication was intended for the state of Massachusetts (references are made to specific schools), but the suggestions offered are applicable to any school.

Just the Facts about Sexual Orientation and Youth: A Primer for Principals, Educators, and School Personnel
American Academy of Pediatrics and Others
http://www.pflag.org/education/schools/docs/justthefacts.pdf

Ten reputable associations developed this fact sheet to provide school professionals with accurate, science-based information about gay, lesbian, and bisexual youth. The twelve-page document includes information about sexual orientation development, reparative therapy, transformational ministries, and legal principles. An outline of resources follows the content.

PERSON Project Organizing Handbook
PERSON Project
http://www.youth.org

This 1995 handbook was created to reform school curricula and policies so that information about people with diverse sexualities is provided to students accurately, fairly, and continually. Discussions about youth, educational equity, textbook adoption, legal issues, and other topics ensue in this resourceful document. The website allows users to download state-specific documents.

Preventing Youth Hate Crime: A Manual for Schools and Communities
Safe and Drug Free Schools
http://www.ed.gov/pubs/HateCrime/start.html

This document provides readers with ideas for preventing and reducing intolerance and violence among youth. It discusses the prevalence of hate crimes in society, elements of effective programs, and programs in operation, and it concludes with classroom activities. A resource list and a bibliography of curricula and instructional material, books, and videos are found at the end of the document.

The PROJECT 10 East GSA Handbook
PROJECT 10 East
http://www.project10east.org/handbook.html

This handbook was created for gay-straight alliances needing a starting point from which to draw ideas and for school personnel interested in creating safe places for GLBT youth. The content is divided into twelve areas, including definitions, frequently asked questions, assistance with coming out, suggestions for reducing homophobia, and counseling considerations. Youth testimonies and information about PROJECT 10 East are included.

Protecting Students from Harassment and Hate Crime: A Guide for Schools
Office for Civil Rights, Department of Education
http://www.ed.gov/pubs/Harassment/harass_intro.html

This two-part document provides a comprehensive overview of harassment and hate crimes in schools. Part one explains that schools must develop and implement policies that prohibit harassment, provides procedures for identifying and responding to such violence, and offers recommendations that create supportive school climates. Part two discusses development of an antiharassment policy, response to incidents, complaint/grievance procedures, climates that appreciate diversity, and how to address hate crimes and conflicts. This document is critical for schools that have weak antiharassment policies.

Resource Guide to Coming Out
Human Rights Campaign (HRC)
http://www.hrc.org/ncop/guide/index.asp

Because disclosing one's sexual orientation can be a challenging event, the HRC has created this document to help those contemplating coming out. *Coming Out* is supportive of readers, offering practical information about sexuality, gender identity, and the coming-out process and giving encouragement for the journey ahead. Photographs and brief testimonies of celebrities and common citizens appear throughout the document.

Safe Schools Resource Guide
Safe Schools Coalition
http://www.safeschoolscoalition.org/SSCresource.pdf

This eighty-three-page document is a comprehensive tool for any person searching for resources to help a gay, lesbian, bisexual, or transgender youth. Information includes toll-free hotlines, organizations, resources by topic (Boy Scouts, Law and Policy, and so forth), and resources by type (postcards, brochures, and so forth).

School Shouldn't Hurt: Lifting the Burden from Gay, Lesbian, Bisexual, and Transgendered Youth
Rhode Island Task Force on Gay, Lesbian, Bisexual and Transgendered Youth
http://members.tripod.com

The Rhode Island Task Force gathered the testimonies of students and parents at a public forum to determine the level of discrimination aimed at youth with diverse sexualities. These testimonies are presented in this two-part report. The first part, Identifying the Problems, investigates verbal harassment, violence against students, gay and lesbian visibility, suicide and isolation, drop-out rates and school performance, and school personnel indifference. The second part, Recommendations, calls for policies protecting gay and lesbian students, professional development for teachers, increased resources pertaining to gay and lesbian issues, better support systems, and further dialogue on the matter.

Stopping Anti-Gay Abuse of Students in Public Schools:
A Legal Perspective
Lambda Legal Defense and Education Fund
http://www.lambdalegal.org/sections/library/stopping.pdf

The content is presented in a "how-to" format and is appropriate for students who are experiencing antigay harassment at school. This document explains how students should report the abuse, whom to contact for help, how to document the harassment, and how to file complaints, while encouraging readers to be ready with solutions. The information is straightforward, practical, and resourceful.

Taking the Lead: How School Administrators Can Provide
the Leadership Necessary to Creating Schools Where All People
Are Valued, Regardless of Sexual Orientation
Gay, Lesbian, and Straight Education Network
http://www.glsen.org/templates/resources/record.
html?section=14&record=384

The information in this document is designed to help administrators create climates where all students are welcomed, respected, valued, and supported. Author Charles Todd, a school head and a GLSEN board president, explains the need for these climates and outlines ten steps for administrators to follow. Three of the accompanying appendixes are personal views shared by practicing school leaders.

They Don't Even Know Me! Understanding Anti-Gay
Harassment and Violence in Schools
Safe Schools Coalition
http://www.safeschoolscoalition.org/theydontevenknowme.pdf

This publication is the executive report of the Safe Schools Coalition of Washington State's five-year research project. The project investigated antigay harassment and violence in kindergarten through twelfth grades. Analysis of 111 reported antigay abuse incidents is presented in this eighty-two-page document.

Understanding Gay and Lesbian Students through Diversity
National Education Association (NEA)
http://www.nea.org/bt/1-students/gayles.pdf

This document serves as the NEA's diversity resolution, which addresses the need to eliminate all forms of racial, sexual, and sexual orientation discrimination. The resolution also discusses developmental, academic, social, and discrimination issues as they relate to gay and lesbian youth. Recommendations for NEA members and other professional organizations conclude the document.

WEBSITES

The following websites are ideal for youth who are GLBT as well as those who are questioning their sexual orientation. Although some of these websites are community specific, most post current news for and about youth with diverse sexualities; offer pen pal and communication services; have links to other support networks; provide online magazines; offer advice, tips, or online peer consulting; have search buttons to locate issues of concern; and answer questions about sex, relationships, sexually transmitted diseases, and HIV/AIDS. The websites are sponsored by reputable organizations and sincerely extend their support and resources to youth. All youth should, however, exercise caution when interacting with others on the Internet as law enforcement agencies have found that some adults disguise themselves as youth and prey on adolescents' naïveté.

Bear Youth
http://www.bearyouth.org/start.htm

Books for and about Gay/Lesbian Teens and Youth
http://www.softlord.com/glbbooks

Boston Alliance of GLBT Youth
http://www.bagly.org

Boston GLASS Community Center
http://www.bostonglass.org

Café Pride: Chicago's Gay-Friendly, Youth Coffeehouses
http://www.cafepride.com

Cool Page for Queer Teens
http://www.bidstrup.com/cool.htm

Day of Silence Project
http://www.dayofsilence.org

Dignity USA
http://www.dignityusa.org

District 202: Creating Safe Space for Queer Youth
http://www.dist202.org

Elight!
http://www.elight.org

Financial Aid for Lesbian, Gay, and Bisexual Students
http://www.finaid.org/otheraid/gay.phtml

Gay and Lesbian National Hotline
http://www.glnh.org/home.htm

Gay.com Youth Zone
http://www.gay.com/chat/promo/youth_psa.html

Gay, Lesbian, Bisexual, and Transgender Scholarship Resources
http://www.washburn.edu/sobu/broach/glbt-scholar.html

Gay Teen Resource
http://www.gayteenresource.com

Gayteens.org
http://www.gayteens.org

Gay Youth Community
http://www.geocities.com/WestHollywood/3785

GLBT Years Book
http://www.gayyearbook.com

Go Ask Alice
Columbia University's health question and answer Internet services
http://www.goaskalice.columbia.edu/index.html

Horizons Community Services
http://www.horizonsonline.org/main.html

Jewish Queer Youth Home Page
http://www.jqyouth.com

Lambda Foundation for Excellence
http://www.lambdafoundation.com

LAMBDA 10
http://www.lambda10.org

LAMBDA Youth Project
http://www.gayprom.org/lypinfo.html

Lambert House
http://www.lamberthouse.org

Lavender Youth Recreation and Information Center
A community center for GLBT youth twenty-three and under
http://thecity.sfsu.edu/~lyric

Mogenic
http://www.mogenic.com/index.asp

National Association of Lesbian, Gay, Bisexual, and Transgender Community Centers
http://www.lgbtcenters.org

OASIS Magazine
A writing community for queer and questioning youth
http://www.oasismag.com

One-in-Teen
http://members.tripod.com/oneinteen

Outminds.com
http://www.outminds.com/pridebeta/prideindex.cfm

OutProud: Be Yourself
http://www.outproud.org

Out Youth Austin
http://www.outyouth.org/index.html

A Place for Asian and Pacific Islander LGBT Youth
http://groups.yahoo.com/clubs/apilgbtyouth

Positive Images
http://www.posimages.org

Pride Street
http://www.pridestreet.net/Community/youth.html

Pride Zone: GLBTQA Youth Center
http://www.pridezone.org/home.html

PRYSM (Protecting the Rights of Young Sexual Minorities)
http://www.safeschoolsmc.org

Queer America: Find Your Way
http://www.queeramerica.com

Queer Resources Directory
http://www.qrd.org/QRD

Queertoday.com
http://www.queertoday.com

Rainbowlinks.com: Youth Resources
http://www.rainbowlinks.com

Safer Sex Page
http://www.safersex.org

Scouting for All
http://www.scoutingforall.org

Sex, etc.
http://www.sxetc.org/library

Sexual Minority Youth Assistance League
http://www.smyal.org

Soc.support.youth.gay-lesbian-bi FAQ
http://www.ssyglb.org

Soulforce
http://www.soulforce.org

Teenwire.com
http://www.teenwire.com/index.asp

Trevor Project
http://www.thetrevorproject.org

True Colors
http://www.ourtruecolors.org

Unity through Diversity
http://www.geocities.com/unity_through_diversity_1999

University LGBT/Queer Programs
http://www.people.ku.edu/~jyounger/lgbtqprogs.html

Wingspan's Youth Services
http://www.wingspanaz.org

www.iwannaknow.org
http://www.iwannaknow.org

XY Magazine
http://www.xymag.com/index2.php

Young Gay America
http://www.younggayamerica.com/index.shtml

Young Gay and Lesbian Talking
http://www.avert.org/ygmt.htm

Youth Guardian Services: Electronic Mail Lists
http://www.youth-guard.org/youth

Youth Resource
http://www.youthresource.com

Chapter Eight

•← Afterword

I was always treated badly by the girls. The boys were okay. They never bothered me. But the girls, I swear they could be running around and playing tag or jumping rope or something like that, but they would see me coming, and I swear they would want to play house or Barbies or beauty shop. Girl things. . . . It's almost like they had a radar that told them, "She hates this stuff, so let's make her play this way," and they did. . . . I never did like it. It bothered me a little bit as a kid, but I just went along with it because I was scared I would get into trouble. We were all about the same age, and when we got to like around twelve, they wanted to change me. They told me I was fat, that I needed to get on a diet. They wanted me to wear makeup and nail polish and tight clothes and get my hair done. I had so much pressure from them. And then I don't know what happened. I got ballsy and let everyone know: "You know something, I'm not going to do what you want me to do. I'm going to do what I want. I know me better than you know me." And from then on nobody bothered me anymore. Only two of the girls still tell me stuff, but one of them got pregnant. How can she judge me and be a big ho?

—Caitlyn, Seventeen, Tampa, Florida

Caitlyn is a well-mannered adolescent, respectful of those around her, free in many ways, and seemingly unaffected by the fact that she is a lesbian. She knows herself well enough to know that she is not going to let others' opinions about her life influence her in any way. I hope for the day when all GLBT youth can feel as freely as Caitlyn does—so open about their sexuality, accepted and supported for who they are, living in a society where sexual orientation does not matter. I know this hope is currently unrealistic because we still live in a homophobic society where openly GLBT youth are often subjected by their peers, families, and teachers to derogatory remarks, prejudice, harassment, abuse, and violence.

I set out to write this text after I had written *Sex, Youth, and Sex Education*. In that book, I had written a chapter on sexual orientation, and thereafter I became more attentive to national and local news about these youth. In these reports I noticed consistent patterns—these youth had additional challenges in their lives, many schools ignored these youth altogether or denied them their rights, and some youth who could no longer stand feelings of alienation or isolation committed suicide. I found one story (in 2000) particularly distressing.

Police officers found Marcus Wayman, an eighteen-year-old high school football player in Philadelphia, in a parked car with a seventeen-year-old male. The officers questioned the youth and searched their car. They found condoms and ultimately arrested the adolescents for underage drinking. As the story goes, the two were told that homosexuality is immoral, against Christian teachings, and that the Bible condemns homosexuality. The officers then threatened Marcus by saying they were going to tell his grandfather that he is gay. This was apparently too much for Marcus because on his release from policy custody, he committed suicide.

I cannot believe that some adults would abuse their power and violate someone's constitutional right to privacy. Imagine Marcus's pain: to be threatened with exposing something so private, so intimate that he was driven to take his life. There are other disturbing stories, some of which are outlined in Sidebar 1.2, but since early 2002, other troubling events have occurred. One California father did not want his daughter to share a bathroom with lesbian students during PE, so he sued his district. A school board in Florida called homosexuality "a sin" and would not support "homosexual" issues. A high school lesbian was denied the opportunity to run for prom king. A principal who supported the Day of Silence (mentioned in Chapter 2) was reassigned to a central administration position. Two lesbian teachers in Connecticut were dismissed when their administrators learned they were going to have a commitment ceremony. The stories go on.

Readers may believe that I intentionally chose to discuss the negative aspects of growing up with a diverse sexuality or focused too much attention on the negative repercussions of living openly as gay, lesbian, bisexual, or transgender. But the fact remains that there seem to be more challenges in being a sexually diverse youth than there are rewards. Society tends to have a hard time with diverse sexual orientations—most adults believe that these youth are going through a phase they will outgrow; others believe that those "people" are complete "sinners" and will end up in hell; still others find diverse sexualities completely foreign, frightening, or sick; and adolescents in general tend to expect conformity from one another. One well-known comedian asserted, "No one ever gives you a cake that reads, 'Congratulations on being gay,'" and rarely does a parent or teacher pat a youth on the back and declare, "I'm glad you're gay."

It goes without saying that not all discussions about this topic are doom and gloom. There are many stories and testimonies about heterosexual allies, school administrators demanding gay-straight alliances, openly gay and lesbian youth accepted by their peers, and parents embracing their child's sexual orientation. There are also some very courageous youth who offer no apologies for their sexual orientation; refuse to kowtow to conservative, traditional authorities; and survive comfortably in their homes and schools. Society is slowly changing, and in the last several years I have noticed

- more gay and lesbian characters and themes on TV
- more magazines about and for the gay and lesbian community in grocery store aisles and bookstore racks
- more gay-straight alliances in schools across the country
- more gay celebrities and public figures living openly

Moreover, some news items (outlined in Sidebar 8.1) reflect how youth are being supported. These items lead me to believe that schools will become more tolerant and accepting of these youth. One day, I hope sooner rather than later, this topic will be merely historical, a reference to a time when social injustice was directed toward the GLBT community. In the meantime, these youth will reach adulthood as generations before have, surviving challenges imposed on them by ignorant people and standing strong—no different from any other U.S. citizen.

In one short year, I have developed a new understanding and respect for gay, lesbian, bisexual, and transgender youth. In writing this text, reading the literature on this population, and interviewing some youths and their teachers, I have also made some discoveries. I will discuss here the distinct population, historical perspective of the research, youth interviews, and three schools today.

THE DISTINCT POPULATION

I started working on this text shortly after the September 11th tragedy. I had gathered some of my resources before the Trade Center attack and knew that GLBT youth (and adults) were often targets of hate crimes, discrimination, and so forth. But on that day I saw dramatic footage of

Sidebar 8.1 Recent Media Reports of GLBT Youth

Title	Date	Source
"School Considers Classroom Participation on Day of Silence"	March 28, 2002	*Journal Sentinel,* Wisconsin
"Governor Signs School Bully Bill"	March 28, 2002	*Seattle Post-Intelligencer,* Washington
"LGBT Books Soon to Find Place in High School"	April 1, 2002	*Trenton Times*, New Jersey
"Gay-Straight Clubs Growing in Schools"	April 1, 2002	cnn.com
"Schools to Widen Civil Rights Policy"	April 2, 2002	*Times-Union,* Florida
"Silence Speaks Out about LGBT Bias"	April 5, 2002	*Nashville Tennesean,* Tennessee
"Students at 16 Indiana Schools Silently Protest"	April 11, 2002	*Memphis Commercial Appeal,* Indiana
"Broward School Board Considers Pact with GLSEN"	April 18, 2002	*South Florida Sun-Sentinel,* Florida
"Local Teens Honored for LGBT Activism"	May 2, 2002	*Santa Cruz Sentinel,* California
"Residents Pack Forum on Keeping Students Safe"	May 3, 2002	*Cape Cod Times,* Massachusetts
"New Gay-Straight Alliance Promotes Acceptance"	May 15, 2002	*Dallas Morning News,* Texas
"No Taunts at LGBT Proms"	May 23, 2002	Miami Herald, Florida
"School Lets Transgender Student Graduate in Drag"	June 8, 2002	*Honolulu Star-Bulletin,* Hawaii
"Star Athlete Comes Out to Peers"	June 11, 2002	*Waterbury Republican-American,* Connecticut
"LGBT at Prom: Less of an Issue than Ever"	June 14, 2002	*Washington Post,* Washington D.C.
"Colleges Increasingly Look to Attract LGBT Applicants"	June 19, 2002	*Education Week*

people working together, helping and supporting one another—race, ethnicity, gender, occupation, and such did not matter. That is the way it should be—it should not matter that someone is gay or lesbian or straight. We are all complex human beings who deserve equal treatment and rights, and youth especially deserve to feel safe, accepted, and supported at school and in their community.

As I wrote Chapter 1, I was reminded about youth with disabilities and the way they have been treated by schools. (I am not making comparisons between people with disabilities and GLBT persons; these are two distinct cultures with different histories.) For years they were made to feel inferior, were treated as second-class citizens, and had very little protection prior to 1975. I thought back to some of my experiences with youth with disabilities and remembered some of the comments they and their parents had made:

- "I just want to be like everybody else."
- "I want to be treated like a normal kid."
- "I want to have friends."
- "I want teachers to respect her."
- "I want him to have the same experiences as all the other students."
- "I want to live with my family."
- "I wish other kids would befriend him."

These statements sounded familiar to those made by some GLBT youth. Moreover, it seems that many youth also make fun of, avoid, or shun youth with disabilities, and despite advances in the field, some teachers do very little to accommodate youth with disabilities. All of this seemed analogous to GLBT youth. A statement is often made in special education—"It's not the kid with the problem; it's the way society responds to them"—that is applicable to GLBT youth: it is not the gay or lesbian kid with the problem; it is the way heterosexual youth and school personnel deal with them that is the problem. Therefore, it only makes sense that school personnel be trained to work effectively with GLBT youth and learn ways to create classrooms that accept diversity. I have discovered that teachers are often reluctant to work with youth with disabilities because these students are unfamiliar territory. But after some professional development and work with the students, teachers change their attitudes and are more receptive to special education. I think the same would hold true for many school personnel and their perceptions of GLBT youth. With learning and exposure, school personnel would become more supportive of these students.

I am reminded of the 2002 season of the MTV reality show *Real World*. The show brings youth together from all walks of life and has them live together for months, documenting the issues presented in their lives. Among the male housemates in this season were two straight and one gay. The friendship that develops throughout the show between Theo (straight) and Chris (gay) is a lesson for all of us. At the beginning of the show, Theo is not readily accepting of Chris, informing him that homosexuality is immoral and homosexuals go to hell. He becomes uncomfortable and disturbed when Chris enters into a relationship and is publicly affectionate with his boyfriend. Throughout the show, however, viewers notice Theo making an emotional transformation as he becomes more accepting of Chris and his life. Theo even goes to a gay and lesbian party hosted by Chris's friends. By the end of the show, Theo has made a complete turnaround and calls Chris his brother. How could the seemingly homophobic Theo change his attitude in a few months and become accepting of gay and lesbian people? The answer is simple, really: through his interactions with Chris, Theo realizes that Chris is a good person whose love, hate, and passions are not so different from those of anyone else. If school personnel and youth just took the time to get to know more GLBT people, they would understand that these youth are no different from heterosexual youth. This would be a critical first step toward having school environments free of antigay harassment.

HISTORICAL RESEARCH

Significant strides have been made in this field of research. In just forty years, we went from occasional research on homosexual adults and impressions about their childhood to large-scale surveys of school environments. Research had overlooked this population of youth seemingly because homosexuality was a taboo topic, the American Psychiatric Association (APA) believed it was a sickness, society believed that youth could not possibly know their sexual identity, and adults in general hid their sexual orientation. Society seemed to presume for a significant part of its history that adults simply awaken one day with an attraction for the same sex. This could not have been further from the truth.

The Stonewall riots, demonstrations against the APA, and national marches paved the way for youth-serving professionals to investigate GLBT youth experience. These professionals knew that these youth existed, probably because they had encountered some who had been victimized and others who had attempted or committed suicide. As early as 1970, one researcher published some information on homosexuality and recommendations for teachers. Martin Hoffman (1970) advised:

> It's hard for a teacher to keep an effeminate boy's peers from making him feel like a worthless human being, but if it can be done it should be. . . . I believe that what the student really needs is acceptance from the family, and in many cases this is only possible if the parents are told (by someone they will listen to) that they cannot change their child's sexual preference. The only choice they have at this stage is how much guilt they will burden the child with. (48)

For nearly thirty years, journal articles have covered an array of topics on this subject, and the consensus has been the same: these youth have challenges in their lives, and schools must support them. The articles all have similar recommendations, including more teacher training, better protection policies, more support services, more resources in the libraries, and more discussions in the classrooms. It is unfortunate and somewhat ironic that school communities, despite their increasing acceptance of GLBT youth, are slow to digest this information and implement the recommendations. School officials and personnel could certainly do more to keep GLBT youth from falling through the cracks.

YOUTH INTERVIEWS

Sexually diverse youth are alike in many ways and different in so many others. I interviewed youth who had "in-your-face" attitudes, others who seemed unaffected by their sexual orientation, and others who wished they could be heterosexual. I saw gay boys and lesbian girls who could pass for Ralph Lauren all-American models, and I saw gay boys who wore makeup and lesbian girls who wore ties. Some of the youth came from middle-class families, and others were living in poverty and foster care. Some had parents who supported them, and others were estranged from their parents. This population is as heterogeneous as can be. The one core element all these youth shared, however, was that they wished for a society more accepting of them and more understanding of their plight.

From my observations, gay boys tended to be more affected by their sexual orientation than lesbian girls were. More often than not, the boys said that they wanted to be heterosexual (not one girl mentioned this desire). The girls were more often accepted by their school community and family than were the boys. The boys seemed to be picked on, harassed, and teased more often than the girls. Perhaps this is because society has different (and maybe stricter) standards and expectations for men. One graduate student whom I met during my visit to Walt Whitman Community School remarked that she found that gay and lesbian youth who were more traditional ("straight acting") in their mannerisms, dress, and behavior were more likely to be accepted by their school community. It could very well be that gay and lesbian youth are tolerated and accepted as long as they conform to traditional norms and are quiet about their sexual orientation.

In my interviews I saw remarkable youth with so much spirit and potential in their lives. In Angel, a biological girl, I learned that someone so young could be so determined to conform her body to her sexual identity: a boy. She knew her transgender community well, understood the process to physically transform her body, and embraced the repercussions of taking testosterone and having her breasts removed. Most people might have been intimidated by Angel and her thirty-seven piercings, the tattoos all over her body, and her blue hair, but she was a sincere, respectful youth who would "tone down" her appearance if it made people uncomfortable. School life had not been easy for her. Girls were scared of her, teachers thought she should not be playing with boys, and she was constantly harassed and barraged with questions about her sexuality. Her biggest vexation in school was that her teachers would stifle her whenever she discussed her personal life. Teachers who stymie openly GLBT youth send a powerful message to their students—the voices of sexually diverse people are gross, inappropriate, and inconsequential.

William and Jericka were a couple to behold. In their short lives they met, got married, and had a child. This is not an unusual circumstance in today's society until one factors in that they had both questioned their sexuality prior to getting married. Even though William is bisexual and Jericka is lesbian, they love each other dearly, are the best of friends, will remain married, and plan to have another child. They just seem to do whatever feels right to them, regardless of what others might think. From them I learned that some openly gay and lesbian youth tend to distinguish gay and lesbian culture from the greater culture and that there are great differences between the two. William and Jericka's experiences led them to believe that there is a lot more drama and drugs among gay and lesbian youth (at least in their social circle) than there is among straight youth. William is adamant that he did not have problems until he entered the "gay world." For him, gay boys were superficial, catty, promiscuous, and craved his attention. In one relationship, William found that his boyfriend would bicker with his two-year-old daughter, and it was an ex-lover who got him addicted to drugs. For Jericka, the lesbian girls were aggressive and possessive even after the relationships were over, and she remained bothered by the fact that lesbian girls pursued physically attractive lovers. They both found it absurd that the straight world believes that the gay world "recruits."

Jeremy was nearing the end of his stay at a psychiatric hospital. He had known he was gay his whole life, but fear kept him from accepting or acting on that knowledge. He had attempted suicide when his parents realized that he was gay—it was too much strain on his already weak relationship with them. From Jeremy (and another gay youth) I learned that some youth hate being gay or feminine and do not want to expose their sexual orientation at all. They understand their sexuality but struggle with being different from others. School life had not been difficult for Jeremy considering that he excelled in academics and had a small circle of friends. He had been teased about his mannerisms but not to a degree that required some attention. He accepted the fact that homophobic comments were an everyday occurrence among his peers.

Samantha was a courageous youth who had overcome one hardship after another. From Samantha I learned that schools can be the downfall in the life of a GLBT youth. In her case, her family and community had accepted her, but her teachers made her life miserable. They never appreciated her, they never allowed her to talk about her personal life, and one teacher stripped her of a rainbow flag necklace. All of this distressed Samantha to the point that she became truant and had no academic success whatsoever. Had it not been for the foresight of a school counselor who thought Harvey Milk School would turn her life around, Samantha's future would have been bleak. Because of Harvey Milk School, Samantha has a newfound relationship, is close to earning her high school diploma, and has a support network encouraging her to pursue her goals and ambitions.

THE THREE SCHOOLS

Before *Sex, Youth, and Sex Education,* I never knew that there were public and private schools that catered to gay and lesbian youth. It never occurred to me that some youth would need an alternative placement because their school life had become an overwhelmingly negative experience. I am glad that some advocates had the gumption to fight for and create safe havens where youth could regain their high school experience. These advocates simply want to save adolescent lives. I learned some valuable lessons from these institutions.

First, these youth are considered at risk for developing cognitive and emotional problems. Youth in general are at risk for developing future problems when they live in poverty; were exposed in utero to alcohol, drugs, cigarette smoke, and diseases; have been abused physically or emotionally; live in single-parent homes; have teen parents; are homeless; and/or are stressed (Kaplan 1996). Understandably, many of the students at the three schools were at risk because they lived in poverty, were abused by adults and peers, had been homeless, and/or were stressed about their lives. I was surprised to learn that students often enroll with very low academic and social skills—some students had third- or fourth-grade reading and math skills. But, then, how are they to acquire better skills if most of their time has been spent worrying about their safety? or wondering about their next meal? or wondering where to find a warm place to sleep? or believing that suicide might resolve their problems? They have so many issues to contend with that they are often emotionally unstable, distrusting of youth and adults, and on the defensive. I now understand why they are taught how to be nice and are asked to "tone down the gay attitude." Their teachers have many roles to fulfill—teacher, counselor, social worker, and therapist—in order to get them through the academic programs.

Prior to visiting the schools, I imagined that gay and lesbian studies were prominent in the curriculum—discussed in every course every day. I could not have been more mistaken. The students have academic courses to complete, and gay and lesbian studies seem to take a back seat to standard curricula and basic skills/concepts acquisition. Discussions about gay and lesbian issues do occur, but they are not a common practice for every subject. The teachers emphasized that the students have enough gay and lesbian issues in their lives and they need more time for the basics. Another mentioned that she could barely get them to read about gay and lesbian history. The students are interested in the topic but not to the point of pursuit.

Lastly, I knew that some conservative factions opposed the schools and their creators calling them agents of the "homosexual agenda," but I was not prepared for the most common complaint against the schools: segregation. Gay and heterosexual people alike tend to believe that it is wrong to have schools solely for these youth. They assert that these youth will not learn how the real world is and therefore do not become skilled at working with intolerance and discrimination. They believe that GLBT youth become accustomed to associating only with their own kind and will not seek out diversity in their lives. Moreover, they believe that heterosexual youth miss out on the opportunity to interact with GLBT youth. But these youth know intolerance and discrimination. They have encountered and continue to encounter both in school and outside of school, in the magazines they read, in the TV programs they watch, and from their family members. Not only do the students learn the skills from their experiences in the community but also all three schools teach their students the skills to work effectively with all people. Moreover, these youth had been segregated their whole lives when schools ignored and failed to support and protect them from hostile environments. In all, the three schools educate about 140 students each year. If there are 246,000 gay and lesbian youth (a very conservative estimate; see Chapter 1) in the nation's schools today, it seems that 24.6 million heterosexual youth (between thirteen and nineteen) would hardly notice that there are fewer gay and lesbian youth to interact with.

SUMMARY

Gay, lesbian, bisexual, and transgender youth are in our schools and in our communities. Some are more out than others, but those who are denied support, affirmation, or validation of any kind are in for an arduous journey into adulthood. How completely ignored, invisible, and isolated these youth must feel. Despite many problems and challenges, most of these youth will grow up to be independent, well-functioning adults at the severe price of alienation, harassment, abuse, and so forth. We have come a long way in this field, but we need to do more for gay, lesbian, bisexual, and transgender youth.

REFERENCES

Hoffman, Martin. 1970. "The Searching Mind: Homosexuality." *Today's Education* 59(8): 46–48.

Kaplan, Paul S. 1996. *Pathways for Exceptional Children: School, Home, and Culture.* New York: West Publishing.

✎ Appendix

Sidebar A.1 Bullying Behaviors and Reporting Process, School District of Hillsborough County, Florida

Bullying

1. Bullying is a form of aggression and occurs when a person(s) who perceives a power imbalance, willfully subjects another person (victim), whoever he or she may be, to an intentional, unwanted and unprovoked hurtful verbal and/or physical actions(s) which result(s) in the victim feeling oppressed (stress, injury, discomfort) at any school site or school board–sponsored activity or event. Bullying may also occur as various forms of hazing, including initiation rites perpetrated against a new student or a new member of a team. Students who engage in such conduct shall be subject to a range of punishment to include verbal or written reprimand, in-school or out-of-school suspension, change of placement and/or expulsion.

2. Examples of types of bullying may include, but are not limited to:
- ✎ physical bullying—punching, shoving, poking, strangling, hair-pulling, beating, biting and excessive tickling;
- ✎ verbal bullying—such acts as hurtful name-calling, teasing and gossip;
- ✎ emotional (psychological) bullying—rejecting, terrorizing, extorting, defaming, humiliating, blackmailing, rating/ranking of personal characteristics such as race, disability, ethnicity, or perceived sexual orientation, manipulating friendships, isolating, ostracizing and peer pressure;
- ✎ sexual bullying—many of the actions listed above as well as exhibitionism, voyeurism, sexual propositioning, sexual harassment and abuse involving actual physical contact and sexual assault. In many cases, gender and cross-gender sexual harassment may also qualify as bullying.

3. Although boys are more often the perpetrators and victims of bullying, girls tend to bully in more indirect ways (manipulating friendships, obstructing classmates and spreading malicious rumors). However, it is quite possible for bullying to occur in many different types of interpersonal relationships in a school setting.

4. Bullying may be limited to a single incident. However, in most cases, the bullying is characterized by repeated harmful actions on the part of the bully(ies).

5. Personnel at all levels are responsible for taking corrective action to prevent bullying at any of the school board sites or activities. Information relative to the prevention and correction of bullying shall be provided in writing to district personnel, students and parents.

6. An individual has the legal right to report an incident(s) of bullying without fear of reprisal or retaliation at any time. Retaliation is defined in the dictionary as meaning "to pay back (an injury) in kind." When a person is accused of having engaged in an inappropriate fashion, especially bullying, the common reaction of that person is to be angry and want to pay the "victim" back (retaliate). *Retaliation must not occur.*

Some examples of retaliations are:

➻ attempting to discuss the matter in any way while it is under investigation
➻ spreading rumors
➻ following the person
➻ becoming physical in any way
➻ destroying property
➻ using the telephone or any other electronic or written form of communication to retaliate in any way
➻ ostracizing

Therefore, allegations of bullying shall be promptly investigated, giving due regard to the need for confidentiality and the safety of the victim and/or individual(s) who report an incident(s) of bullying.

7. Proven allegations of bullying can have serious consequences for the party deemed guilty, including but not limited to the following:

If the party deemed guilty is a student, the range of punishment could include verbal and written reprimand, in-school or out-of-school suspension, change of placement and/or expulsion;

If the party deemed guilty is a school board employee, the range of punishment could include a letter of caution, written reprimand, suspension with pay and/or termination;

If the party deemed guilty is neither a student nor a school board employee, appropriate steps shall be taken, which could include limiting the access of this party to a school board property and any other action deemed necessary, including criminal prosecution.

If You Are the Victim of Bullying:
➻ Clearly tell the "bully(ies)" to stop;
➻ Don't ignore the incident. Immediately report the incident to someone at school or seek peer mediation at school. Tell your parent(s)/guardian(s);
➻ If the bullying continues after you have clearly told the bully(ies) to stop, make a written record of the incident including date, time,

witness or witnesses and parties involved in the incident. Report the incident immediately to an adult who has authority over the bully(ies); for example: teacher, guidance counselor, assistant principal, or principal;

•→ Avoid being alone with the person(s) who have attempted to bully you in the past.

If you are the victim of bullying and you feel uncomfortable reporting this fact to adult personnel at your school, contact someone on the following list:

•→ Guidance Services;
•→ School Social Work Services;
•→ School Psychological/Diagnostic Service;
•→ General Director of Employee Relations and Hillsborough County School Equity Coordinator;
•→ Director of Professional Standards;
•→ Supervisor of Professional Standards;
•→ General Director of Human Resources.

To Minimize the Risk of Being Accused of Bullying
Do:
•→ Keep your hands to yourself.
•→ Remember that *NO* one has a right to harm another person in any way.
•→ Think before you speak.
•→ Immediately apologize if you accidentally say or do something that has made another person feel oppressed.
•→ Report all incidents of bullying behavior you have witnessed to appropriate school personnel.

Don't:
•→ Touch anyone without his or her permission and especially in an inappropriate way.
•→ Keep interacting with a person after he or she had perceived your behavior toward him or her as being "inappropriate" and has clearly told you to "stop."
•→ Make remarks that may cause another person to feel "oppressed" (stressful, scared, or intimidated).

Source: "School District of Hillsborough County, Florida: Student Handbook 2001–2002," 8a–9a. Reprinted with permission.

⚫◆ Index

❧ About the Author

David Campos is assistant professor of elementary education in the College of Education at Roosevelt University. His experiences include teaching second grade and conducting corporate training and development for Advanced Micro Devices and Guiltless Gourmet, Inc. He has supervised student teachers and taught undergraduate and graduate courses in special education, multicultural education, and curriculum methods. In addition to his duties as an assistant professor, he has served as an assistant dean of academic affairs and as a project coordinator for a Title II Teacher Quality Enhancement Grant.